A History of the Smithsonian American Art Museum

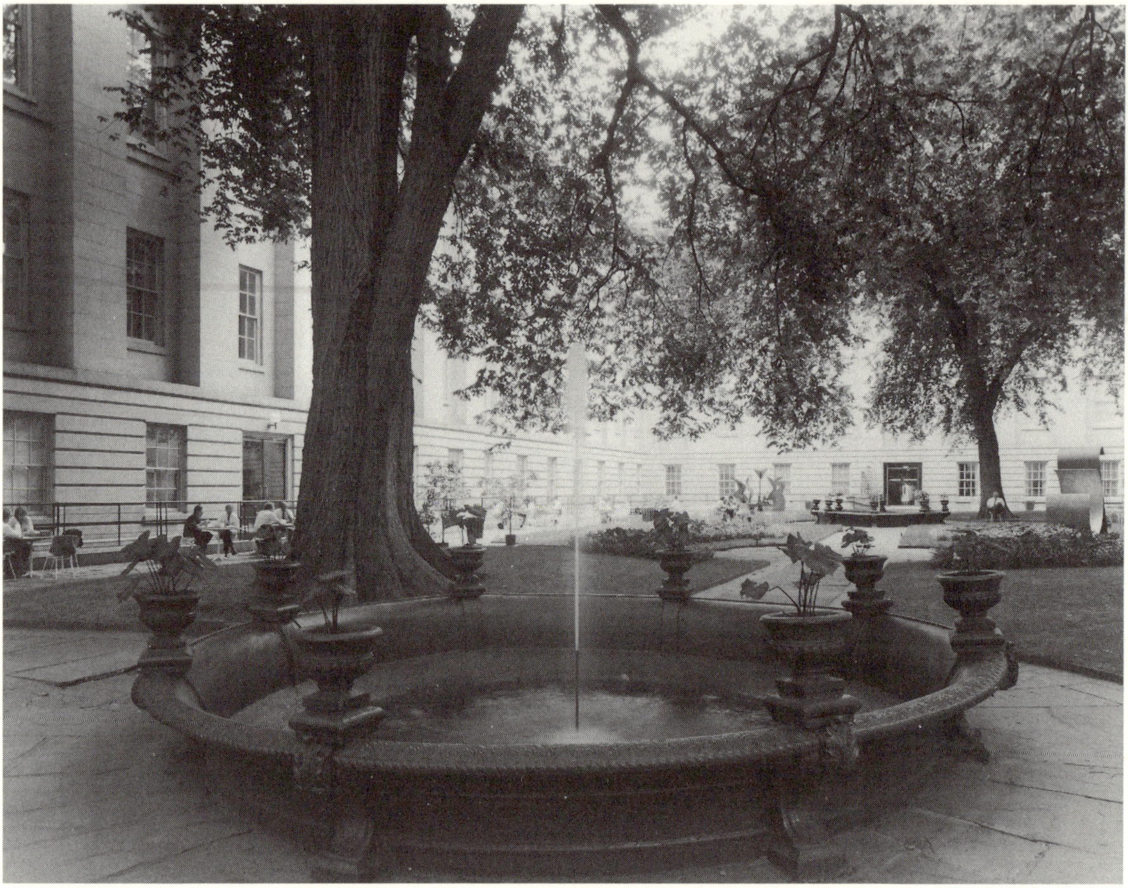

A History of the Smithsonian American Art Museum

THE INTERSECTION OF ART, SCIENCE, AND BUREAUCRACY

Lois Marie Fink

University of Massachusetts Press
AMHERST AND BOSTON

Printed in the United States of America.

LC 2007024293
ISBN 978-1-55849-616-3

Designed by Dennis Anderson
Set in Janson Text by BookComp, Inc.
Printed and bound by Sheridan Books, Inc.

Library of Congress Cataloging-in-Publication Data

Fink, Lois Marie.
A history of the Smithsonian American Art Museum : the intersection of art, science, and bureaucracy / Lois Marie Fink.
p. cm.
Includes bibliographical references and index.
ISBN 978-1-55849-616-3 (cloth : alk. paper)
1. Smithsonian American Art Museum—History. I. Title. N857.F56 2007
709.73'074753—dc22
2007024293

British Library Cataloguing in Publication data are available.

Frontispiece: Robert Lautman, *Courtyard of National Museum of American Art (now Smithsonian American Art Museum) and National Portrait Gallery, Washington, D.C.*, 1980s. Smithsonian American Art Museum. Sculpture in right center background: Alexander Calder, *Nenuphar* (name of a Water Lily), Smithsonian American Art Museum, Gift of the Artist; sculpture at right background: Lila Katzen, *Curled Up C*, Smithsonian American Art Museum, Gift of Dr. and Mrs. Reuben Hoppenstein. Elm trees shade turn-of-the-century water fountains.

Dedicated to the
Staff Members, Docents, Fellows, and Interns
of NCFA/NMAA

CONTENTS

ILLUSTRATIONS

PREFACE

My involvement in the history of the Smithsonian American Art Museum is personal, for I was a member of the staff for twenty-three years—although I had not planned a museum career. I was teaching at Roosevelt University when my former professor at the University of Chicago, Joshua C. Taylor, in 1970 was appointed director of the National Collection of Fine Arts (the title at that time). He invited me to head a program for Smithsonian Fellows in residence at NCFA to research American art, a role similar in some ways to the responsibilities of teaching. I decided to try it for two or three years and stayed for a couple of decades. Taylor's curiosity about NCFA's history initiated forays into archival files to gather material about the earliest acquisitions. We both believed in the need for a published history of the museum because of its confused identity in the mind of the public and even members of the staff. The proposed project was put on hold for various reasons until shortly before my retirement, when I once again took up the research.

Studying a museum of which I have been a part has necessarily affected my perception. Being a staff member made me aware of the human side of museum operations. We often speak of museums as if they were abstract entities with a single mind and will, but in reality, of course, they involve many individuals who daily work with the public, donors, artists, and works of art.

I appreciate the interest my former colleagues have taken in the prolonged progress of this book and for sharing with me their experiences and memories. I had interviews with Patricia H. Chieffo, director of intern programs; Margaret P. Cogswell, of the office of exhibitions abroad; George Gurney, curator; Lloyd Herman, former director of the Renwick Gallery; W. Robert Johnston, former registrar; Val E. Lewton, exhibition designer; Michael W. Monroe, former curator in charge of the Renwick Gallery; Richard N. Murray, curator; Ellen M. Myett, exhibitions coordinator of the Renwick; Nora M. Panzer, head of the education department; and William H. Truettner, curator. I also held conversations with former directors Thomas M. Beggs,

David W. Scott, and Charles C. Eldredge, current director Elizabeth Broun, former assistant and acting director, Harry Lowe, and deputy director Charles J. Robertson.

For the time-consuming task of closely reading early drafts of the entire manuscript I am deeply grateful to Neil Harris and the late Lillian B. Miller, both of whom offered invaluable critiques and encouragement. Drafts of particular chapters were read by Smithsonian colleagues Nancy E. Gwinn, Smithsonian Institution Libraries; Pamela M. Henson, Institutional History Division of the Smithsonian Institution Archives; Richard N. Murray and William H. Truettner, SAAM curators; Ellis L. Yochelson, Department of Paleobiology at the National Museum of Natural History; and alumni Fellows of the museum, Francis V. O'Connor, Frances Pohl, and Gabriel Weisberg. Special thanks go to alumni Fellows Doug Adams, David Bjelajac, Elizabeth Johns, Gerald D. Silk, and Roberta K. Tarbell, who evaluated a controversial chapter at a critical juncture.

The Smithsonian has a wealth of research resources which I used extensively. At the American Art/Portrait Gallery Library, Cecilia H. Chin, librarian, and Patricia M. Lynagh, assistant librarian, Martin R. Kalfatovic, and Stephanie Moye efficiently helped with a variety of questions. Courtney De Angelis, Andrew L. Thomas, Joan R. Stahl, and Richard Sorenson assisted with the gathering of photographs. At the Smithsonian Institution Archives, where I camped for weeks at a time, the staff was unfailingly helpful: Alan L. Bain, William E. Cox, William A. Deiss, Susan Glenn, R. Shawn Johnstone, Bruce R. Kirby, Kathleen Robinson, Tracy Robinson, James A. Steed, Paul Theerman, and Kathleen M. Williams of the Archives Division counseled me on sources and kept me supplied with boxes of file papers; Pamela M. Henson shared her extensive research on the chronology and history of the Smithsonian. At the Archives of American Art, Judy Throm directed me to relevant materials. Individuals who shared their research projects with me include Cynthia R. Field of the Smithsonian Office of Architectural History and Historic Preservation, who helped with sources on the Smithsonian Building; Ellis L. Yochelson provided notes on Secretary Walcott and the National Museum of Natural History Building (where the art collection was shown for decades); Merl Moore, legendary among scholars of American art, often deposited on my desk relevant materials from his extensive research in nineteenth-century newspapers. Other useful materials were found in the National Archives and the Gallery Archives of the National Gallery of Art.

At the beginning of my project a grant from Smithsonian Studies funded research assistance in the person of Susan Bollendorf, who enriched my study on the early period; Diane Dardis and Kinsey Katcha, volunteer research assistants, helped with a variety of points raised by the material.

I am grateful for permission to publish photographs from the following collections: at the institution, the Smithsonian American Art Museum, the Slide and Photo Archives of the Smithsonian American Art Museum, the Smithsonian Institution Archives, the National Portrait Gallery, and the American Art/Portrait Gallery Library; and beyond, the Historical Society of Washington, D.C.; the Lyndon Baines Johnson Museum and Library, Austin, Texas; and individuals Margaret Price Cogswell and Merl M. Moore.

Finally, because I encountered unending difficulties in trying to get this book published, my heartfelt gratitude goes to colleagues in the scholarly community who were willing to lend their names in support of my publication effort: Madeleine Fidell Beaufort, David Bjelajac, Michele H. Bogart, Ruth Bohan, Norma Broude, Petra ten-Doesschate Chu, Betsy Fahlman, Cassandra Langer, Theresa Leininger-Miller, Patricia Mainardi, Janet Marstine, Francis V. O'Connor, Elizabeth L. O'Leary, Frances Pohl, Roger B. Stein, Alan Wallach, Sally Webster, Gabriel Weisberg, Cécile Whiting, and James L. Yarnall.

It's a pleasure to acknowledge the contributions of all the foregoing individuals and institutions to my work on this book.

INTRODUCTION

A History of the Smithsonian American Art Museum: The Intersection of Art, Science, and Bureaucracy follows the nation's first art collection from its origins in private and government holdings of the early nineteenth to the late twentieth century. My aim is to convey a sense of the historic continuity of the museum and its identity as a collection that has developed for over 150 years within the context of national ideals and Washington realities. Like the museum itself, this book is intended for the general public as well as for scholars of art history and American studies.

Histories of art museums commonly trace a straightforward course from their founding to unwavering growth in collections and programs. Quite a contrast, the subject of this history has followed a meandering, circuitous path through time and space, wandering literally (moving from one building to another for a total of four different locations, ending up where it started) and figuratively (searching for an identity through name changes, altogether four official titles) as of this date. Made custodian of the nation's art, for decades it received little support for that purpose from the federal government or from the renowned institution of which it is a part. Its history reads like a nineteenth-century melodrama: there are villains and heroes, destruction by fire, dashed hopes, and subsistence survival. And true to the literary prototype, after all the perils a happy ending ensues as the museum emerges with renewed strength to follow its original mission of promoting the nation's own art and artists.

Originating as the art gallery stipulated in the 1846 founding legislation of the Smithsonian, SAAM developed within an institution that was essentially under the control of scientists. From the mid-nineteenth century and well into the twentieth, the relation of art and science at the Smithsonian played a major role in the museum's history for it largely determined possibilities for accessions and exhibitions. The significance of this vis-à-vis encounter goes beyond events in Washington, for it also suggests the impact of science on concepts of art and museum practices elsewhere in the nation. Bureaucracy, the other defining relationship as indicated by the subtitle of this book, refers to levels of institutional authority and power. Unique circumstances of the Smithsonian's origin determined its distinctive kind of governance, which differs from that of other museums in the United States.

Most institutions with collections—particularly art collections—have been initiated through efforts of private citizens who desired to bring cultural opportunities to their communities. Consisting of individuals with wealth and political power, these groups or their representatives ordinarily remain in control as trustees or boards of directors to determine museum policies. In these institutions the professional staff to some degree is subject to nonprofessionals of an elite social class. Scholars of sociological theories about museums have questioned the purposes served by this manner of founding and style of governance; some conclude that the intent and result is to reinforce class distinctions.[1]

The Smithsonian was established without obligations to a group of wealthy patrons. In his bequest the donor, James Smithson, stated briefly that his gift to the United States was to be used "for the increase and diffusion of knowledge among men." No restrictions or further explanations were given. Without external obligatory ties, the power base of the Smithsonian became internal. Its management system—and that of today's SAAM—is based on gradated levels of responsibility that advance through levels of bureaucratic authority: the Smithsonian American Art Musem is a bureaucracy under the bureaucracy of the Smithsonian, which is under the bureaucracy of the federal government.

At the first level of the art museum itself, the director as head official makes decisions of policy, sets priorities for the staff, determines the tenor of relationship to the public, and, with the curators and other administrative heads, provides directions and sets goals for exhibitions and programs. Working with the director, an advisory group called the Commission functions as a sounding board, provides advice and initiates action on specific issues, and is invested with power for certain responsibilities, such as approval of accessions over a stipulated value. In keeping with a tradition established by the original advisory group, which consisted entirely of artists, the commissioners include practicing artists along with collectors and other art-minded citizens.

The museum's director reports to an undersecretary in the office of the Smithsonian secretary. Appointed as head authority over the entire operation, the Smithsonian secretary determines the direction and priorities of the institution at large. In charge of funding and exercising the capacity to impose policies for the Smithsonian generally and for each museum or agency specifically as occasions may warrant, the secretary has enormous power. Major changes in the destiny of the art collection have been determined by Smithsonian secretaries.

The secretary reports to the Board of Regents, which constitutes the institution's highest and final authority. Members of this board are appointed from all three branches of the federal government together with private citizens. They finalize decisions and initiate actions on behalf of the institution, question or approve museum policies, and make conclusive determinations about controversial issues. Regents select and have authority over the secretary; however, they rarely disagree with or criticize the secretary. The Board of Regents is required to send to the Congress annual reports on the activities of the Smithsonian. These publications contain submissions by directors of the museums, curators, and other administrators, in addition to the report of the secretary, and constitute useful sources for the history of the institution.

The federal government represents the uppermost authoritative level that governs the Smithsonian. Congress ultimately holds the purse strings, for much of the institution's funding is federal in origin. Through legislation, Congress initially established the Smithsonian, is called upon to approve major decisions or actions, and occasionally undertakes investigation of practices. From time to time congressional committee members have become involved in specific issues affecting SAAM and have made substantial contributions to its development. Certain federal agencies have control over particular policies, such as the hiring of personnel. The office of the president has also acted on behalf of the art museum, sometimes asking Congress for specific action or giving approval and encouragement to the museum and its programs.

Consistent with the benefactor's intent to foster "the increase and diffusion of knowledge," at the1846 founding the Regents appointed a scholar of science as secretary. With the exception of the current period, beginning in the year 2000, this position has always been held by a scholar—usually a scholar of science. Control by scholars of the institution's direction and programs enabled the Smithsonian from its earliest years to attain international recognition for scholarship. The first secretary, Joseph Henry, established a policy of sponsoring and publishing original research, regularly producing publications that were sent to scientific organizations on every continent in an ambitious and successful exchange program.[2] This activity established the institution's renown for expertise and the sharing of expertise—which it still holds today. It also promoted the emergence of a powerful "elite" that differs considerably from wealthy benefactors: an elite of scholars.

From the late 1960s, when the art museum at last, as the National Collection of Fine Arts, received adequate funding to support staffing and programs, its directors have been art historians with Ph.Ds. Under their direction the art collection began to forge its own reputation with public education programs, accessions, and exhibitions that celebrated contemporary art along with historical and traditional works, and a research community for graduate and postdoctoral scholars. Exhibitions in American art became memorable productions for their subjects, manner of presentation, and accompanying publications of original research by scholar-curators.

The significance of scholars for setting the institution's agenda was corroborated with the appointment in January 2000 of a secretary with credentials instead as a banker and corporation chief executive officer. The institution began an aggressive policy of seeking and engaging obligatory ties to wealthy benefactors, both individuals and corporations—the same sort of relationship that had taken place earlier but now was much more actively pursued. A consequential debilitating effect on the institution's traditional scholarly emphasis provoked controversy within and beyond the Smithsonian. An event of January 2002 dramatized the protests and illustrates the extraordinary authority invested in the role of secretary. An open letter to the Regents, signed by 170 scholars from across the nation, contended that the current secretary was "unwilling or unable to carry out the mission of the Smithsonian, or to safeguard its integrity." In a subsequent meeting with the secretary, however, the Regents applauded his policies.[3]

All aspects of SAAM's formation and growth or lack thereof has taken place within the shadow of the three-tiered authoritative structure of the museum itself, the Smithsonian Institution at large, and the federal government. But although shadows may protect and nurture, they can impede as well. This system explains why major decisions about the art museum were often made with little or no involvement of officials in charge of the art collection, especially during the period before the late 1960s.

The bureaucratic trio has produced a cornucopia of memos, letters, minutes of meetings, committee reports, budget estimates, five-year plans, ten-year plans, annual reports, and so on and on. By winnowing through a great deal of this material, I have tried to spare the reader endless facts—dates, names, proposals, and the like—though such material necessarily forms the backbone of my study. Wherever possible I have tried to keep a narrative flow to lighten the burden of reading about bureaucratic machinations. Copious notes are provided for those who wish to pursue particular points in further depth.

The experience of working in the museum gave me insights into certain areas of institutional life, and my earlier studies in American art within the context of French art and art institutions provided points of comparison. Consequently, I take a different approach from that of most scholars writing on museums today, for whom the methodology of choice is often based on sociological theory. Their studies largely dismiss historical references to seek commonalities in institutional goals and programs, whether discussing museums of nineteenth-century Paris or twentieth-century Washington, D.C.[4] My text is based on the archival files and other primary sources that I searched for specifics of the events that formed the historical development of SAAM. I then related this material to concepts of art and science that defined collection and exhibition strategies, to philosophical backgrounds that connect the museum's activities to the wider world of beliefs and theory, and to ongoing issues about museum practices.

I have organized the chapters around turning points in the history of the museum's collection, with particular attention to those that relate to shifts in museum practices elsewhere and to issues of our own time. Chapter 1, "Art as Knowledge," describes how the significance of collections in the Western world determined their function in the youngest nation. Exhibition practices of that day are related to a theory of epistemology that posited a harmonious relationship between art and science. Modeled after earlier institutions in Washington, the Smithsonian was established and inherited extensive collections of art and science from private and government holdings, assuring its future as a museum with diverse collections.

Chapter 2, "Exhibiting the Evolution of Culture," shows public education becoming the raison d'être for museums, partly because of the experiences of the great international expositions. The overwhelming impact of Darwinian theory provided new structures and vocabulary for the organization of both collections and exhibitions—particularly at the Smithsonian.

Chapter 3, "Defining Art for the Nation in Two National Galleries," 1906 and 1937, relates progressive growth of the collection and hopeful plans for the future as the museum acquired a prestigious title and a dedicated gallery space. The loss of the title "the National Gallery of Art" to the Mellon collection in 1937 is the basis for considering different expectations held by two generations for a national gallery of art and the function of nationalism in relation to art museums.

Attitudes toward American art, a theme throughout the text, emerge more emphatically in chapter 4, "Rejecting Modern Art for Washington, 1930s–1960s," as the Smithsonian's own indifference toward its National Collection of Fine Arts (the new title) reflected the low esteem in which the nation's own art was generally held. The unrelenting conservative taste of NCFA officials was reinforced by political repression of art and artists during the McCarthy era.

Chapter 5, "Opening a New Era for Art at the Smithsonian, 1960s–1980," after all the reversals and disappointments of the past, shows NCFA escaping from the jaws of dinosaurs (almost literally) to settle at last into its own space within the building where the collection had first been shown a century earlier. Momentous strides were made during a period of national upheaval as the museum itself became embroiled in the politics of international exhibitions. Two dynamic directors articulated new approaches to museum policies and practices, with funding and encouragement from a creative Smithsonian secretary.

This study of SAAM from its pre-Smithsonian origins concludes in 1980 with the bestowal of the title the National Museum of American Art. (The current name, the Smithsonian American Art Museum, was acquired in 2000.) Accounts of subsequent years will require viewpoints from longer distances in time, and besides, major documents for the post-1980 period are not yet accessible. The names of succeeding directors and Smithsonian secretaries, however, are listed in the appendix.

A brief coda relates connections from the past to ongoing activities of the present, and, in the manner of the wandering collection itself, returns to the original starting point of the museum's history, more than 150 years earlier.

ABBREVIATIONS

AAA	Archives of American Art, Smithsonian Institution
AA/PG Library	American Art/Portrait Gallery Library
Annual Report	*Annual Report of the Board of Regents of the Smithsonian Institution*
NCFA	National Collection of Fine Arts
NGA	National Gallery of Art
NMAA	National Museum of American Art
NPG	National Portrait Gallery
RU	Record Unit (in the Smithsonian Institution Archives)
SAAM	Smithsonian American Art Museum
SI	Smithsonian Institution
SIA	Smithsonian Institution Archives

A History of the Smithsonian American Art Museum

1
Art as Knowledge

Within a year after the nation's political center had moved to Washington—when roads were still little more than paths through the trees, government buildings stood half-built, private housing was grossly inadequate, and no established water or sewage system existed—one resident declared that what the city really needed was a museum. "Nothing would tend more to benefit this city and the nation at large than that the seat of the general government should be in the depository of the arts and sciences," insisted this anonymous writer, who speculated on turning the president's house "into a National Museum, where, as in Paris and London, a National Institute might be established and lectures read."[1] The word "museum" here referred to an institution devoted to scholarly activities as well as the display of collections.[2]

In previous locations of the capital, such amenities already existed. In Philadelphia the American Philosophical Society had maintained from colonial days diverse collections and an interest in all kinds of knowledge, and Charles Willson Peale's "Philadelphia Museum" was thriving. In New York the Tammany Society's "American Museum" had opened in 1790, four years after Peale's enterprise, with the aim to collect and preserve everything "relating to the history of America, likewise every production of nature or art."[3] If the federal government had remained in either of those lively urban centers, national collections of the arts and sciences could have continued on established foundations, but Washington City beside the Potomac was a swampy, mosquito-ridden village without such signs of civilization. In 1800 the population totaled 3,219, consisting of 2,464 whites, 123 "all other free persons," and 632 slaves. The only outstanding manmade structures to be seen were the unfinished president's house and the Capitol Building, standing a long mile and a half apart. "The Capitol is situated on an eminence, which I should suppose was near the centre of the *immense country here called the city*," Secretary of the Treasury Oliver Wolcott wrote with a bit of sarcasm when first viewing Washington.[4] Here visionary planners would have to start from scratch.

Proposals for cultural institutions in the early republic carried a sense of urgency, for by the time of the nation's founding, national collections and their accessibility to scholars and the general public had become important sources of power and international prestige, inspiring Americans to consider the establishment of museums a priority in their anticipation of creating a world-class capital. By the mid-nineteenth century an institution combining scholarship and extensive collections of art and science would take form in Washington, established partly through the efforts and determination of private citizens—such as the author of the 1801 statement—and partly through sheer happenstance. It was destined to become the most renowned and largest museum complex in the world.

Objects as the Key to Knowledge

A visit to a typical art or science museum today involves either walking through gallery after gallery of paintings and seeing still more paintings through each open doorway, or encountering endless displays of objects pertaining to natural history or technology. Quite a different experience awaited visitors to the first museums established in the American hemisphere and many of those in European countries as well. While looking at a landscape painting they might see, just beyond, a mounted grizzly bear, canoe paddles and tomahawks, the model of a steamboat, a display of mineral crystals, Franklin's printing press. These early museums presented to visitors the astonishing expansion of knowledge in their own time through encounters with real things. Objects from near and far and from ancient times to the present, products of nature and of human minds and hands collected and shown together, revealed to viewers a sense of how they related, as individuals and as a nation, to history and nature and human cultures throughout the world.

Collections were not merely acquired for the sake of curiosity or as impressive displays of riches, as had been true of earlier *Wunderkammern* or "cabinets of curiosity" but represented a belief in knowledge as the chief means to power and progress, plus the conviction that knowledge required access to objects. Members of academies and institutes in European countries were turning away from traditional theories and dogma inherited from philosophers and theologians to engage scientific methods that centered on material things and observable phenomena. Such an awareness, beginning as early as the writings of Roger Bacon in the thirteenth century, had become more viable by the late sixteenth century in the generation of Galileo. A catalogue of 1655 describing the collection of a Danish medical professor proudly proclaimed that it had been formed "with the clear intention to lead towards knowledge by direct observation and away from hollow verbiage."[5] New methods of pedagogy began to involve the use of objects as the basis of learning experiences, most notably from 1769 in the writings and classrooms of Johann Heinrich Pestalozzi, the Swiss educational reformer. This approach to the interpretation of the real world, constituting a radical change in Western thought and marking a great watershed between the medieval and modern eras, made collections an absolute necessity.

An emphasis on objects also brought higher status and power to scholars, for organizing and utilizing collections required the expertise that only they possessed.[6] As authorities in their fields, scholars could use collections to convey interpretations of history, propose means of utilizing natural resources, devise new techniques in warfare, promote medical science, and make decisions affecting other areas crucial to Western nations. At the future Smithsonian, scientists and historians would be appointed as chief executive officers of the institution and directors of the museums of science, history, and art.

In explorations throughout the world, European encounters with previously unknown flora and fauna and human beings spurred the amassing of nature specimens and cultural artifacts. Columbus's voyages were soon followed by further explorations of the American hemisphere by John and Sebastian Cabot, Amerigo Vespucci, and other adventurers. Ferdinand Magellan set out to circumnavigate the globe in 1519, extending curiosity and knowledge far beyond previous limits. Diverse types of collections gathered through such expeditions gave pleasure to viewers, but more important, they served purposes of research, resulting in advances in medicine, mineralogy, knowledge of the sea, inventions of mechanical devices, the promotion of agriculture, trade, and industry.

Concurrently, archaeological discoveries in Italy and elsewhere in the Mediterranean area enriched humanistic studies of the Renaissance and stimulated a taste for art of the past. Private holdings of antiquities had become common in Rome by the fifteenth century; the young Michelangelo is known to have been powerfully affected by the Laocoön, a Hellenistic figure group excavated in 1506. Collections of art made possible the conceptualization of the history of art—beginning with sculptures from ancient Greece and Rome—and the sense of a nation's own distinctive tradition.

In the late eighteenth century, France opened state collections to the public, extending their educational benefits as befitted the era's democratic sentiments. Other nations began to follow that example. Philosophical concepts of the Enlightenment had promoted education as an important value to a civilized society, connected to a major preoccupation with the systematic organization of knowledge. Acquisition of hundreds of thousands of objects stimulated such endeavors; public museums and encyclopedias appeared about the same time. Royal collections at the Luxembourg in Paris opened contemporaneously with the first publication of the program of the Encyclopedists.[7] Throughout the articles of twenty-eight volumes, completed in 1772, Denis Diderot and his colleagues emphasized empirical inquiry, the modern approach to learning.

Pre-Smithsonian Scholarly Organizations and Collections

On the other side of the Atlantic, citizens of the United States, infected with the era's mania for collecting, cast a wide net over items of nature, science, history, and art to acquire the "useful knowledge" that would promote the nation's economic and moral progress, according to Charles Willson Peale. While Peale in Philadelphia and collectors-turned-entrepreneurs in New York and other cities were first to open exhibits of their holdings to the public, nowhere were such efforts more ardent than in the capital city.

In Washington, individuals and private organizations engaged in two kinds of activities: gathering and exhibiting collections, and trying to persuade Congress to assist their efforts. Joel Barlow, a frequent visitor to France who was impressed by the generous government patronage of art and scientific endeavors in that country, submitted to Congress in 1806 his *Prospectus of a National Institution*, which was to include a central university, laboratories and libraries for the sciences and the arts, and botanical gardens for agricultural experiments. "This is the moment in America," he declared (with an arrogance already well developed in the brash young nation), "to give such a direction to poetry, painting and the other fine arts, that true and useful ideas of glory may be implanted in the minds of men here, to take the place of the false and destructive ones that have degraded the species in other countries." As a convincing argument for federal funding, he listed in an appendix institutions in France supported by the state.[8] Barlow's proposal was introduced in the Senate but became mired in committee. He had expected the government to establish and maintain such an organization, but more successful efforts would begin with private funds and afterward seek government assistance.[9]

Repeated requests to Congress for aid from the Columbian Institute for the Promotion of Arts and Sciences, founded in 1816, and the National Institution for the Promotion of Science, established in 1840, resulted in allotments of space in government buildings but no funds. Several attempts to secure assistance for Peale's museum and a proposal to move it from Philadelphia to Washington had likewise been unsuccessful.[10] Like Pierre-Charles L'Enfant's plan for Washington, successful efforts to obtain federal funding for support of national cultural institutions would have to wait. But these early organizations did serve the important purpose—similar to the broad sweep of the French architect's design—of providing visions for the future. In the breadth of their intellectual interests and collections, the Columbian Institute and National Institution set important precedents for the founding of the Smithsonian.

Members of the Columbian Institute initiated their collection with a cabinet of minerals, expanding to specimens pertaining to zoology and botany, historical memorabilia (George Washington's uniform as commander in chief was a prized item), and technological and archaeological studies. Works of art included drawings, sculptures, engravings, and casts, several of which reflected current interest in ancient Greece and Pompeii. Although the organization's goals were worthy of a learned society, without a community of scholars or financial support outside its own membership, the Columbian Institute fell into an irreversible decline before its charter expired in 1838.

Officials of the National Institution sought to create a politically powerful organization that would promote American science, art, and history at a national level. By establishing membership among scientists, historians, artists, and writers in the United States and abroad, the society became internationally recognized as worthy of respect. Through the appointment to the Board of Directors of cabinet members—the attorney general, and postmaster general—and commissioner of patents and by naming the president as its patron, members created the illusion of government sanction, producing a confident expectation of federal funding—which was to prove illusory. Internal organization, modeled after the French Institute, defined eight departments comprising specialized fields in science, history, and the arts which were represented in the group's collections, public lectures, and other scholarly projects. Founders believed, as had Barlow, that a general taste in art on the part of the public was essential for the preservation of republican principles. In an address given in 1841, Joel R. Poinsett, founding director and first president, expounded on the significance of art for the nation—and on the need for federal support. Observing that art in Europe was patronized by church and state, he asserted that "in a free country, *literature* may and will flourish by the well-directed efforts of individuals; but *the arts* require the protecting hand of Government."[11]

In spite of congressional rebuffs for funding, the federal government itself—almost unaware—was slipping into the museum business. At least two offices were deliberately collecting and exhibiting specific types of objects. The United States Patent Office throughout much of the nineteenth century required applicants for patents to submit drawings and models of their inventions; these were retained, whether or not the patent was granted, and from 1812 were exhibited as examples of native genius and technological progress. The agency's first location, a building known as Blodgett's Hotel, gained a unique notoriety as the only public structure the British did not burn in 1814—reportedly because of the significance of the displayed patent models for posterity. But alas! the precious exhibits were destined for destruction by fire on December 15, 1836, when all the models (about 7,000), drawings, and records (with the exception of one volume), were reduced to ashes. Only six months earlier, Congress had appropriated funds for construction of a new building for the Patent Office, stipulating that the design should include an exhibition hall for patent models and other government collections. As a further indication of the importance placed on inventions and their public display, Congress now supplied a grant to the commissioner of patents to have the destroyed models replaced.

At the War Department, Thomas L. McKenney, head of the Bureau of Indian Affairs, in 1817 began a collection that became a gallery of Indian portraits and relics. Most of the portrait subjects, approximately 145 in all, were painted from life by Washington artist Charles Bird King as the chieftans and delegates came to the capital to represent their people. Shown in the War Department building located next to the White House, the Indian Gallery displayed war clubs, bows and arrows, pipes, and other artifacts of Indian life along with the paintings.[12]

Government-sponsored explorations to the Far West and elsewhere produced massive quantities of nature specimens and ethnological objects. Most impressive of these adventures, an exploring and scientific expedition left in August 1838 for a four-year voyage to South America, the South Pacific, and the northwest coast of North America under the command of Captain Charles Wilkes of the U.S. Navy. Scholars of natural history on board were commissioned to collect and identify natural specimens and objects related to ethnology.[13] Great quantities of materials were sent back even before the enterprise ended, to be stored temporarily in Philadelphia until the Patent Officc Building was completed.

One other source of exhibits that would join these private and public collections in the new exhibition hall was John Varden's Washington Museum. Unlike the more assertive members of the Columbian Institute and National Institution, entrepreneur Varden made no attempt to secure federal support. He opened his museum in June 1836 after spending almost ten years in gathering materials. As the Columbian Institute had become virtually defunct by this time, he was assured of an audience for the two large exhibition rooms attached to his home on Fifth Street, where he displayed "a sharkes jaw bone, a Chinese Umbrella," coins, butterflies, coral rock, shells, Egyptian mummies, guns, plaster busts, oil paintings, engravings, and drawings.[14] Within three years the popularity and size of the collections outgrew the original rooms, encouraging the proprietor to procure a larger exhibition space in the nearby Masonic Hall. Like other small museums in the United States, Varden's was formed after the image of Charles Willson Peale's famous project; most likely he patterned the name "Washington Museum" after Peale's "Philadelphia Museum."

Realizing that he could not possibly compete with the National Institution's extensive display of nature, history, and art objects that was to open in 1840 in the Patent Office Building—an exhibition, moreover, that would be free to the public, whereas he had to charge an admission fee—Varden sold his holdings to his rival and went along as curator and jack of all trades. The National Institution had already absorbed the collections and membership of the Columbian Institute and, besides, was given charge of gatherings from the Wilkes expedition.

Incorporating items from these federal offices, government-sponsored explorations, and private organizations, the largest and most varied exhibition in the nation opened to the public in the new Patent Office Building soon after completion of the first unit in 1840, the F Street or south facade (figure 1). Created by William Parker

Elliot and Ithiel Town, with the execution and parts of the interior design carried out by Robert Mills, it was only the second government building constructed after the sack by the British in 1814 (the Treasury Building, designed by Mills, being the first). The central portico of a double row of eight Doric columns supporting an entablature and unadorned pediment was inspired by the Parthenon. Designed for showing the collections of the Patent Office and other government bureaus, the display area

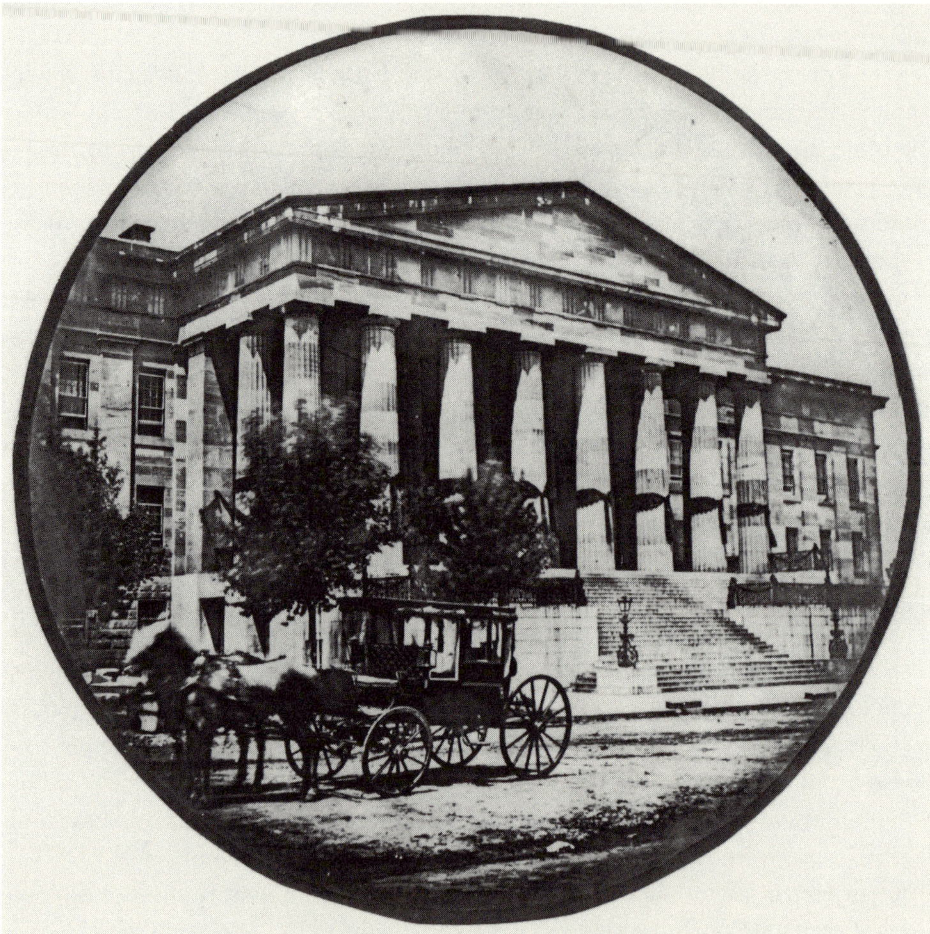

Figure 1. *Patent Office, South Facade,* 1850. Mourning bands commemorate the death of President Zachary Taylor on July 9, 1850. The Historical Society of Washington, D.C./City Museum.

on the top floor constituted a spacious hall, 243 feet long and 63 feet wide, beneath a barrel vault 40 feet from the floor, its grandeur indicating the importance Congress placed on public exhibitions (figure 2).[15]

Called by several names—the Museum of the United States Patent Office, the National Cabinet of Curiosities, the Hall of the National Institute, the National Museum, the National Gallery—this wealth of displays included such exotic items as kangaroos and Hawaiian feather garments, boomerangs, forty cases of beetles, minerals, and corals from Tahiti, fish spears from Tierra del Fuego, war weapons of Siam, Indian cradles and snowshoes, all gathered by scientists on the Wilkes voyage; models of mechanical contrivances displayed by the Patent Office; portraits of Indians commissioned by the War Department; gifts resulting from Admiral Matthew Perry's mission of 1852–54 to Japan (among later additions to the exhibits); the original Declaration of Independence (bleaching out in the sun), and other documents from the State Department. Holdings originating with private Washington organizations included marble sculptures, small statues of Ceres and Flora (the Roman goddesses of agriculture and flowers), and a head of Ceres, from the Columbian Institute; two seventeenth-century oil paintings, *The Massacre of the Innocents* and *Portrait of a Cardinal* (artists unidentified); and other paintings and prints from John Varden's Washington Museum.

Images of famous men gathered by the National Institute included the full-length portraits *Washington at Princeton* by Charles Willson Peale and *François Pierre Guillaume Guizot* by George Peter Alexander Healy. Guizot, a historian and prime minister to Louis Philippe of France, had endeared himself to Americans by spreading the fame of their first president among the French through historical accounts and translations of Washington's writings; consequently, a group of Americans in Paris had commissioned his portrait from Healy. A statue of George Washington, one of the finest works shown by Ferdinand F. A. Pettrich, a German sculptor who worked for a time in the United States, was probably a model for a proposed figure for Washington Square in Philadelphia; the larger-than-life figure was made of plaster treated to look like bronze. Pettrich and American sculptor Clark Mills together presented at least twenty-five of their portrait busts and other sculptures to the National Institute. Several catalogues of the exhibits were published, none of which, however, gave a complete list.[16]

American and foreign visitors to the "National Museum" (said to number 10,000 a year by the 1850s) had cause to wonder at the high level of expertise and power displayed by so young a nation. Objects representing vast reaches through time and

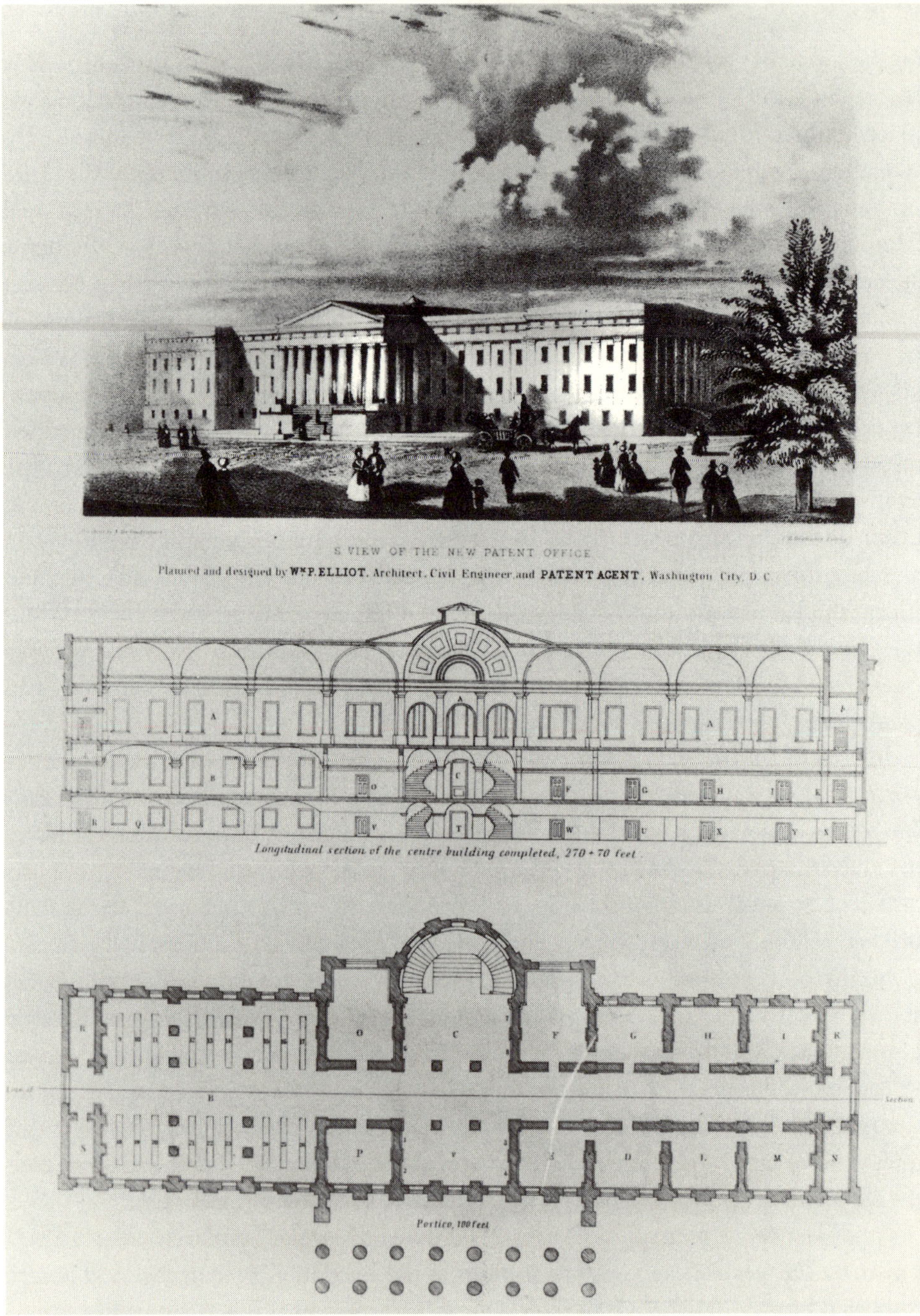

Figure 2. *Patent Office, Plan of Exhibition Hall: Elevation, Facade*. From "Pictorial History Notebook," American Art/Portrait Gallery Library, Smithsonian Institution.

space, collected and shown together, implied dominance over nature and human cultures. Displayed in a government building and composed in large part of government collections, this early national exhibit hall set an important precedent in the United States for the role of museums in projecting a national identity—and for their subsequent federal support.

Except for the patent models, the bulk of items shown were to become core collections of the Smithsonian Institution. Works of art displayed in this hall constitute the origin of the nation's first art collcction, known today as the Smithsonian American Art Museum. An exception is the Peale portrait of Washington, which, after a controversy about ownership, was afterward sent to the Capitol Building. Curiously, paintings and sculptures inherited by the Smithsonian were first exhibited together in the building that a century later would once again become their home.

Understanding Nature through Art and Science

From the perspective of the twenty-first century, the exhibition at the Patent Office with its flotsam and jetsam of art, science, and nature might seem to be a hodgepodge, but for nineteenth-century viewers in Washington, such juxtapositions created areas where they could move easily—mentally and physically—from one class of material objects to another. In galleries today we ordinarily see art within the context of art, as an isolated enterprise unrelated to nature and apart from science and human history. The nineteenth-century arrangement presented objects from all of these fields together in an essentially holistic conception of knowledge, implying a relationship among the diversity of objects on view and underscoring their mutual function as interpreters of reality and experience.

Before its professionalization and specialization, science was considered to be accessible and understandable to a literate public. Indeed, the word "scientist" did not exist before about 1834, when it was coined by British historian William Whewell as an analogue to "artist." Whewell "had no intention of fragmenting that public space upon which sharable human knowledge depends" and was committed to "an idealistic, unitary theory of knowledge and reality [that] made it impossible to conceive of any irreconcilable conflict between science and the humanities."[17]

Practioneers of both art and science perceived and described the natural world in essentially the same way. Natural objects were rendered in works of art and in scientific illustrations not with the specificities of particular specimens but as generalized forms that best represented characteristic types. British painter Joshua Reynolds wrote that an artist should regard "the invariable and general ideas of Nature [and avoid being distracted by] minute particularities and acccidental discriminations." Reynolds was the most influential authority on art in the English-speaking world until the middle of the nineteenth century. Publications of his *Discourses*, originally given as lectures at the Royal Academy in London between 1769 and 1790, were attentively read by artists in the United States. In a similar manner, descriptions and representations by scientists during this era focused on general characteristics of a natural form, rather than recording those aspects that might pertain only to an individual subject.[18]

The proximity of art and science displays at the Patent Office and other early museums reflected additional qualities shared by those vocations. Practioneers had no difficulty in developing abilities in both fields: they studied nature specimens or experimented with chemistry and mechanics, and also honed skills for creating paintings and sculptures. The careers of Charles Willson Peale and Samuel F. B. Morse exemplify this practice, which was not uncommon among their contemporaries. The character of art made these transitions manageable.

Works of art required skills and techniques that had to be learned; certain of these were also basic to the sciences, such as the study of human anatomy and the craft of drawing to depict actual objects or spatial relations. Like scientists, artists based their endeavors on ideas, knowledge, and observation. Defined primarily as produced by mental activity, a work of art derived its significance from the conception of its subject, rather than the manipulation of clay, marble, paint, and other materials. Academies of art had operated in Europe for over two centuries to promote this principle, seeking to elevate artists to the level of poets and savants—that is, those whose creations proceed from their minds—above unskilled laborers who work with their hands.[19] Ideas of morality and national glory, and knowledge about history and the natural world became a part of the education of artists and visible aspects of their creations.

Americans accepted these European concepts about art without question. From the founding of the nation, leaders believed that art could expand the mind to great ideas, to virtues, and to nationalistic aspirations, as Barlow had asserted, making it—like the sciences—essential to a democratic nation. Moreover, exposure to paintings and sculptures was widely perceived as having the power to promote morality among the general public, intensifying efforts to establish accessible collections.[20]

During the nineteenth century, nature as object and phenomenon intrigued both artist and scientist, especially in the Americas, where the overwhelming pres-

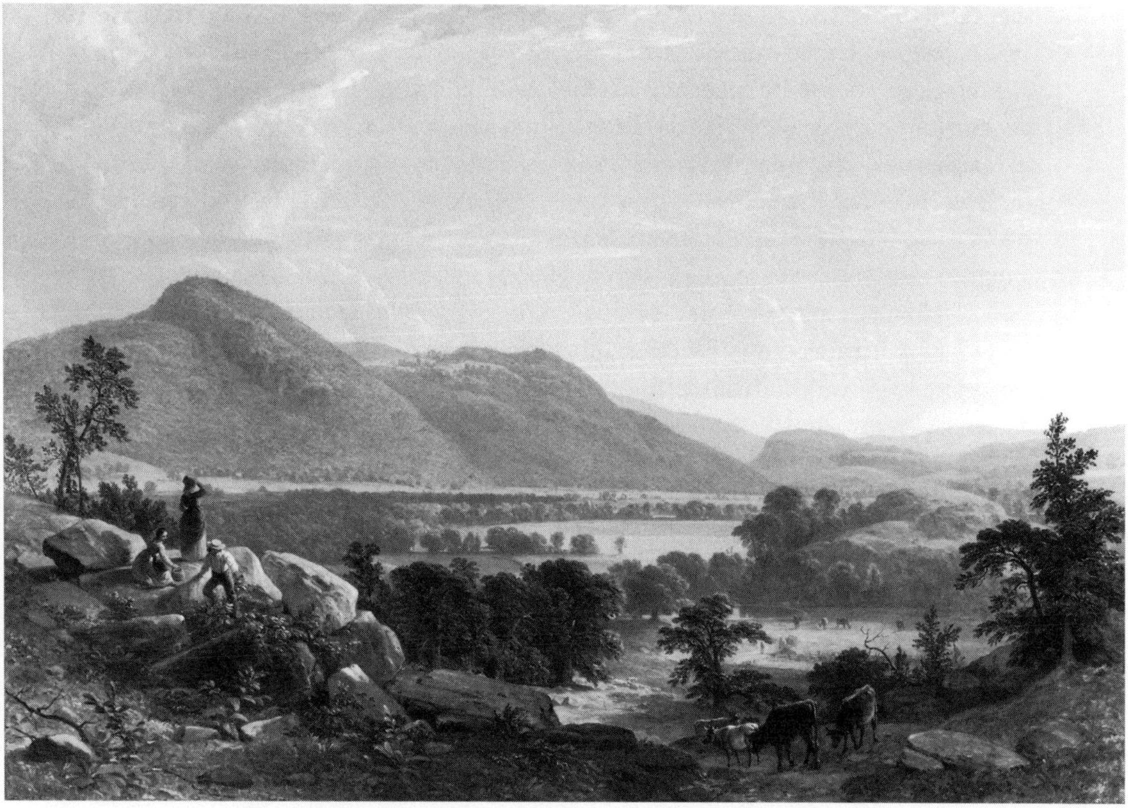

Figure 3. Asher B. Durand, *Dover Plain, Dutchess County, New York*, 1848. Smithsonian American Art Museum, Gift of Thomas M. Evans and museum purchase through the Smithsonian Institution Collections Acquisition Program.

ence of untrodden nature in the hemisphere assured its dominance in both the arts and the sciences. Studies for painters in the United States, as was true abroad, emphasized awareness and close observation of specific types of trees and other plants, geological formations, clouds, and rainbows. Asher B. Durand admonished aspiring young artists to go "directly to Nature" to observe a particular tree, "wherein it differs from those of other species, . . . the termination of its foliage, best seen when relieved on the sky, . . . the character of its trunk and branches, . . . their direction, curves and angles." A painting by the artist from the 1840s (figure 3) shows careful attention to foreground plants and rocks, silhouettes of trees, and contours of distant mountains. At the prestigious Ecole des Beaux-Arts in Paris, students of landscape painting were expected to be able to paint particular species of trees from memory.[21] Sculptor Henry Kirke Brown, returning in the 1840s from Italy to the United States, determined also to focus his study upon nature rather than on classical works of the past.

The significance of an empirical approach to the natural world reached beyond mere accuracy of description, for nature was thought to give access not only to factual data but also to moral and spiritual truths that could be disclosed by both art and science. European and American poets used forests, rivers, mountains, and the sea as metaphors for individual and national experiences. "The groves were God's first temples," wrote William Cullen Bryant in "A Forest Hymn," epitomizing a generation that was awash in sentiment about nature. Ralph Waldo Emerson's essay of 1836, *Nature*, regarded as uplifting experience an awareness of natural wonders from snowflakes to stars. Many Americans responded with almost religious reverence to the beauty and diversity of nature as revelations of a higher Truth, finding in rocks and mountains, in every flower or twig or blade of grass, manifestations of the divine Creator. "Yet another motive for referring you to the study of Nature early—its influence on the mind and heart," Durand continued in his remarks to young painters. "It is impossible to contemplate with right-minded, reverent feeling, its inexpressible beauty and grandeur . . . without arriving at the conviction . . . that the Great Designer of these glorious pictures has placed them before us as types of the Divine attributes."[22]

Theologians and clerics who promoted this creed of "natural revelation"—joined by not a few scientists—considered themselves to be empiricists who carefully observed nature to reach a deeper understanding of both the natural world and the Creator's wisdom. Facts and observations about nature served to advance both faith and science; speculation and theory were avoided as useless impediments.[23] Philosophical support for this emphasis derived from Auguste Comte, advocate of positivism, which essentially limited the pursuit of knowledge to that which is observable and measurable. Within this intellectual and spiritual framework, a prepared mind perceived objects in an exhibition gallery pertaining to art, science, and nature not as bizarre juxtapositions but as aspects of the real world in all its relations to the meaningful life of the viewer.

An Institution for the "Increase and Diffusion of Knowledge"

While visitors milled about exhibits at the Patent Office, Congress engaged in an extended debate over types of knowledge and their potential usefulness. An astounding gift had arrived in Washington in 1838, virtually out of the blue: a half-million dollars in gold from an Englishman who had never seen the nation that emerged from an upstart colony of his own country, "to found at Washington, under the name of the Smithsonian Institution, an Establishment for the increase and diffusion of knowledge among men." Inherited from Enlightenment ideology, the phrase defining the intent of James Smithson, "the increase and diffusion of knowledge," was in common use during the donor's lifetime. Washington himself, in his farewell address of 1796, had written of the need to promote "institutions for the general diffusion of knowledge."[24] Controversy over how to implement Smithson's brief and vague mandate initiated an eight-year discussion by congressmen and other interested citizens. What kinds of "knowledge" had Smithson in mind, and in what manner was the "increase and diffusion" to take place? Did the phrase "among men" refer to a worldwide constituency? Proposals ranged through establishing a library (the Library of Congress was then a modest operation), a national university (renewing a fond hope of Washington, Jefferson, and Madison), an agricultural school (there was as yet no department of agriculture), an astronomical observatory (John Quincy Adams's favorite plan), to a teacher-training school (promoted by Robert Dale Owen, representative from Indiana). Insisting that such projects would merely diffuse knowledge without increasing it, Joseph Henry, a physicist and professor at the College of New Jersey (later Princeton University), urged applying the fund to research as a means of increasing knowledge and to publications which, through international distribution, would diffuse it. This suggestion defined basic functions for the proposed institution without limiting its scope. It became the modus operandi for the Smithsonian, and Henry was appointed as the institution's first secretary, its highest administrative officer.

The importance of earlier organizational models in Washington to the formation of the Smithsonian cannot be overemphasized, particularly to the inclusion in the founding legislation of an art gallery and collections of science and natural history, for Smithson's bequest contained no such references and no details beyond the donor's generalized intent. Moreover, the influential Professor Henry opposed such enterprises. As a physicist whose discoveries and inventions made electricity practical, he had little need of collections in his own research. But a museum culture had taken root in American life; athenaeums and exhibition halls flourished in Baltimore, Boston, Charleston, Cincinnati, New York, Philadelphia, and elsewhere. And less than a mile from the Capitol the exhibition hall at the Patent Office exemplified the value of collections in the arts and sciences for national pride and progress. Besides, most of the items there belonged to the federal government, and objects still privately held by what had been the National Institution for the Promotion of Science were slated to be turned over to the government by 1862.

Ironically, the most direct shaping of the future Smithsonian Institution came from citizens who had founded an organization for the express purpose of gaining control of the Smithson bequest. The original name of their group, the National *Institution* for the Promotion of Science, was changed in 1842 to the National *Institute* in order to imply a superior status, according to their plan, for the parent organization over the Smithsonian *Institution*, whose title was determined by Smithson's will. Although members failed in their initial objective, they provided an invaluable and practical model for the Smithsonian. With a breadth of interests based on the scholarly institutions of Paris and London, the National Institute extended patronage to the sciences, technology, American history, and the arts in an organization devoted to both scholarship and collections. It was the most immediate and significant prototype for the congressional act of August 10, 1846, which founded the Smithsonian Institution. George Brown Goode, assistant secretary in the 1880s, was convinced that the Smithsonian would have taken a different form without the example of the National Institute and the persuasiveness of its president, Joel R. Poinsett, to whom was due "the plan for a national museum of science and art, with a staff of curators."[25]

Smithsonian Regent Samuel S. Cox, observing in 1862 an omission that today catches our eye, noted that Smithson's aim was "to diffuse useful knowledge among men—and women also." When Cox, a representative from Ohio, made this statement on the floor of the House, his congressional colleagues burst into laughter.[26]

Soon after the official founding of the institution, a committee of Smithsonian Regents chaired by Robert Dale Owen drafted plans for the proposed Smithsonian gallery of art. They applied the principles of "increase and diffusion" to the arts by dedicating programs and collections primarily to the careers of living artists. "It is desirable to have," they reported, "one or more studios, in which young artists might copy without interruption." In cooperation with artists' organizations in other cities, they proposed mounting exhibitions of "the best results of talent in the fine arts" during the periods when Congress is in session.[27]

Owen and his committee members recognized the implicit obligation of gallery proprietors toward the art profession, for at this time most public art collections in the Western world served an educational function for art students, who learned to draw and paint by copying works of art. An important precedent, the Louvre, when first opened to the public in the 1790s, reserved the galleries for artists to copy five days of each *décade* (a ten-day week in the French republican calendar). Throughout the nineteenth century, art museums in the United States commonly pursued artist-oriented policies. Art schools were founded as parts of major museums, and into the early twentieth century, exhibits of recent works—regional shows or events open to artists across the nation (and in some cases beyond)—were regularly held in several urban areas, events that were selected and judged by artists, not curators. Owen's planners also realized the potential value of making members of Congress aware of contemporary American art; regular exhibitions in Washington could result in congressional support for the nation's cultural life. A concern for artists was doubtless strengthed by the size and growth of the local art community, for the capital city increasingly attracted painters and sculptors who sought possibilities of commissions and portrait opportunities from government officials.[28]

Conveying Ideas through Copies and Casts

The committee's advice for acquiring a permanent collection focused on the fine arts of painting and sculpture, and on engravings as reproductive substitutes for inaccessible famous works. They also recommended the acquisition of architectural designs and models, appropriate in a city that aspired to buildings of monumental grandeur. A subsequent report emphasized the need to acquire "casts of the most celebrated articles of ancient and modern sculpture" and "models of antiquities, such as those of the remains of ancient temples, etc."[29]

Casts of sculptures, copies of paintings, and reproductive engravings were widely exhibited in public art galleries at this time—and not only in the provincial art world of the United States with its dearth of original art. In France in the 1840s, more than half of official painting commissions were for copies, and in Paris a museum of copies was proposed to serve as an educational experience for the public as well as artists. Until 1888, copies were accepted at the Paris Salons—annual exhibitions of contemporary art—with the qualification that they must be in a technique other than that of the original work.

From the standpoint of our own era, obsessed with originality and authenticity as foremost qualities in works of art, these practices may seem naive, but when an artwork was considered primarily as a conception of the artist's mind, it did not have to be a unique product of the artist's hands. In order to evoke a response, the idea behind the image was more important than the process of its creation, and the idea could be conveyed in a good copy of a painting, a reproductive engraving, or a cast of a sculpture.

Exhibiting copies and casts also gave viewers the opportunity of becoming familiar with renowned works located elsewhere, and the practice was necessary in order to present a complete chronology of the history of art—the ultimate goal for an art collection—beginning with the ancient Classical world and leading up to the present. If a sense of connection to a cultural heritage was important for Europeans, how much more so for Americans who, for all their pride in independence, had a sense of discontinuity from a nurturing past? Casts of ancient and Renaissance sculptures, and engravings and copies of famous paintings—like the Classic mode of architecture chosen for government buildings in Washington—related this nation to the highest ideals and attainments in Western history.

Smithsonian Secretary Henry and Assistant Secretary Charles Coffin Jewett (the librarian, who was also in charge of the art collection) believed that famous original works of the past could never become part of gallery holdings on their side of the Atlantic because, they reasoned, virtually all of those objects were already accounted for in European private and public collections. (Great fortunes that could pry loose such items did not yet exist in the United States.) "The formation of a gallery of the best paintings, is, in this country almost hopeless," Jewett pointed out to the Smithsonian Regents. "Engravings furnish us with translations, authentic and masterly, of the best creations of genius in painting and sculpture, the originals of which are utterly beyond our reach."[30] This conviction added incentive to obtaining copies of paintings, casts of sculptures, and reproductive as well as original engravings. In 1850 the institution made its first purchase of art, the George Perkins Marsh collection of engravings and etchings, a superb gathering of prints and art books.

Acquisition of works of art through reproductions persisted in the United States through the turn of the twentieth century. When the Fogg Museum at Harvard was being planned in 1895, Martin Brimmer and Edward W. Hooper wrote that the collections should "be limited to things of great importance, and must, of course, always largely consist of photographs, casts, and other secondary evidence as to the greatest works of art which belong to the European governments and religious houses. . . . [T]he most valuable of such original works can never come into our possession."[31]

For artists, copies and casts served a practical purpose. Whereas they could study trees and other natural specimens within the setting of nature, they learned how to compose these objects into a picture by studying works of art. Painters and sculptors of figure subjects began their careers by drawing from engravings and casts to gain a basic learning experience for studying the complexities of the human body. The idealized proportions and repertoire of poses found in sculptures from ancient Greece and Rome and the Italian Renaissance offered a first step toward developing aptitude in depicting that most difficult of subjects.

The stated mission of the new institution, the increase and diffusion of knowledge, might today be more exclusively associated with the sciences. But because art in the nineteenth century was perceived as a form of knowledge—a product of the mind and compatible with science—it appropriately related to Smithsonian goals along with scholarship and collections in the sciences.

Controversy over how the interest from Smithson's bequest of a half-million dollars (the sole support for programs of the institution) was to be apportioned had ended with a compromise stipulated in the founding legislation that divided the income into two parts "after deducting general expenses": one part to be devoted "to the formation of a museum, a library, and a gallery of art, and the other to publications, researches, and other active operations." If this directive had been carried out, the gallery of art would have consistently received an apportionment of funds and its fair share of attention from Smithsonian officials, but within a decade of the founding, in May 1854, the plan was rescinded by the Regents in response to Henry's urging. Concerned that the provision would handicap research and publications in science by spreading limited income too thin, the secretary had become involved with Jewett in a power struggle over the allocation of funds. The decision of the Regents to side with Secretary Henry resulted in the firing of Jewett and a drastic change in support for the programs of the institution as defined in the 1846 legislation by virtually eliminating from the budget the projects of a museum, library, and gallery of art.[32] This action was the first major setback for art programs in deference to the scientific side of the institution.

Chapter One

Exhibiting Art in the Smithsonian Castle

No matter what the secretary's attitude toward museum objects, the fact remained that collections already existed, for the sizable gatherings of art objects, nature specimens, and ethnological items shown in the Patent Office exhibition hall had been handed over to the care of the new institution. In the summer of 1857 workmen began moving these assorted objects of "Extraordinary Curiosity," which had informed and entertained visitors for almost twenty years, to another building, a picturesque red sandstone structure of turrets and towers that seemed to belong to another world (figure 4). While the Classic order of columns, entablature, and pediment of the Patent Office announced the clarity of process and rational purposes that inspired the mechanical inventions displayed by that agency, the Smithsonian was to develop as an entirely different sort of enterprise, without the imprint of a focused purpose. With towers that sprout from hidden corners of the roof, a facade that gives no hint of what lies beyond, and doors that open to rooms where almost an entire wall is a round window, architect James Renwick's Smithsonian Building, commonly called "the Castle," appropriately houses an organization designed by Congress with idealistic and ambiguous goals rather than definitive expectations, an institution free to grow in multiple and unforeseen directions.

The inherited collection of art numbered hundreds of paintings and prints (both originals and copies) and dozens of sculptures and casts formerly belonging to private organizations, in addition to the extensive government collections (the Smithson bequest itself had included a sculpture and a painting). This group of works—portraits and sculptured busts, engravings, European works dubiously attributed to old masters, contemporary works by American artists, original marbles and casts of sculptures—constituted in general what could be found in other American institutions in the first half of the nineteenth century. Private galleries of the antebellum era were more focused than those open to the public, according to the taste of each collector, but even the finest of these were modest affairs in comparison with the riches that would mark American collections in the next generation. Some of the important private collections of the earlier period were eventually absorbed into institutional museums, the New-York Historical Society, Yale University, and elsewhere, a practice that would continue in the United States. About the time of the Smithsonian's founding, Robert Gilmor Jr. of Baltimore, one of the most significant art collectors in the United States before 1850, had envisioned

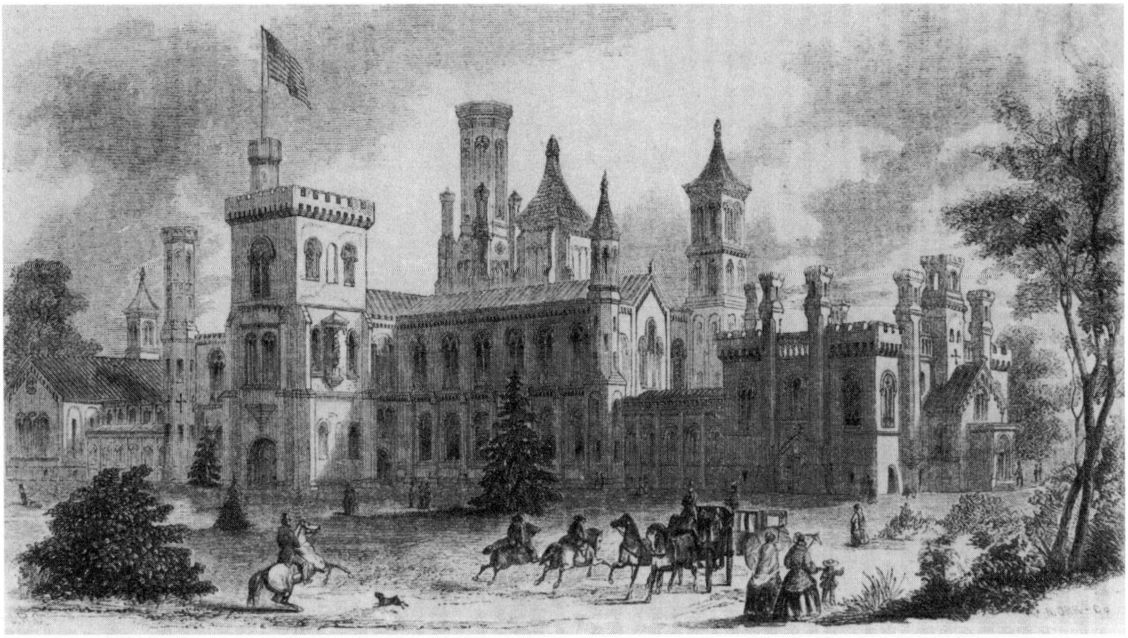

Figure 4. *Smithsonian Institution from the South-West.* From *The United States Magazine*, 1857. Merl M. Moore Collection.

his collection becoming a part of the new institution, yet his diverse holdings, spanning Classical pieces and old master paintings to contemporary works—which would have considerably strengthened the role of art at the Smithsonian—were never received.[33]

The majority of art objects transferred from the Patent Office were portraits: images of Indians and distinguished American and European men (mostly) in oil, marble, and plaster. Together these works provided visible links to the heritage of the past—to the indigenous people of the continent and to individuals who represented great accomplishments in Western history. Throughout the nineteenth century, the adulation of scientists, inventors, military officers, statesmen, musicians, and artists promoted the writing of biography and the production of portraits on canvas and in marble or bronze. The National Institute had made a practice of collecting busts and commissioning oil portraits, and the organization had served as the depository for such works presented to the nation.

Works of art were placed in several areas of the Castle Building. Prints from the Marsh collection and a group of busts occupied the library in the west wing (sometimes called the chapel because of an apselike vault at one end). Connecting this room to the central part of the building was a long, rectangular reading room, the west range or cloister. Here Healy's solemn *Guizot* presided over a gallery of Indian portraits (figure 5). Adjoining exhibition cabinets may have contained natural

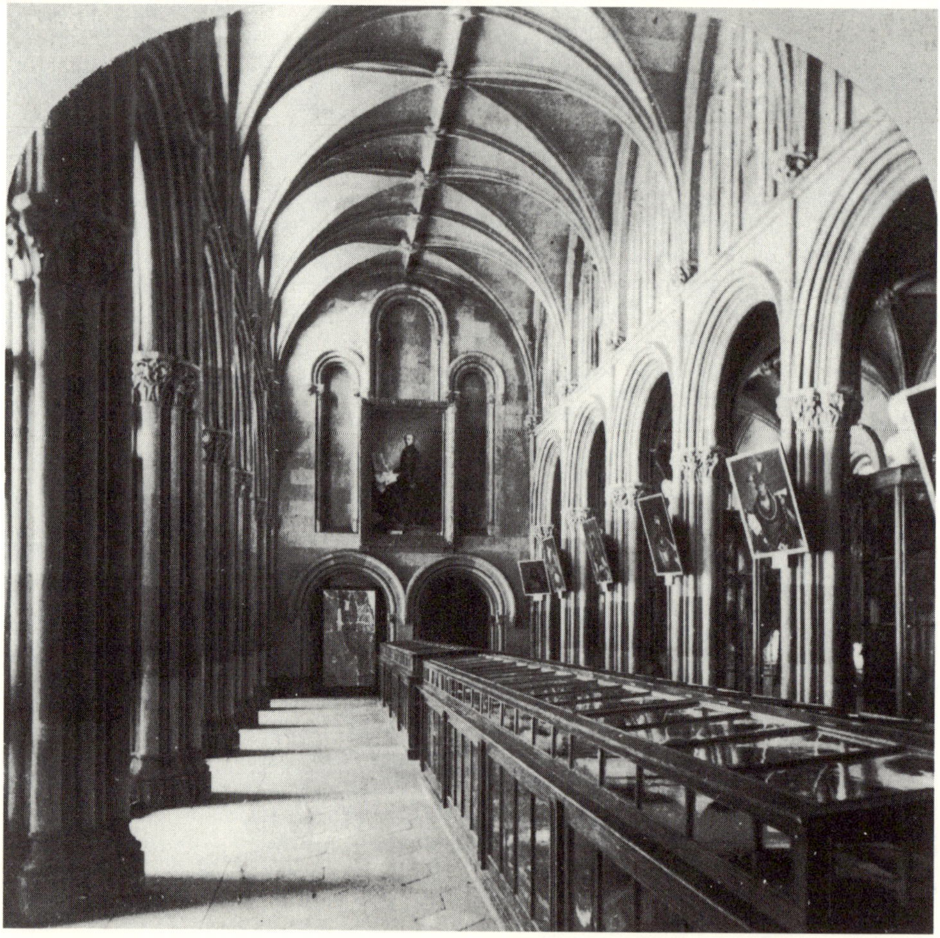

Figure 5. *West Range, Smithsonian Building*, ca. 1860. Smithsonian Institution Archives, neg. no. 60144.

history specimens or artifacts relating to the life and culture of North American natives. Several paintings from John Varden's Washington Museum and several of the Marsh prints could also be viewed here. On the other side of the hall, oil portraits hung above an array of portrait busts and casts of antique works (figure 6). Ferdinand Pettrich's sculpture of Joel Poinsett is fifth from the right among other celebrated individuals and busts of children by Pettrich and Clark Mills. At the far end of the row the head of the *Apollo Belvedere* looks reproachfully toward a canine visitor. The pair of figures at the end of the gallery are probably Pettrich's *Justice and Minerva: Wisdom Guided by Justice*.

The largest group of paintings received from the Patent Office consisted of the approximately 145 portraits of Indians by Charles Bird King from the War Department collection. Together with another large group of portraits and scenes of Indian life, 152 paintings by John Mix Stanley on loan from the artist, these works were mounted in a large upper room in the central section of the building designated as the Gallery of Art (figure 7). Hung in five tiers, almost 300 paintings of Indians surrounded display cases of Indian costumes and war implements and nature specimens; a marble sculpture, *The Dying Gladiator*, by contemporary English sculptor John Gott (on loan from a Washington collector) occupied the center of the gallery. (This work might have been *The Dying Spartacus*, shown by Gott at the Royal Academy in 1820 as a portrayal of the rebel slave falling upon a Roman he had slain.) Thus a gladiator from a distant time and place eternally expired in the midst of New World warriors—who themselves were perceived as belonging to a culture that would shortly see its own demise.

Secretary Henry viewed the Indian images as significant ethnological records, an invaluable source of knowledge about the first inhabitants of the continent. He felt strongly that Stanley's paintings, like those of King, should properly belong to the nation. "It is the most complete collection of the kind now in existence, and it would be a matter of lasting regret were the pictures sold to individuals, and thus separated," he asserted, in an unsuccessful attempt to persuade Congress to fund their purchase.[34]

By 1860 these Smithsonian exhibits of art, natural history, and ethnology were on view in the Castle, where they served as education and diversion to the thousands who swelled the population of the capital city during the war years. The Smithsonian Building, isolated in the long stretch between the truncated (incomplete) Washington monument and the Capitol, must have seemed like the entry to a world apart from the confusion and anxieties visible in other parts of the city, teeming with boisterous crowds of Union soldiers, while makeshift hospitals throughout the District tended to their wounded and dying comrades. "During the past year Washington has been visited by a greater number of strangers than ever before since the commencement of its history," Henry reported in 1861. "The Museum has consequently been continually thronged with visitors and has been a

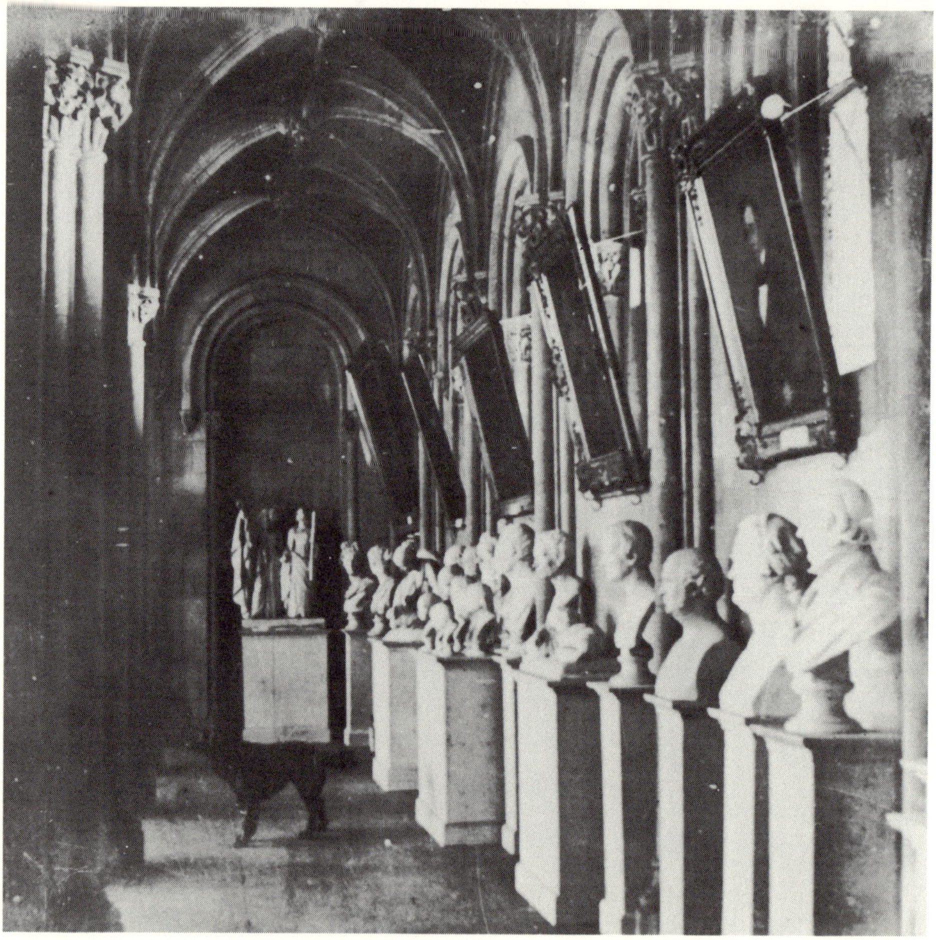

Figure 6. *West Range, North Side, Smithsonian Building*, ca. 1860. Smithsonian Institution Archives, neg. no. 18-B.

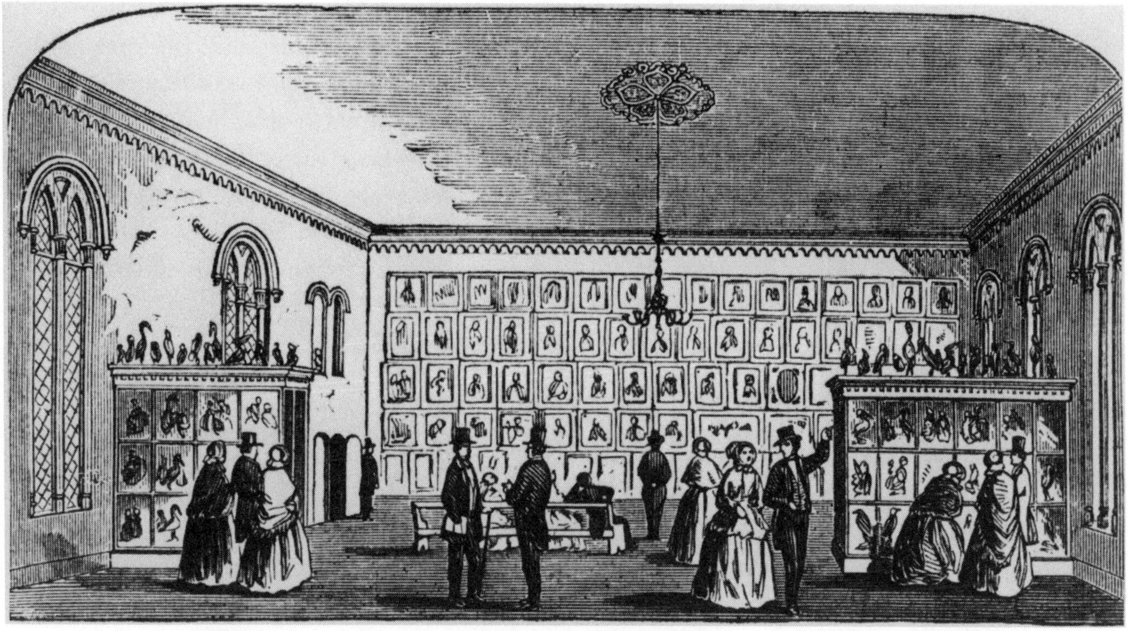

Figure 7. *The Gallery of Art, The Smithsonian Institution,* before 1865. Smithsonian Institution Archives, neg. no. 43804-D.

never-failing source of pleasure and instruction to the soldiers of the army of the United States quartered in the city or its vicinity. Encouragement has been given them to visit it as often as their duties would permit them to devote the time for this purpose."[35]

Because the institution was open only on weekdays, eliminating most government employees and other workers, the museum audience must have been composed mainly of newcomers to the city—military men and civilian consultants, businessmen and women drawn by opportunities in the expansion of hotels, restaurants, and prostitution. The faces that returned Guizot's piercing glance and peered at walls covered with images of noble savages were overwhelmingly white. A large contingent of free blacks lived in the city, but they did not enjoy freedom of circulation, and bitter controversies over the issue of slavery did not improve their situation. Though the slave trade had been abolished in the capital city in 1850, and slaves in the District emancipated in April 1862, "colored people" continued to be identified as a separate class with few privileges. Secretary Henry was criticized for giving permission (reluctantly) for the use of the Smithsonian's lecture hall for a series of talks by abolitionists Henry Ward Beecher, Horace Greeley, and Wendell Phillips, where, it was reported, the audience included colored people.[36]

Viewers of exhibits could refer to guidebooks by William J. Rhees for an account of the founding of the institution and descriptions of displays throughout the building. A tall, distinguished visitor was spotted in the galleries on March 24, 1863; President Lincoln had taken time from his frustration over Union generals and the Congress to ponder museum exhibits at the Smithsonian.[37]

Fire!

With the short-range intent of saving money, Congress had not allowed for fireproofing the central section of the Castle. At three o'clock on Tuesday afternoon, January 24, 1865, a fire broke out in the west end of that area and was quickly spread by the wind to engulf the entire upper center of the structure. When the smoke cleared, a crowd of bystanders was awed by the devastation: the top story at the building's center and three adjacent towers had been totally destroyed. This meant that the art gallery—with the paintings by King and Stanley and the marble *Gladiator*—was reduced to ashes. Another grievous loss was the destruction of personal papers and memorabilia of James Smithson, which, of course, held great sentimental value for the institution. Among destroyed objects of the Smithson bequest was a bust of Saint Cecilia by Danish sculptor Bertel Thorwaldsen.

Charles Bird King had died three years before his government-owned paintings burned, but an enormous personal loss was sustained by John Mix Stanley, who still owned his works—a sizable portion of his oeuvre. Coincidentally, Stanley had sent a letter to Henry from Detroit on January 24, 1865, noting that the Michigan legislature was considering the purchase of his Indian gallery for the state university and proposing to sell the works to the Smithsonian for $20,000, to be payable in three equal installments.

"The loss has fallen very heavily upon Mr. Stanley, the painter and owner of this collection," Secretary Henry reported to the Regents. "It was the result of the labor of many years among the Indians; it constituted the pride, as it has been the crowning effort, of his life, and he ardently desired that it might be transmitted to posterity."[38] A small group of the artist's paintings hanging elsewhere in the building did survive the flames. *Hunter's Escape* was the prescient title of two of the canvases; another was *Buffalo Hunt on the Southwestern Prairies.*

The future of art at the Smithsonian was all but consumed in the fire, for doubts were raised as to whether the institution could properly care for unique objects of intrinsic value such as those that constitute an art collection. Taking immediate action, the Regents, following Henry's proposal, authorized that the principal part of the library (which had not been touched by the flames), including the art volumes and many of the prints in the Marsh collection, be transferred for temporary safekeeping to the Library of Congress. The question of relocating the remaining works of art scattered throughout the Castle Building was also a matter of grave concern.

As early as 1859, when William Wilson Corcoran first made public his intent of founding a gallery in Washington, Henry had suggested that the Smithsonian share the responsibilities of its art gallery with Corcoran's projected museum. Two years after the fire, he proposed an actual transfer of the Smithsonian collection and again included this recommendation in his reports for 1868 and 1869.

The Corcoran Gallery, however, failed to open as expected in 1869—which was only the latest delay experienced by the Washington collector in inaugurating his art museum. The project had been abruptly put on hold after his first announcement when war clouds began to gather over the capital city. Because Corcoran was perceived as an overt sympathizer for the southern cause, his presence in Washington was not appreciated by the federal government, making Paris a more expedient place for him to wait out the war years. Meanwhile, the building designed by James Renwick for his gallery, located on Pennsylvania Avenue near the White House, was confiscated by federal officials for use as a Union Army supply depot. Government occupation continued after the end of the war, and Corcoran did not succeed in repossessing his building until 1869. Not until five years later, in January 1874, did the Corcoran Gallery open to the public, providing a potential location for the Smithsonian works of art.[39]

Among Henry's 1874 transfer of paintings, statues, and prints to the Corcoran Gallery were an antique marble head (probably the *Ceres*), eleven etchings by Rembrandt, and three portraits by George Peter Alexander Healy, including the *Guizot*, which now hung in the new surroundings of the Corcoran's Grand Salon. In 1879 another deposit was made of plaster busts, marble figure groups by Pettrich, and a model of Clark Mills's equestrian statue of Jackson. In both cases, the transfers were recorded with the qualification that the Smithsonian works of art "are not presented to the Gallery, but simply deposited, and are subject to reclamation at any time." Occasional pieces continued to be sent to the Corcoran in subsequent years.[40]

In spite of these efforts for removal of the collection, new acquisitions of art continued without interruption. There seemed to be no way to turn off the constant flow of objects from enthusiastic citizens as well as worldwide organizations and individuals, for the Smithsonian's scientific publications had brought the institution international fame. Donors of art objects responded to the breadth of interests identified with the Smithsonian and to nineteenth-century explorations and studies of world cultures. Casts newly received ranged from those of Chaldean figures in the Louvre to plaster models of American statues; Thomas Crawford's *Freedom* on the Capitol dome could now be viewed close at hand. A group of nine genre subjects in sculpture, given by the commercial enterprise of John Rogers and Son, and Joseph Mozier's marble statue *Il Pensero*, received by transfer from the Capitol, suggest other sources of new accessions. Even as action was pending on depositing artworks in the Corcoran and after the transfers had taken place, the Smithsonian acquired sculptures, casts, paintings, prints, porcelains, and china, by purchase and transfer as well as by gift or loan. Obviously, the institution had moved beyond the initial plan for a collection composed of paintings, sculptures, prints, and architectural models. Many newly acquired pieces came from the 1876 Centennial Exposition in Philadelphia.

Culminating years of effort that had begun with a proposed amendment to the bill that established the Smithsonian, more than 500 of George Catlin's paintings of Indians became part of the Institution's collections in 1879 as a gift of Mrs. Joseph Harrison Jr. of Philadelphia.[41] This particular acquisition would have pleased Henry, for he had repeatedly attempted to convince Congress to purchase the artist's Indian gallery. The paintings were accessioned as ethnological items, not as works of art, in accord with the judgment of institution officials.

Within three decades after the founding, plans for the role of art at the Smithsonian had suffered serious setbacks, withdrawal of funding, and the calamity of fire. Lacking staff and a budget to implement programs, recommendations of the Owen committee languished, and transfers of art to the Library of Congress and the Corcoran understandably caused a loss of confidence in maintaining an art gallery or museum activity in general, for Henry had also removed and transferred groups of items from other collections. But under a new secretary, Spencer Fullerton Baird, a biologist who succeeded Henry at his death in 1878, museum collections would become an acceptable and unalterable part of the institution.

A scholar of natural history, Baird was an obsessive collector. During his tenure as assistant secretary, he had filled the Castle with barrels and crates and piles of fish, birds, and pelts of mammals (occasioning an infestation of fleas). He encouraged the study of natural history throughout the nation, and instructed government expeditions to the West on the collecting of specimens. Through the acceptance of carloads of all kinds of objects from the 1876 Philadelphia Exposition, Baird irretrievably established the character of the Smithsonian as a museum with extensive display collections. This emphasis was to make the presence of an art gallery more logically a part of the institution than had seemed appropriate to Joseph Henry. But because the first secretary's guidance had won recognition for the Smithsonian as a major center for scientific research and publication, subsequent development could take place within its identification as a scholarly institution of international renown.

About 1880 in the chapel of the Castle, visitors could see casts of sculptures and architectural decorations that had been shown at the Philadelphia Centennial Exposition. Occupying the most prominent position at the center of the gallery, a full-size reproduction of *America* from John Bell's *Albert Memorial* in London symbolized the taming of the continent's original savage beasts and inhabitants under the civilizing guidance of lithe, bare-bosomed personifications. Directly in front of *America*, a baptismal font featured Renaissance sculpture and, behind it, a terra-cotta reproduction of a pulpit. Similar casts of European monumental sculptures and details of buildings formed conspicuous attractions at major art museums in the United States and European countries into the early decades of the twentieth century. Almost all these works in American museums have been destroyed or removed to storage, but at the Victoria and Albert Museum in London, visitors can still experience the bizarre wonderment of ancient, medieval, and Renaissance sculptures and architectural monuments compressed in the time and space of a single glance.

Pettrich's statue of Washington also stood forth here, and more than thirty portrait busts lined the tops of cases under the windows. Atop display cabinets at the other side of the room, pottery and porcelain pieces represented crafts of Europe, Asia, the Middle East, South America, and works by native ceramists of Arizona and New Mexico. Because of the predominance of exhibits in terra-cotta and porcelain, this wing of the Castle was sometimes referred to as Ceramic Hall. Prominently displayed above the door, a portrait of Joseph Henry by Thomas LeClear (figure 8) looked out—perhaps resignedly—upon this exhibition of arts and craft objects.

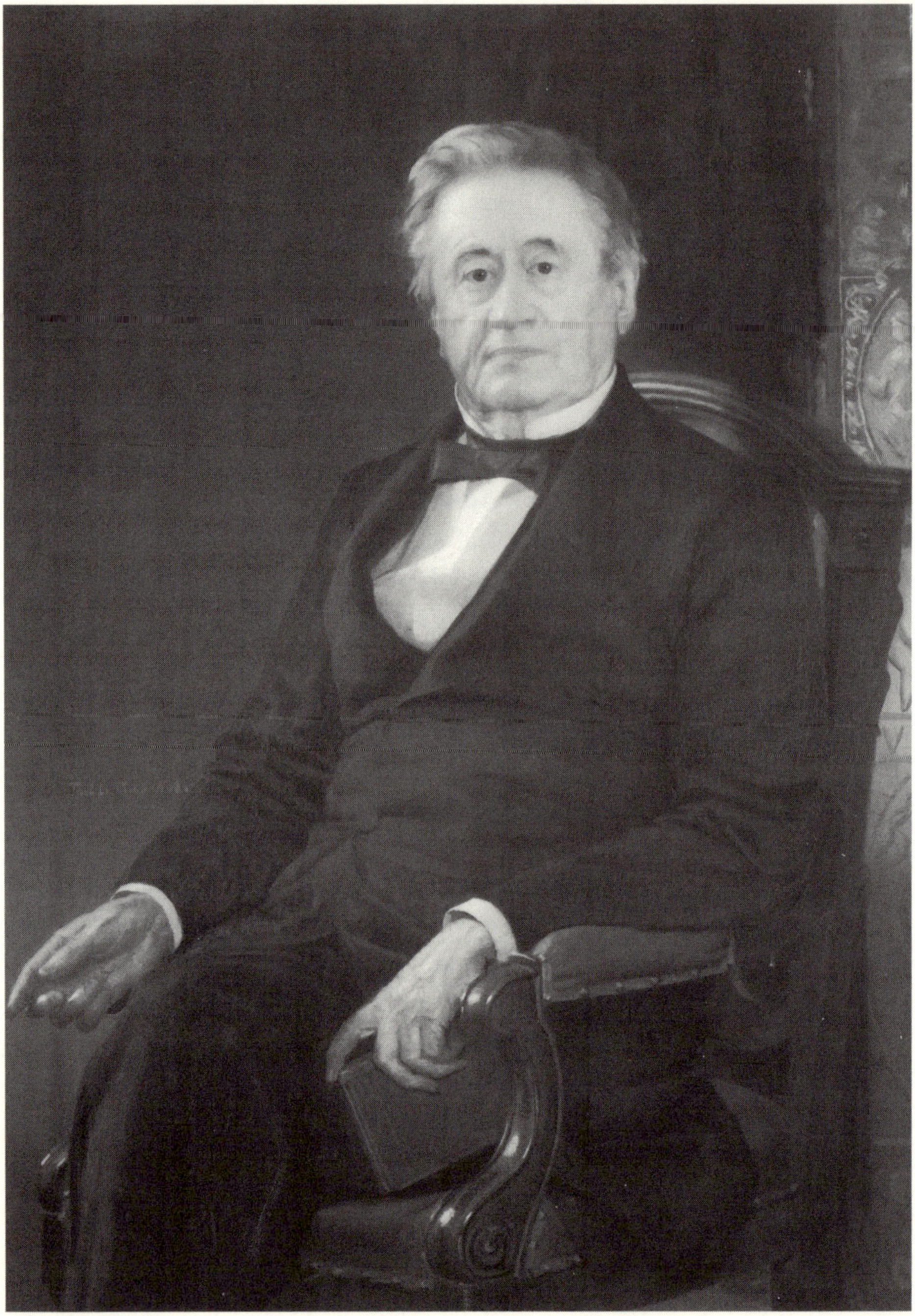

Figure 8. Thomas Le Clear, *Joseph Henry*, 1877. National Portrait Gallery, Smithsonian Institution, Transfer from the National Museum of American Art.

2
Exhibiting the Evolution of Culture

TWO MAJOR INNOVATIONS IN THEORY AND practice changed the museum experience of viewers in the late nineteenth century—and still determine our own in the twenty-first. Education became a primary aim, and objects on exhibition began to be presented systematically. A shift toward reaching a popular audience joined other nationwide movements in public education: establishing tax-supported public schools and universities in many states; opening higher education to women; and introducing new theories and reforms by American and European educators.

Officials of earlier collections had stated the intent of reaching out to lay visitors, but not until this period was that goal widely emphasized and carried out. At the Smithsonian it constituted a major departure from institutional policy, for at its founding the Regents committee on the proposed gallery of art had addressed the needs of artists, not a general public, and when the collections of nature and science at the Patent Office were transferred to the Castle Building, they were arranged primarily for the benefit of scholars in science. In addition, the secretary's ambiguous attitudes about museum displays had not favored popular education.

A significant change in the manner of mounting exhibits related to this educational trend. Curators began to organize exhibitions to convey specific meanings that could be understood by the public. Museum visitors of the previous generation had wandered through the Patent Office exhibition hall in random fashion, without any suggestion of a direction to follow or a pattern that marked the arrangement of displays. They could read explanatory labels about the individual items they saw but had to interpret for themselves relationships within the diversity of objects.

A new type of event, the great international expositions held in European capitals and cities in the United States from the 1850s through the turn of the century, served as catalysts to the development of educational museum displays. They offered visible proof of the appeal of exhibits to the public and demonstrated their potential for commercial profits and national prestige.

Making up a second factor that operated to change the organization of museum exhibitions were new theories in biological science. Darwin's publication of *The Origin of Species* in 1859 produced a great upheaval in the field of biology with aftershocks felt in every area of thought and activity. Scientific focus on nature shifted from nature as object to nature as process, continually in flux and manifesting the interdependence of all life—in which humankind itself was an inextricable part. Although biological research continued to center on actual specimens, emphasis now turned to theories about their relationship to one another and to their environment. These principles affected the organization of many museum accessions and exhibits but nowhere so visibly as at the Smithsonian, where collections and exhibitions were in the hands of a scientist.

Impact of the International Expositions

Initiated by the 1851 Crystal Palace Exposition in London and the Exposition Universelle of 1855 in Paris, these enormous and wildly popular international fairs attracted visitors from all over the world. In the United States the 1876 Centennial Exposition in Philadelphia and the 1893 World's Columbian Exposition in Chicago highlighted a series that took place in cities throughout the country. Kings and queens, presidents, farmers, fishermen, scientists, artists, laborers, homemakers, children, servants—all professions and classes—poured through entrance gates to marvel at the latest wonders of science and technology, shown together with agricultural products, ethnology exhibits, handicrafts, manufactured goods, and the fine arts. The gathering together of many different kinds of things spurred the founding of new museums and swelled the holdings of others, for great quantities of the thousands of items exhibited became incorporated into the collections of permanent institutions. Tons of objects from the Philadelphia centennial celebration were afterward shipped to the Smithsonian.

These extravaganzas were designed to promote commerce and trade while enhancing the prestige of participating nations. Exhibitors vied for attention amid throngs of competitive displays, each with a vested interest in presenting products in a clearly descriptive, attractive format that could appeal to the diversity of visitors. Educational and aesthetic display modes developed for the expositions impressed museum professionals who participated in the events. Smithsonian curators mounted instructive materials pertaining to science, technology, and art, the latter consisting of original paintings and prints from the collection and autotypes of famous works by European masters. (Characterized by delicate nuances of light and shadow, autotypes are prints produced by a carbon process from photographic negatives.)

In spite of competition among participants, the mingling of people from every nation in the West and beyond in a peaceful and useful enterprise engendered a sense of international harmony, put into song for the 1855 Paris event:

Chantons, célébrons l'industrie,
Chantons, célébrons les beaux-arts!
N'ayons qu' une mème patrie
Sans frontiérs et sans remparts![1]

(We sing, we celebrate industry, / We sing, we celebrate the fine arts! / We would have but one country / Without borders and without ramparts!) Such idealistic praise for a world without national boundaries could well serve as an anthem for the World Trade Organization in the twenty-first century—with a crucial difference. Today no one would think of putting the fine arts on a level of importance with industry, for art in our own time in many ways is deemed superfluous to useful productivity. But in the nineteenth century the arts were coupled with industry and science as essential to progress in a modern nation, and up to the middle of the century the arts were understood to be leading the way. A turnabout in this position had apparently taken place by the late 1860s. Whereas at the 1851 Crystal Palace Exhibition it was taken for granted that creative initiatives came first in the arts with science following in a natural sequence, at the Paris Exposition of 1867 the impressive exhibits of technology were attributed to innovations of science, now perceived as the primary agent of advancement in industry.[2]

Responsible for spatial arrangements of a plethora of many different kinds of things, the Royal Commission for the Crystal Palace event settled on four main divisions: raw materials, machinery, manufacturers, and fine art—categories that would be adopted by subsequent exposition managers. An emphasis on materials and processes used in production suggested qualities that were to distinguish late-century art and museum exhibitions.

Reflecting on the London displays, German architect Gottfried Semper in 1852 observed the significance of this emphasis: "The basic form, as the simplest expression of the idea, is modified by the *materials* that are used in developing the form as well as by the *tools* that fashion it" (the emphasis is his). Viewing ethnology exhibits that presented native artifacts and the inhabitants themselves from European colonies in the Pacific and Africa, and natives and crafts from the Americas, Semper perceived illustrations of the concept of cultural evolution (which preceded the theory of biological evolution). "What rich material for its understanding, comparison, and reflection was offered in the London exhibition by the works already noted by people still living in the earlier stages of cultural development," he observed, in reference to the belief that culture progresses in evolutionary steps from simple to complex.[3] The international exhibitions appeared to confirm the validity of this interpretation through contrasts of simple tools and methods of production in preliterate societies with the sophistication and complexities of Western art and machinery.

A direct descendant of the 1851 Great Exhibition at the Crystal Palace in London, the South Kensington Museum (today known as the Victoria and Albert) was established in 1857 as a demonstration of connections between the fine arts and manufactured goods. Two lofty goals inspired the founding: the improvement of national products—to enable the British to compete successfully in the international market—and the elevation of public taste. To attain those ends, the museum's emphatic mission was education. Exhibits presented the materials, tools, and techniques used in a particular sort of fine art or manufacturing—such as etching or ceramics, for example—and illustrated, step by step, how an end product is formed.[4] Originating with objects from the 1851 Great Exhibition, the collection continued to expand with casts, textiles, ceramics, porcelains, prints, and original paintings and sculptures, among other items, all intended to serve as resources for designers and manufacturers and as educational experiences for the public.

South Kensington made a tremendous impact upon the museum world and inspired the founding of museums of applied or industrial art throughout western and central Europe. Collections of these specialized institutions consisted of furniture, porcelains, enamels, glassware, silver utensils, and other objects that combine the art of design with techniques of manufacturing. Displays illustrated the several processes necessary to create an object. Strictly speaking, this was not a new kind of museum.

Some fifty years earlier, in 1799 in Paris, the newly founded Conservatoire des Arts et Métiers included in its collection graphic and textile arts, tools of mechanical trades, and scientific instruments. It was the sort of museum first proposed by Descartes.

A purposeful relationship of the fine arts with mechanical processes developed as products made by machines for a mass market began to replace those made by the centuries-old methods of individual craftsmen who created for an elite clientele. South Kensington and its lineage intended to address a major problem of this momentous change: "aesthetic deterioration." Through collections and exhibits they meant to promote good design in the applied arts and, in the role of educators, teach consumers how to recognize the better products.[5] Nostalgia over the demise of craftsmanship encouraged an interest in works of the past, causing such objects as fine handcrafted furniture, porcelains, enamels, and textiles to be sought after and collected by the new museums.

Aesthetic decay was hardly the worst problem brought on by the new economic order in industrial nations. Unemployment and grossly underpaid workers who labored under dreadful conditions resulted in widespread poverty and crime, made graphically familiar to us in nineteenth-century British novels. Certain idealistic schemes for reform involved the arts as a major factor. John Ruskin lent his persuasive prose to the cause, extolling medieval society as an exemplary model for its integration of artists and craftspersons into the community as useful and respected members, in contrast to modern life with its spirit-crushing industrial employment that deprived workers of involvement or pride in their products. A dedicated reformer, William Morris in an 1884 lecture to the Traders' Guild of Learning declared, "I do not want art for a few, any more than education for a few, or freedom for a few," thus putting art in a democratic society on a level with other basic needs.[6] Morris passionately believed that objects of beauty in everyday life—ideally produced by handicraft methods—provided a means to physical and spiritual development, that the very form of common household furnishings and the spatial relations of living conditions affected mental and physical well-being—and probably morals as well, thus making good design imperative.

Though the theories of Ruskin and Morris rang true to the social and economic problems caused by the new order of production, their impracticality could not lead to solutions; however, they did add to a renewed enthusiasm for handicrafts. William Morris's own designs for wallpaper, furniture, and other articles mark the applied or industrial arts of the era, while creative new approaches to ceramics, furniture design, and textiles fostered by arts and crafts organizations in Europe and on the American continents produced wares for middle-class consumers, objects that were to become prized museum possessions.

In the United States fewer specialized museums of industrial art were established than abroad. More commonly, collections of applied or decorative art became departments within art museums, as was the case at the great institutions founded in the 1870s in New York, Boston, Philadelphia, and Chicago. In common with the European institutions, however, a relationship of art collections to manufactured objects was a concern. The charter of the Metropolitan Museum of Art, for example, noted among its purposes "encouraging and developing the study of the fine arts, and the appreciation of arts to manufactures and practical life, of advancing the general knowledge of kindred subjects, and to that end, of furnishing popular instruction and recreation." At the Newark Museum, John Cotton Dana, who became director at the museum's founding in 1909, argued for relating fine art collections and exhibitions to industrial products, citing European museums as models. Several organizations in Chicago promoted the idea and practice of good design applied to industrial products. One of the most active, the Association of Arts and Industries, subsidized the School of the Art Institute of Chicago for this purpose. At the Smithsonian, collections of ceramics and glass and other machine-produced objects expanded with acquisitions from the nation's developing industries. Items acquired from manufacturing companies and placed on exhibition, however, often represented expensive merchandise designed for a limited clientele, rather than the greater part of commercial consumer goods, intended for the mass of ordinary buyers.[7]

"The Most Comprehensive and Instructive Museum in the World"

The opening of a new Smithsonian building in 1881, the National Museum Building designed by Adolph Cluss, later called the Arts and Industries Building (figure 9) coincided with the appointment of George Brown Goode (figure 10) as assistant director of the National Museum.[8] (Baird as secretary carried the title of director.) The building and the man were to play key roles in transforming Smithsonian collections into educational public exhibits. Carloads of items received from the 1876 centennial necessitated this second Smithsonian structure, which spread over more than 100,000 square feet, its spacious halls visibly embodying the new preoccupation with exhibitions.

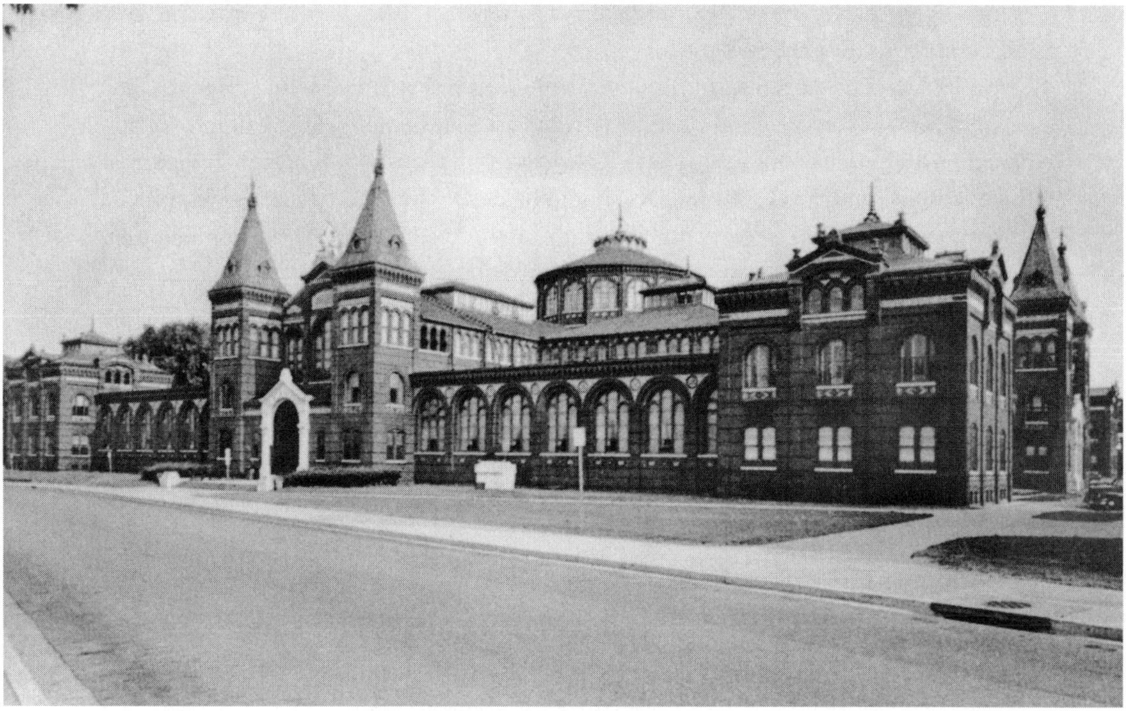

Figure 9. *The National Museum Building (Arts and Industries)*, Smithsonian Institution. Smithsonian Institution Archives, neg. no. 44606-a.

An ichthyologist who began at the institution as a curator in zoology, Goode encompassed much wider interests than his own field. Through visits and correspondence he studied every aspect of museums in Europe and, as a result of his writings and his work at the Smithsonian, became one of the most influential museum professionals of his time and is still quoted in studies of museum theory. One of his major contributions to the Smithsonian was to reconcile opposing views of the purposes of collections and exhibitions: whether they should primarily serve the needs of specialists—scientists, artists, and connoisseurs—or instead focus on the education of the general public.

Certain museums abroad had earlier weighed the respective benefits of the two approaches; in Berlin the debate entered into plans for the 1822–30 architectural design of the Altes Museum. As a scholar, Goode was committed to the Smithsonian emphasis on professional research and study, insisting that "no museum can grow and be respected which does not each year give additional proofs of its claims to be considered a center of learning," but he also believed that "the public museum is, first of all, for the benefit of the public." As a practical administrator, he did not ignore the reality of a museum experience: "Colors of walls, cases, and labels must be restful and quiet, and comfortable seats should be everywhere accessible, for the task of the museum visitor is a weary one at best."[9] Museum audiences of our own time can testify to the disregard by major museums of his latter point.

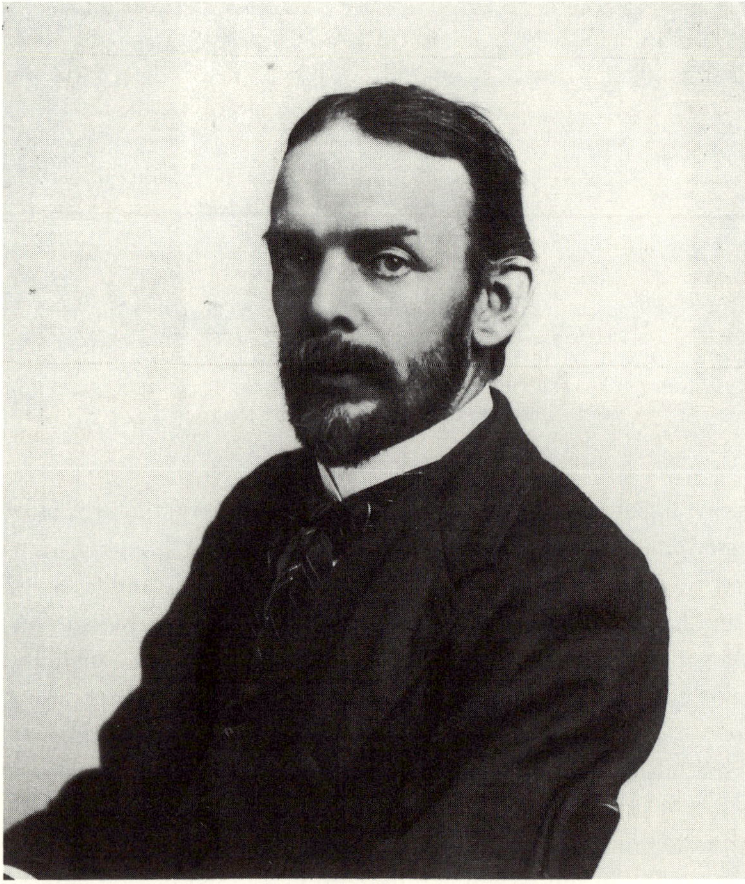

Figure 10. *George Brown Goode*. Smithsonian Institution Archives, neg. no. 11776.

Goode matured in the era of the great worldwide expositions. He much admired the program at South Kensington, assessing the British museum system of presenting science and art with an educational approach as a worthy model for the United States to follow. His conclusion after studying it and other European institutions, however, reveals his own higher ambitions for the National Museum in Washington:

> The museum is yet to be organized which shall show, arranged according to one consistent plan, the resources of the earth and the results of human activity in every direction. This has not yet been done, even for a single country.
>
> There can be little question that the National Museum of the United States can be made, in the course of a few years, the most comprehensive and instructive museum in the world. . . . [E]xamples of every kind of object known to man may be acquired, and . . . this museum may be able, by means of a thorough classification . . . to illustrate the history of human culture better than has ever before been done.[10]

Biology, the dominant science of the nineteenth century and Goode's own field, supplied the concepts to implement key phrases in his proposal, "one consistent plan" and "a thorough classification." Within an overall system the biological sciences designate a particular place for each specimen in nature, a position that reveals its developmental history and its relation to other kinds of specimens. By imposing this basic type of plan on objects in a museum, Goode expected to arrive similarly at a structure of meaning that would derive from the organization of the exhibition itself. The enormous breadth of his vision—to utilize "every kind of object known to man"—indicates his absolute confidence in these principles.

Turning his attention first to organizing the collections, Goode placed art under Anthropology, one of five major divisions of the museum along with Zoology, Botany, Geology, and Exploration and Experiment. Works of art were subdivided into three departments of the Anthropology Division: Art and Industry (graphic arts, modern pottery, porcelain, bronzes); Races of Men (objects pertaining to ethnology, such as portraits of Indians and native American pottery and other crafts); and Antiquities (glass, ceramics, casts, sculptures, and other pieces representing the ancient world). Each of the three departments also included other items besides the artworks.

Art in proximity to anthropology within the administration of the collections and the arrangement of exhibitions in the galleries was to continue at the Smithsonian for the next half-century, promoting a decided tendency toward conservative art. Anthropology, a new field of science that emerged in the second half of the nineteenth century, comprised two major specialties: physical anthropology, which includes human paleontology, the study of human development through millennia; and cultural anthropology, subdivided into archeology and ethnology, or research into the past and living cultures of humankind. Studies in both fields fit into a pattern of evolutionary development. The physical history of human beings was viewed as proceeding from such brutish forms as Neanderthals to the refinements of mental and physical development in modern humans; similarly, cultural objects were seen as progressing through centuries from the simple and crude to the complex material productions of industrialized Western societies.

Anthropological studies gave credence to the theory of cultural evolution, affecting the organization of museum art collections at the Smithsonian and elsewhere. Objects from preliterate and other non-Western cultures (at times including some Asian art) were categorized under ethnology as artifacts, worthy of study and interest chiefly as they provided insights into the beliefs and customs of premodern or exotic peoples, rather than as works of art with potential for the intellectual and emotional responses engendered by images of the European tradition. Administrative organization of the collections was reflected in the way they were exhibited.

In Goode's galleries the significance of his classification scheme was clarified by explanatory labels, essential to his concern for public education: "The objects should be so carefully classified that their relations to each other may be recognized by the visitor, so that, taken together, they suggest certain general conclusions, . . . [and this classification] aided by certain general or collective labels which relate to and describe groups of objects in a manner similar to that in which the individual labels describe separate articles."[11] Designed to become "the most comprehensive and instructive museum in the world," Goode's National Museum was based on a highly structured presentation with each individual object and each group of objects assigned to its proper place, as are flora and fauna in biological nomenclature. By observing items within one classification placed in proximity to related gatherings of larger and more inclusive categories, viewers were meant to understand the significance of how individual objects and particular groups of objects related to other objects and groups within the all-encompassing museum.

Goode's ambitious plan of exhibiting "every object in existence" would be compromised where necessary by the use of pictures, photos, or diagrams. Placing faith in the correctness of the system itself, he concluded that "the chief requisite to success in the development of a great museum is a perfect plan of organization and a philosophical system of classification."[12] These efforts at universal comprehensiveness presented the essential relationship of all things as revealed to modern eyes by scientific truth, which for many had replaced the literal biblical truth revered by an earlier generation. Significantly, there was still a belief in the existence of absolute truth, as Goode's fervor and commitment to his principles illustrates.

Emphasis upon an educational function changed the way Smithsonian holdings were collected and utilized. Previously, objects had been acquired for use in research and for the purpose of record. Now another factor was added: items were accessed specifically for display, with the aim of serving public education.

The idea of separating museum specimens into one part for scholars and another for the public originated in the early 1860s with Louis Agassiz, a Swiss American zoologist and geologist. Developed particularly for museums of natural history, the practice was applied to art collections as well, in both Europe and the United States. At the Kaiser Friedrich Museum in Berlin, opened in 1904, the study collection—which was not intended for public display—consisted of paintings judged to be of lesser value than those by acknowledged masters. These works were made available to serve the "scientific aim" (in the vocabulary of the time) of enlightening specialists such as connoisseurs and collectors. Wilhelm von Bode, director of the museum and an influential figure in the museum world of his time, further drew upon concepts from the biological sciences by classifying and exhibiting artworks according to an adaptation of the law of evolution, arranging them not acording to genres of paintings, sculptures, and so on but according to chronology and geography, as a biologist might arrange specimens of nature. Indeed, this manner of organization borrowed from natural history had preceded Darwinian theory. By the late eighteenth century, collections in Europe, promoted by professional connoisseurs such as Jean-Baptiste-Pierre Lebrun, followed the classification schemes of Swedish botanist Carolus Linnaeus and French naturalist Georges Louis Leclerc de Buffon.

An article of 1906 describes the practice of separating art collections into two parts, one for the benefit of scholars and the other for the public, as "the Boston idea of museum policy" involving "the novel idea that an art museum should serve, not the student but the general public."[13] At the Smithsonian the practice of dividing collections into categories of research, record, and public display would persist, affecting accessions of art into the 1960s. Contemporary art museums that display works within study areas available to interested visitors include the National Gallery in London, which places its entire collection on view with works of lesser importance on the lower floor. In the United States the practice has become more common in recent years, for example, at the Metropolitan Museum in New York, where objects of the American collection not on exhibit in the main halls can be viewed in a special study gallery, and at SAAM, where some three thousand artworks are displayed at the Luce Foundation Center.

Goode considered the museum collections as analogues of biological relationships where interdependence emerges as the significant determinant of individual parts. He believed that the proper organization of parts constituting a whole revealed the function of each individual item and its relationship to others, just as the taxonomic classifications of forms of life denote similarities in members of a species, the relationship of species within a genus, a genus within a family, and so on, along with a mutual dependence upon the ecological setting. "I can remember the delight which it gave him to consider a classification in which the activities of mankind were divided into genera and species subject to the laws of natural history, of evolution, and geographic surroundings," reported one of his curators. "The development of the Department of Arts and Industries has been the result of these early studies."[14]

Goode's plan for "the most comprehensive museum in the world," perfected to a point in theory that could never be embodied in practice, took form in the Arts and Industries Building (figures 11 and 12). We can assume that as far as possible, everything in his exhibition halls was consciously placed with a purpose in mind. At the Patent Office displays the public had been able to wander from one exhibit case to another, seeing different kinds of objects in random sequence; in Goode's museum, the experience of visitors was orchestrated.

The cast of Thomas Crawford's *Freedom* stood in the rotunda, serving as a visual and metaphoric linchpin that connected all other parts. She faced the most important hall in the museum, to which visitors walked directly from the main entrance—the hall of the "History of the United States," the most progressive nation in the world. It contained portraits and statues of great leaders and scientists, models of sailing ships, ceramic wares, and other items denoting American achievement and expertise. Commemorative vases created for the centennial celebration were here, one titled *1776—The Struggle*, the other, *1876—Prosperity*.

The "Hall of Technology," at *Freedom*'s right hand, exhibited essential attributes of modern progress. Units in adjacent galleries, "Water Transportation" and

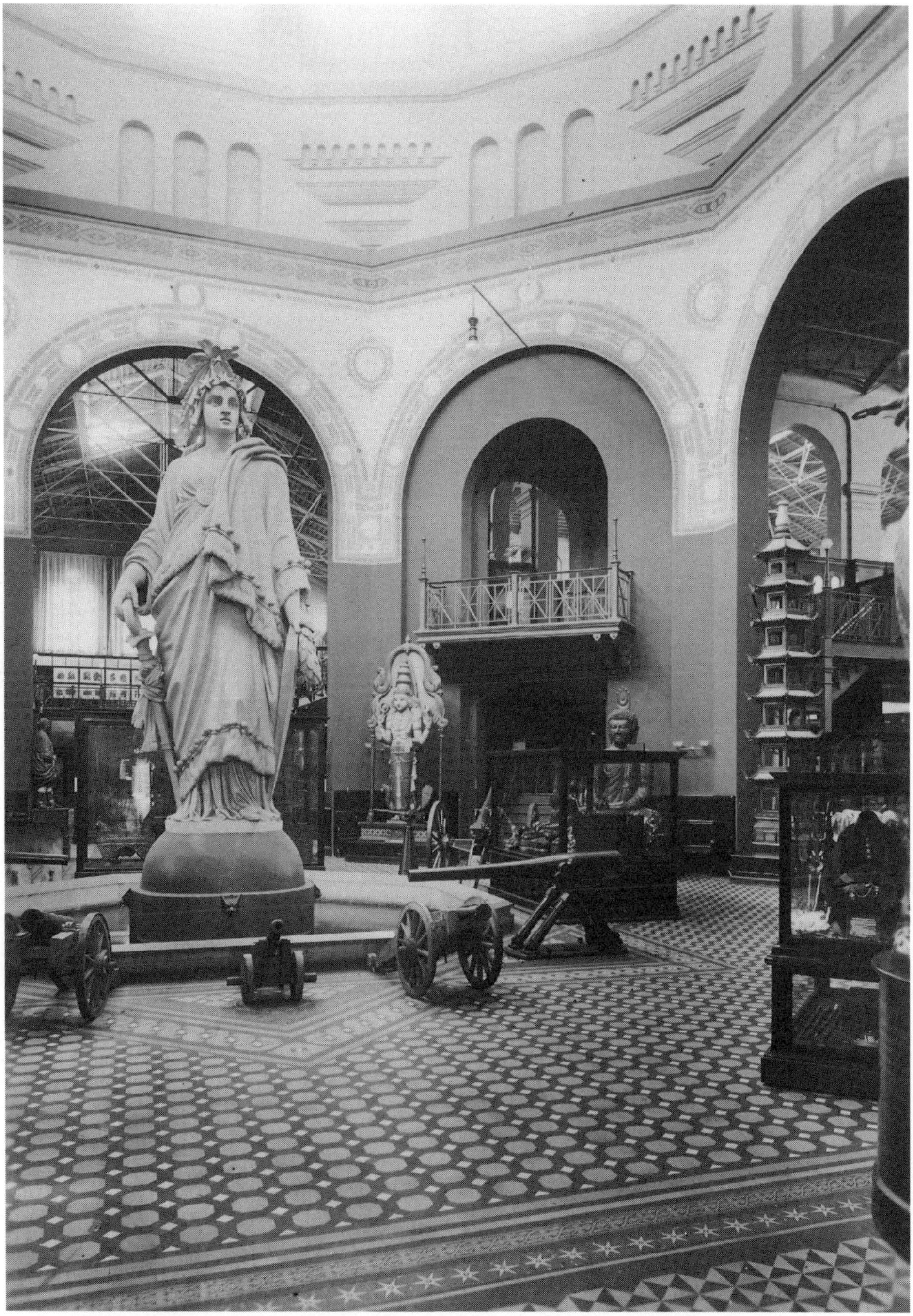

Figure 11. *Rotunda of the National Museum Building*, with Thomas Crawford's *Freedom*. Smithsonian Institution Archives, neg. no. 16852.

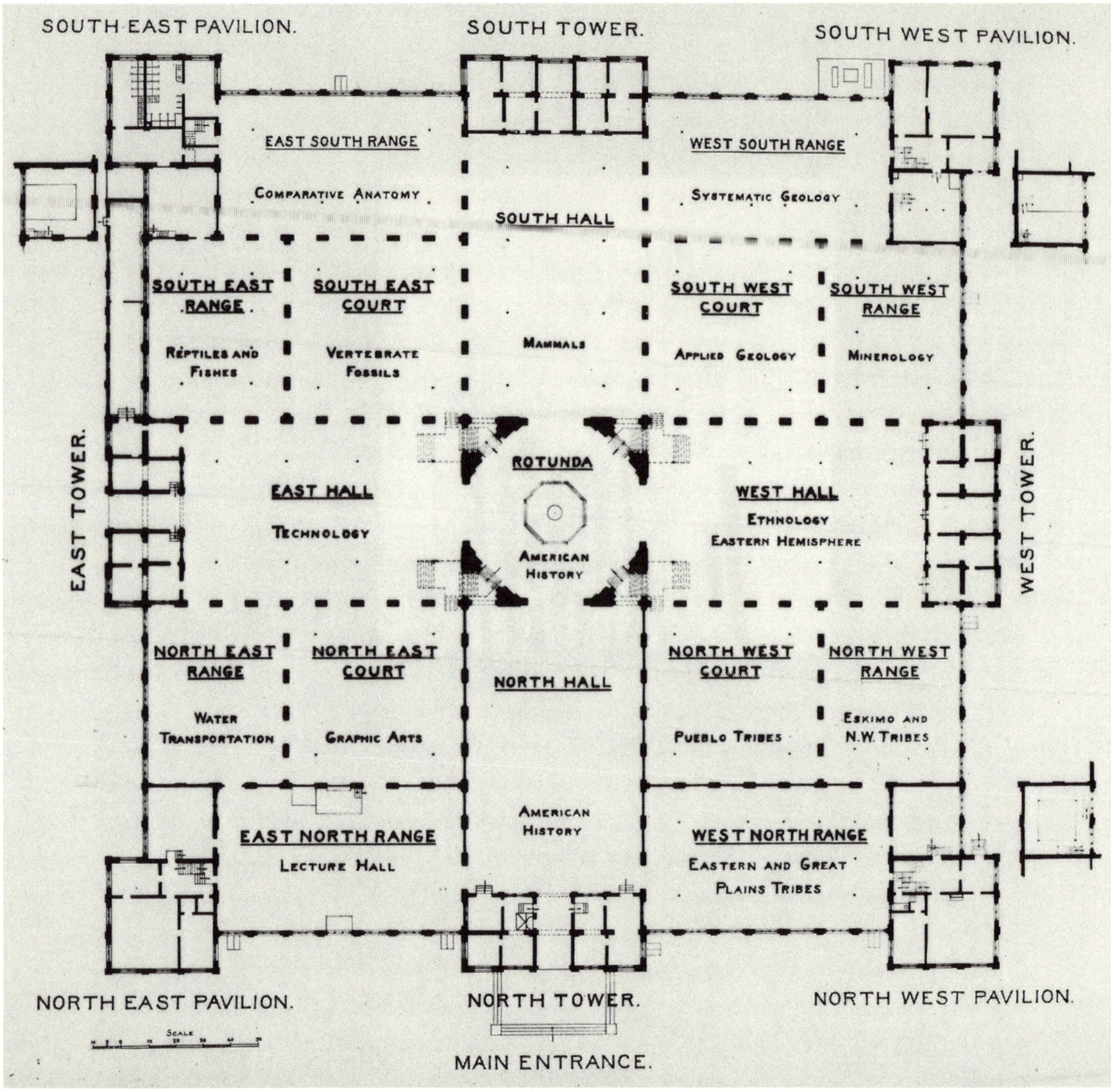

Figure 12. *Plan of the National Museum.* Smithsonian Institution Archives, neg. no. 16181.

"Graphic Arts," related to the Technology display with exhibits that followed an evolutionary pattern, from earlier and relatively simple objects to complex modern products.

The hall to *Freedom*'s left was "Asian Ethnology," at a distance apart from the progressive potential of technological displays. It opened into ethnology exhibits pertaining to natives of the American hemisphere.

Behind *Freedom* the "Hall of Mammals" reconstituted the long history of physical development in the animal world, which chronologically began in adjacent galleries of "Reptiles and Fishes" and "Vertebrate Fossils" and culminated in casts of sculptures of human figures and busts from the ancient classical world. Thus past and distant human history and culture were related to the evolutionary schema of the natural world, culminating in the present day and place. The furthermost hall of the east south range presented an instructive display of "Comparative Anatomy" in the entire gallery, and on the other side, "Systematic Geology" related to the neighboring exhibits of "Applied Geology" and "Minerology."

The underlying reason for exhibits throughout the museum was the education of the general public. Did visitors grasp the significance of the objects on view and their relationship to each other according to the master plan? Verbal assistance through labels, which Goode stressed, must have been helpful. "It is a *Museum of Record*, . . . a *Museum of Research*, . . . an *Educational Museum* of the broadest type, by reason of its policy of illustrating by specimens every kind of natural object and every manifestation of human thought and activity, by displaying descriptive labels adapted to the popular mind," an 1891 visitor's guidebook asserted.[15]

The only measure of viewers' interest comes from attendance figures, which suggest enthusiastic response for a city that was not a major metropolis. During the year ending June 30, 1891, visitors numbered more than 280,000, averaging over 5,000 per week. A clamor for Sunday hours is more convincing than statistics that the National Museum appealed to a diverse audience, including working-class Washington residents. "Hundreds of persons were fooled by a published notice that the Smithsonian Institute [*sic*] was to be opened on Sundays," the *Evening Star* reported as early as 1874. "Yesterday afternoon the rush was very great in that direction." From 1884 to 1897 four petitions placed before Congress requested that the museum be open on Sundays and at least two or three evenings during the week. These proposals were always referred to committees, but no action was taken until 1911, when for the first time the Smithsonian opened on weekends.[16]

Chapter Two

Art as Process and the Artist as Laborer

The location of the Graphic Arts section next to Technology accorded with the organizational principle that determined how works of etching and other prints were shown. Following several years of discussion and correspondence, Goode and Sylvester Rosa Koehler, curator of graphic arts from 1886 to 1900, decided to use the technical aspect of printmaking as the basis for accessions to the collection and its presentation to the public—after the example of industrial art museums. Koehler tried to illustrate as comprehensively as possible the history, tools, and processes of several methods of making prints, ranging from simple gouges to printing presses. Labels explained a pattern of evolutionary development from origins in primitive block printing to the latest nineteenth-century technology. As at South Kensington, installations featured woodblocks, engraving and etching plates, burins, gravers, and other cutting tools, with examples of various types and stages of prints.

Curator of the print department at the Museum of Fine Arts in Boston, author of a book on printmaking, editor of a periodical about American art, and a printmaker himself, Koehler was not unappreciative of prints as works of art. Nor did he lack connoisseurship: the Smithsonian collection contained superb engravings and etchings by celebrated artists. What the German-born Koehler did not accept was the concept of "fine arts," which raises painting and sculpture to the top of a hierarchy above prints and drawings and the applied arts. "The aim of the section of graphic arts is to represent *art as an industry*," he explained, adding that he did not refer to the application of art to industry but rather to the fact that "art productions of all kinds, from the great frescoes of the most distinguished painters to the slightest illustration produced by the latest photo-mechanical process, are here to be considered, primarily, from their material, that is to say, their technical side."

Koehler thus reversed the defining character of art as a mental activity, held in the early decades of the century, to emphasize instead its manual production through the manipulation of materials. "The expression of ideas by artistic means—is not considered directly in the scheme of the section of graphic arts," he pointed out as he assigned to the artist the role of laborer, of a skilled technician who got his or her hands dirty working with paint or ink or clay like a common laborer in a modern industrial nation.[17] He was critical of "ordinary museums of art" because they dealt only with "results"—the finished works—and ignored the materials and processes used to attain those ends. Contrasting his own curatorial approach he wrote:

> Art thus takes its place in the scheme of the Museum, side by side, and on terms of equality, with the other great industries, —agriculture, the fisheries, mining, transportation, etc.—and the artist is recognized, not merely as an ornamental appendage, whose useless labors may be ignored with impunity, but as a valuable member in the social organization of mankind, whose creations answer to a human want, and whose material necessities it is quite as important to understand and minister to as those of the farmer, the wool-grower, the fisher, the engineer, the weaver, and so on. This view of the matter does not in the least degrade art, as those are apt to think who approach it exclusively from the aesthetic side. It simply recognizes the fact that art stands upon a material basis, in common with all other branches of human activity.[18]

According to the projected plan, decorative arts and painting and sculpture (to be displayed with the help of photographs) would eventually be presented in this way also, although because of budget constraints, that was not yet possible. Moreover, major works of painting and sculpture from the collection remained on temporary deposit at the Corcoran.

Designation of the artist as a laborer who plays an integral role within the social structure related to the great mainstream of nineteenth-century economic theory. With an emphasis on material qualities of human life and the interdependence of all factors in society, Marxist philosophy elevated the means of production and the role of laborers above other aspects of a culture.[19] Taken down from an elevated pedestal shared with poets and savants and judged as "an ornamental appendage" who performed "useless labor" (in Koehler's words), the artist actually advanced in status as "a valuable member in the social organization of mankind." In a sense, this conception fulfilled Ruskin's ideal of the artist's essential place within the community, and William Morris's vision of art as an expression of joy in labor. Contemporaneous arts and crafts movements in Britain and the United States also promoted the image of the artist as a creative person engaged in working materials by hand, a process and vocation seen as ultimately redounding to the benefit of a materialistic industrial society.

Emphasis upon the artist's involvement with materials and processes was consistent with the most advanced art practice of the time. Koehler was an enthusiastic promoter of the "Etching Revival" currently in full force among American artists. Along with engravings, etchings by contemporary artists had served mainly a reproductive purpose in George P. Marsh's day, but beginning in the 1850s and

1860s in London and Paris, original designs and experimentation in etching techniques (earlier revived by Francisco Goya, one of the most creative etchers since Rembrandt) began to captivate artists and collectors, replacing the customary use of printmaking primarily as a reproductive means. By the late 1870s the momentum had spread to the United States. In contrast with engraving, which requires the artist to incise a metal plate by pushing a burin, creating an etching is akin to the ease of drawing and painting. An engraving must be carefully planned, for cutting into a metal surface requires precision and leaves little margin for improvisation. Ink spread into gouged-out areas prepares the plate for printing. In etching techniques the design is eaten away in an acid bath. An acid-resistant material can be painted onto a metal plate, or lines and shapes can be drawn into a resistant resin ground spread over the entire surface. Techniques are versatile and changes are easily made. The finished print is more autographic than an engraving, conveying to the viewer a sense of the artist's hand at work more immediately than an awareness of the artist's mind. With potential for personal touch and spontaneity, etchings could also capture a sense of transitory time, a primary interest of many artists of this later generation who no longer wished to record unchanging ideas and values—as was more commonly the case earlier in the century when engraving was the printmaking method of choice.

Technical processes that leave a record of the artist's hand at work also distinguish the painting and sculpture of the era. Whereas many painters earlier in the century concealed their labor by applying paint on canvas so smoothly as to belie the touch of a brush, obvious individual strokes of pigment are a hallmark of paintings in the late-century decades, creating images that cannot be reproduced in an engraving. John Henry Twachtman's *Hemlock Pool*, painted in the 1890s (figure 13), embodies this quality. In common with most landscape painters of his generation, Twachtman implies a human scale and presence in nature in his depiction of an area that could easily be traversed, in contrast with the vastness of Durand's scene from the 1840s (figure 3). The earlier artist shows tiny figures overwhelmed by a great expanse of space and monumental forms of nature, diminishing the human beings as they look out to that which is infinitely greater than themselves. Carefully delineated rocks, trees, and figures stand forth as distinct from each other with the suggestion of immutability in this pre-Darwinian age, when nature seemed to embody the changless perfection of the Creator's plan. Twachtman's sketchy brushwork alludes rather to the constant flux of nature where, at the pool's edge, shapes are

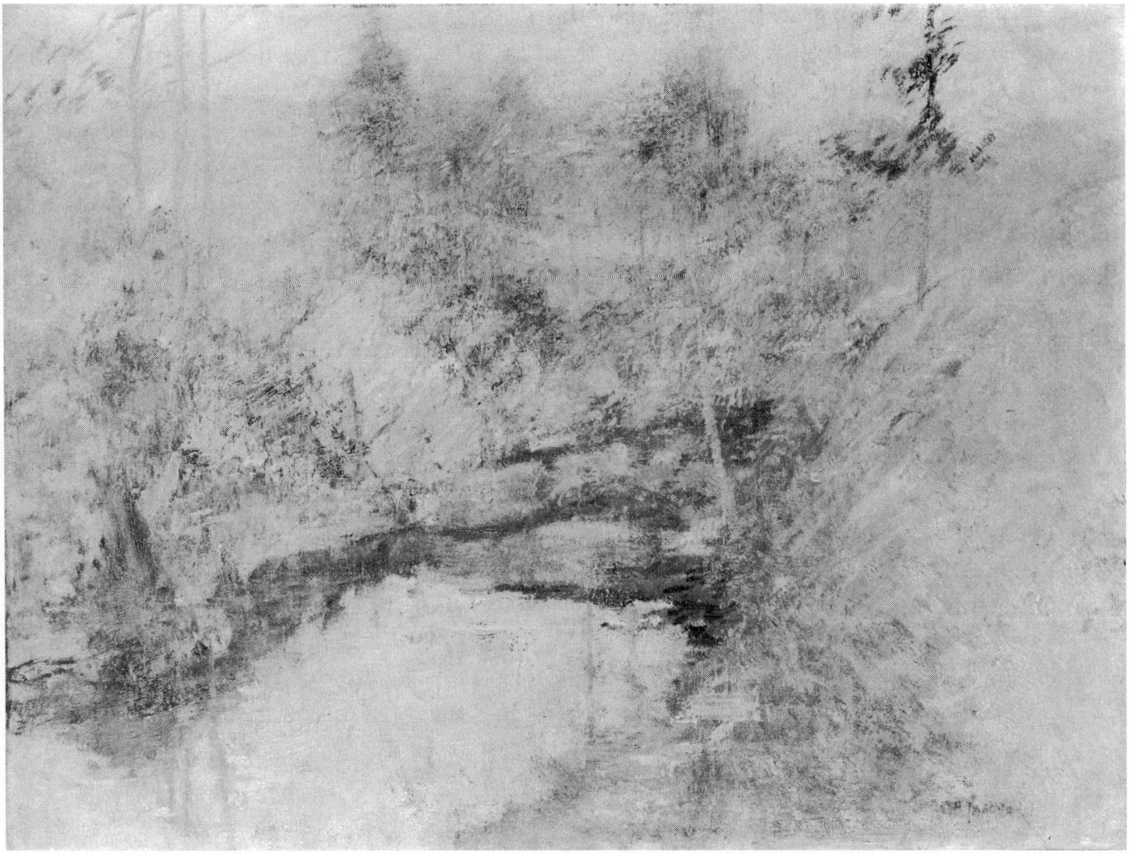

Figure 13. John Henry Twachtman, *Hemlock Pool*, ca. 1890–1900. Smithsonian American Art Museum, Gift of John Gellatly.

constantly hidden and revealed, as unpredictable as human existence. Trees and grass are clearly identifiable as strokes of paint laid on by the artist's hand.

From the 1870s, sculptors similarly took more of a hands-on approach. Marble was supplanted by bronze as the favored material. Originating as malleable clay, the final cast in bronze sometimes reveals a touch as personal as the fingerprints of the sculptor. The previous generation had preferred impersonal, smooth, tool-finished surfaces of marble, with much of the actual work carried out by professional stone carvers rather than the sculptors themselves.

Basic changes in concepts of art and technical methods of the artist contributed toward a change in taste that eventually transformed exhibition halls. Originality and the authenticity of a work, assurance that it came from the artist's own hand, became a major determinant of aesthetic and monetary value, causing the removal of casts of sculpture and other reproductive works to storage or trash bins. Museum art collections thus became more dependent upon wealthy patrons because of the greater expense involved in acquiring original art.[20]

As a scientist, particularly as a biologist, Goode had the capacity and the imagination to conceive of the spheres of nature and human achievements within an organic whole as a totality of culture. But his museum, like the man himself, was destined to be short-lived. After his death at forty-five in 1897, the National Museum at the Smithsonian was reorganized to reflect a more pluralistic approach to objects representing natural and human products. Increasing specialization and new directions in science eroded faith in biological categories as the "one consistent plan" of interpreting nature and human experience. In addition, the practical necessity of dealing with ever expanding collections in all fields was to lead the Smithsonian away from the ideal of a single museum encompassing a related array of cultural objects and nature specimens toward a group of specialized institutions—as was true also of the collections at South Kensington.

Within the fields of art history and art museums, however, certain of these earlier concepts remained viable. Though major art institutions in the United States in the late nineteenth and early twentieth centuries presented fine art in an exclusive role as an end in itself, gallery practices drew upon theories from the field of natural history. Chronology and geography supplied organizational principles of mounting works in the galleries, continuing the example of the Kaiser Friedrich Museum. Label and catalogue texts moved toward stressing the relationship of works to one another and to their social or historical context. The history of modern art borrowed from prototypes in biology by placing individual works of art within stylistic groups according to linear evolutionary patterns that identified their predecessors, forming the basis of an ever expanding body of verbal theory and interpretation.

In the 1880s and 1890s, prints were shown in the Arts and Industries Building and in the Castle acccording to Koehler's principles of process and technique—which to the present day continue as the operative method for accessions and exhibitions in the Smithsonian's Division of Graphic Arts. Shortly after the turn of the century, a display of graphic arts in the chapel of the Castle was presided over by George Washington in his most imperial mode (figure 14). Horatio Greenough's marble sculpture had required removal of a wall to place it in the building after its transfer from the Capitol in 1908. When technology collections were moved in the 1950s to the new Museum of History and Technology (today called the Museum of American History), the Division of Graphic Arts would go there also, along with the monumental enthroned figure of our first president—this time put in place before the building was completed.

The most enduring legacy of late nineteenth-century museum theory was its emphasis upon education of the public. Both Goode and Koehler, like curators at South Kensington and elsewhere, fervently believed that the collections and the expertise of curators should be shared with visitors as well as with scholarly researchers, and to that end they assembled exhibitions in a systematic manner and produced explanatory label texts. The Smithsonian at that point in its history also illustrates the authority exercised by the museum's director and curator in making judgments about the collections and their presentation to the public. Limitations were imposed by inadequate funding, but within those strictures they were able to remain committed to their philosophical principles.

Proposals for National Art Programs

A fervor for public education in art inspired unprecedented efforts to form official links between the nation's art and the federal government, with the Smithsonian as the connecting link. In March 1884 a bill was introduced in the Senate by Wilkinson Call, a Democrat from Florida, to establish an art commission that would be associated with the Smithsonian. That proposal having come to naught, Senator Call tried again in December 1885, introducing a bill to create "in the Smithsonian Institution a Bureau called the Bureau of the Fine Arts, the management of which is intrusted to the Secretary of the Smithsonian Institution." This ambitious proposal aimed to promote "the development of the fine arts in the several States and Territories of the United States," and it called for the reproduction and distribution "of casts of statuary and other objects used in giving instruction in art" and "plans for the construction of buildings and the adaptation of rooms suitable for use as art schools, with printed plans for the organization of various grades of art." The proposed bureau was to hold annual exhibitions in the District of Columbia and

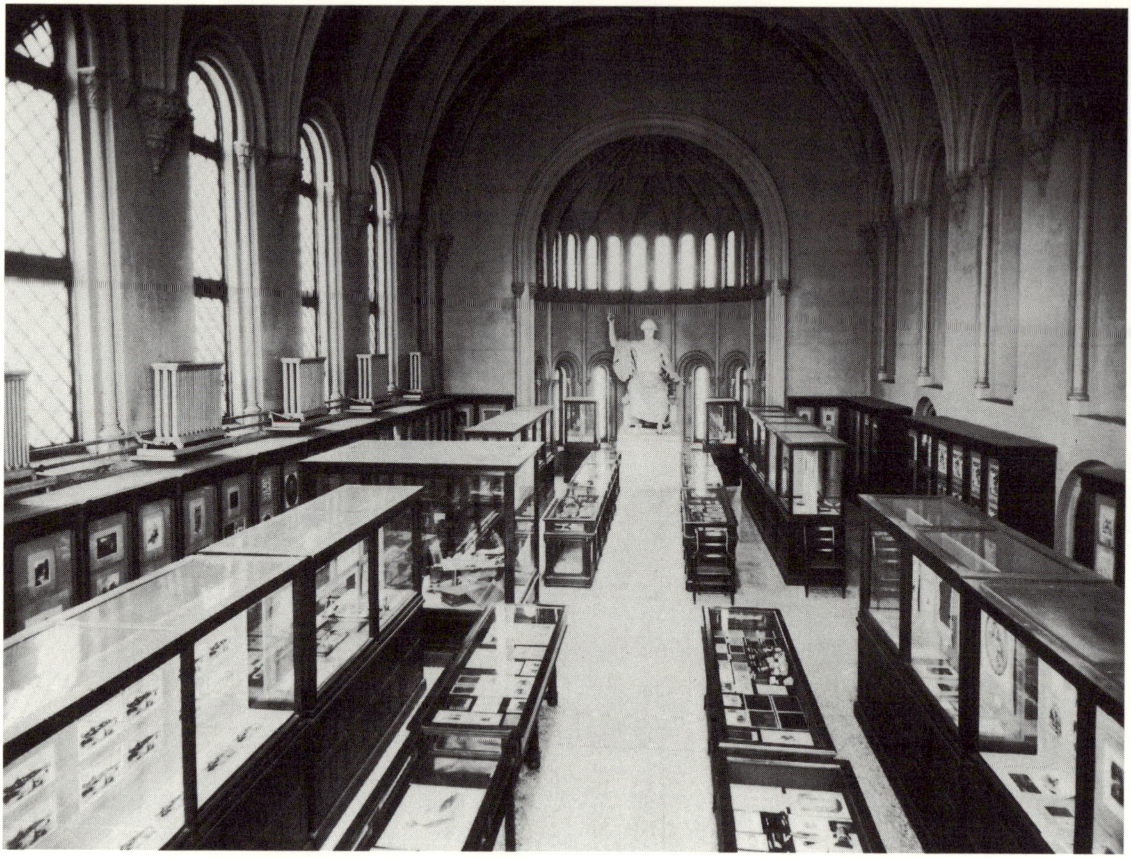

Figure 14. *Graphic Arts Exhibition*, with Horatio Greenough's *George Washington*. Smithsonian Institution Archives, neg. no. 23758.

issue publications on "new discoveries, inventions, and methods of instruction . . . together with a report on the progress of the fine arts in the United States." Like the senator's first effort, this bill never emerged from committee. Several years later, in January 1888, George F. Hoar, a Republican senator from Massachusetts and a Smithsonian regent, proposed a similar bill with the aim of establishing a National Art Commission—again, with no results. The indefatigable Senator Call tried again in December 1889 with an almost identical version of the December 1885 attempt. Still no luck.[21]

In a bizarre scheme to establish a national cultural institution in Washington, Franklin Webster Smith, a Boston architect, proposed to Congress in 1891 the construction of eight full-size replicas of monumental buildings in ancient architectural styles to serve as "the National Galleries of History and Art," aptly subtitled "the Aggrandizement of Washington." Specifying a location on both sides of a special avenue leading from the Capitol to the Potomac River, Smith envisioned these structures as culminating in a "Parthenonic temple to contain a Hall of the Presidents of the United States, an American Walhalla."[22] Planned to extend over sixty acres, his project would appear to be the ultimate boondoggle, but respected architects Paul J. Pelz and Henry Ives Cobb lent their names and advice to the project, while newspapers throughout the country issued glowing reports. Perhaps it was almost impossible not to admire such a grandiose celebration of the United States as the final and most glorious product of the ages. The Smithsonian may be especially fortunate that the "National Galleries of History and Art" were *not* funded by Congress, for if that had happened, envision the transfer papers coming through from the Capitol.

Recalling the earlier plan of Corcoran and other Washingtonians to found a national gallery and academy of art, a group of amateurs and artists banded together in 1892 to establish by congressional act the National Academy of Art, with the intent of forming collections and organizing exhibitions. The kind of academy contemplated was not a school of design but, rather, an umbrella organization under which other institutions could gather. This group, which would take a major role in organizing the American Federation of Arts in 1909, may have been part of the impetus behind the National Loan Exhibition of the National Art Association, presented in the Castle in May 1892. With organizational committees in New York, Boston, Chicago, and Philadelphia as well as Washington, the event was a successful attempt to present a truly national exhibition in the nation's capital. Some one hundred paintings by as many artists represented virtually all the well-known painters of that generation, living or recently deceased, traditional or modern, trained abroad or at home. Arranged alphabetically, the catalogue listed names from Thomas Anschutz to Worthington Whittredge, each exhibitor represented by one work.[23]

These efforts by members of Congress and private individuals indicate a growing awareness of Washington as an appropriate stimulus and center for art—especially for works by the nation's own artists. With the appointment of a new Smithsonian secretary, the stage was set to make the role of art at the institution in the first decade of the new century more nationally viable.

3

Defining Art for the Nation in Two National Galleries

In Washington the title "the National Gallery of Art" was legally conferred upon two collections: the Smithsonian's in 1906, and Andrew W. Mellon's in 1937. Founded a generation apart through very different circumstances, the two institutions evoked contrasting expectations of their potential roles in the nation's cultural life.

When the Smithsonian's art collection received this title, officials and interested citizens believed without question that a national gallery should properly focus on the nation's art. At this time American artists stood at the peak of their recognition at home and abroad. Throughout the previous three decades they had gained renown at exhibitions in Paris and Munich—winning praise and prizes—in competition with the most famous artists of the Western world.[1] Reports of these events regularly appeared in newspapers and popular magazines in the United States, engendering national interest and pride in the achievements of John Singer Sargent, James McNeil Whistler, William Merritt Chase, Mary Cassatt, Augustus Saint-Gaudens, Paul Wayland Bartlett, and a host of others. Important public works—murals and monumental sculptures, in progress or recently completed in Washington and across the country in state capitals and libraries—celebrated national values. The Smithsonian's newly named National Gallery of Art was initiated with an advisory board that consisted entirely of artists, and a solititous federal government in the person of President Theodore Roosevelt enthusiastically promoted the nation's own art.

Inaugurated with a private collection that consisted of Renaissance masterworks, the Mellon National Gallery of Art assembled a board of trustees composed of lawyers and businessmen. The largesse of Andrew Mellon in providing for a building that was to house a premier collection of mostly European works stirred tremendous gratitude from a nation in the depths of economic straits—and another kind of national pride: that the cultural life of the United States would at last be on a par with that of European nations. Although by the late 1930s major galleries in other cities already held impressive works of European and world art, they did not possess the distinctions of the Mellon project—location in Washington, funding by the federal government—or the title of the National Gallery of Art.

The Importance of a Name

At the beginning of the twentieth century the art gallery at the Smithsonian was still in limbo. Established as part of an institution dedicated to all kinds of knowledge, through efforts of Secretary Henry in the 1850s it lost the regular funding that had been stipulated in the founding legislation. In 1865 a disastrous fire destroyed the gallery room and more than three hundred paintings. Many of the remaining paintings, sculptures, casts, and prints remained at the Corcoran Gallery and the Library of Congress, where they had been temporarily deposited. Although the graphic arts collection developed under a knowledgeable curator, a lack of funds and space prohibited systematic acquisitions and other programs. Nevertheless, the Smithsonian Institution itself had been created as the result of an entirely unforseen event—and that is exactly what was to happen for the art collection.

Administratively, a new day dawned in 1887 with the appointment of Samuel Pierpont Langley as secretary of the Smithsonian. An astronomer who is remembered as an inventor of flying machines, Langley took an informed interest in the fine arts and frequented museums abroad; his papers report visits to art galleries and architectural monuments in Athens, Constantinople, Berlin, Dresden, London, Rome, Venice, and elsewhere in Europe. His sister, Anna W. Ciocca, lived in Rome.[2] In an effort to give visibility to art at the Smithsonian, he designated in 1900 a former office in the Castle as "the Art Room." A bas-relief reproduction of the Parthenon frieze and autotypes of famous paintings provided an appropriate setting for the study of prints and art books. The frieze probably came from the original Corcoran Gallery, received by the Smithsonian when the building was purchased by the federal government.

Langley felt that the Smithsonian "should act for the nation in the matter of Art" and accordingly proposed the retrieval of works deposited outside the institution after the fire.[3] In his request to the Regents to bring back the transferred objects, Langley referred to the 1846 founding mandate: "The scientific side of the Institution's activities has been in the past so much greater than its aesthetic that it is well to recall the undoubted fact that it was intended by Congress to be a curator of the national art, and that this function has never been forgotten, though often in abeyance."[4]

Redemption efforts proved to be frustrating, however. At the Library of Congress the Marsh collection of etchings and engravings had been incorporated into the library's own prints, making it impossible to identify many of the Smithsonian holdings. At the Corcoran a search of the storage area revealed that some of the sculptures and casts had been broken or completely destroyed; others could not be found.[5] From both institutions fewer works were returned than had been deposited. Disappointing indeed; however, Langley's resolve had turned Smithsonian attention toward the arts and served as an important point in the court trial that was to bestow the significant title upon the art collection.

On June 8, 1906, Smithsonian administrators found themselves in the Supreme Court of the District of Columbia, confirming the institution's responsibility for works of art owned by the nation. The purpose of this deliberation was to determine the proper recipient for an art collection bequeathed by a Washington resident, Harriet Lane Johnston. Much more was at stake, however, than the potential acquisition of Mrs. Johnston's collection: the important question to be decided was whether the Smithsonian's art collection qualified as the legally constituted "national gallery of art," the title of the beneficiary stated in the bequest. In support of their assertion that it did, officials were required to account for institutional art holdings and exhibitions in the past and to reflect on their vision of an art gallery for the future.

Older Washingtonians could recall the young Harriet Lane as a vivacious First Lady during the antebellum social scene that marked the presidency of her uncle, James Buchanan. Her close ties to Washington's social and political life may have inspired the specific phrase in her bequest that occasioned the 1906 gathering in court. Proceedings centered on a codicil Mrs. Johnston had added to her will in April of 1902, the year before her death, bequeathing her paintings, sculptures, and historic memorabilia to the Corcoran Gallery of Art—with the proviso that the entire collection be given over to "the national gallery of art" in the event that the federal government should establish such an institution in Washington.[6] The bequest also required the Corcoran to build a special annex for the Johnston works.

Not surprisingly, trustees of the Corcoran refused the gift. According to the terms of the will, the objects were then to be sold and the proceeds given to the residuary legatee, the Harriet Lane Home for Invalid Children.

The Johnston collection consists of thirty-four objects, of which about one-third are paintings and engravings by European artists, one-third paintings and sculptures by Americans, and one-third items of historic memorabilia pertaining to President James Buchanan. American painters represented are John Henry Brown, Jacob Eicholtz, Francis B. Mayer, Harper Pennington, Thomas P. Rossiter, and Edward Lord Weeks; sculptors, Henry Dexter and William Henry Rinehart. Scholars' subsequent study of the European works has suggested that probably only three of those works were correctly attributed: paintings by George Romney, Cornelius Jonson, and Bernardino Luini. When Mrs. Johnston acquired her European paintings, misattributions and frauds were common. Although connoiseurship in eighteenth-century British portraiture was not yet highly developed, such works as were included in this collection were selling at high prices, resulting in a flood of copies and false attributions.

Corcoran Thom, president of the Board of Trustees at the Corcoran, suggested to Langley that the Smithsonian lay claim to Mrs. Johnston's collection by establishing a national gallery of art under the aegis of the government. Langley was enthusiastic about the prospect, but it was his belief—based upon the 1846 founding act—that the Smithsonian was already constituted as the national gallery of art and thus fulfilled the conditions of the bequest. Smithsonian Regents shared this point of view. Executors of the estate, however, believed they needed a more binding legal statement that could not be challenged by other heirs. Even though as friends and relatives of Mrs. Johnston most of the trustees of the Harriet Lane Home favored keeping her collection together to honor her wishes, the case had to be established beyond question.

It seemed logical to Secretary Langley that an assurance of legality required going back to Congress to request confirmation of the Smithsonian's status by passage of a bill to include the specific title cited in the Johnston bequest, and he proposed that such a resolution be passed during the current session of Congress. He emphasized that his concern involved more than the acquisition of Mrs. Johnston's collection: "I have had offers of valuable collections, and even of liberal provision for a building to house them," he informed Representative James T. McCleary, chairman of the House Committee on the Library, "and the Institution, being desirous of having some form of legislation which would enable it to constitute a nucleus for these collections, and stimulate donations to the Government, has taken advantage of the offer of Mrs. Johnston's Executors with this in view, more than the immediate value of her paintings, to bring the matter to your attention in a form"—and here he brought out his trump card—"which will cost the Government nothing."[7]

An appropriate resolution was introduced, but no action was taken until President Theodore Roosevelt stepped onto the scene. In contrast to his Rough Rider public image, Harvard-educated Roosevelt was culturally astute (he is the only president besides Woodrow Wilson to have been elected to the National Institute of Arts and Letters), and throughout his presidency he lent persuasive powers to major cultural endeavors (within the year he would actively support the Smithsonian's acquisition of Charles Lang Freer's collection of Asian and American art).[8] Recognizing with Langley the potential significance of the Johnston bequest, Roosevelt in his annual message on December 6, 1904, urged Congress to pass legislation that would enable the institution to accept gifts such as Mrs. Johnston's.[9]

Before Congress could act on the president's urging, Attorney General William Henry Moody considered the case and concluded that rather than seek additional legislation, the institution would be better advised to claim rightful possession of the bequest on the basis that it was already the legally constituted national gallery of art. On behalf of the United States, the attorney general entered the suit filed by the executors in the Supreme Court of the District of Columbia, contending that the trustees of the Corcoran had no authority to decline the Johnston bequest because "at the time of the death of the said Harriet Lane Johnston, there was established and had been established, for a long time prior thereto, a national gallery of art by the Government of the United States."[10]

The decision of the court, rendered on July 18, 1906, in favor of the United States, concluded that the federal government in founding the Smithsonian had the intent of providing for an art gallery; that Congress had recognized the art gallery and had made constant provision for it; that the Smithsonian had developed its art collection from "a *potential* National Art Gallery into an *actual* one, with many collections"; that the art gallery was national in character through its Board of Regents supervised by Congress, the use of the frank in U.S. postage, the deposit of funds in the federal treasury; the fact that all objects of art belonging to the United States are required by law to be properly deposited in the Smithsonian; and last, that Mrs.

Johnston, in writing her will with its codicils, had not known that the Smithsonian Gallery of Art was in existence.[11]

Litigation of the Johnston bequest reinforced the Smithsonian's association with the federal government and, consequently, the government's involvement with the art collection. Support for the institution's case had come from all three branches: a resolution was introduced in Congress; the president made an appeal in his annual address; and the attorney general entered the court case on behalf not of the Smithsonian but of the United States. Thus, the federal government committed itself to an interest in a national gallery of art—specifically to this one—implying that the collections and programs of such an institution were of value to its citizens.

The sense of identity given by the title "the National Gallery of Art" brought immediate response from within and beyond the institution. Richard S. Rathbun, appointed Smithsonian acting secretary after Langley's death in February 1906 (before the successful conclusion of his efforts to acquire the Johnston collection), undertook the essential task of gathering documents that pertained to art acquisitions, giving continuity from the past by tracing origins in pre-Smithsonian sources.[12] William H. Holmes, a Smithsonian anthropologist, an archaeologist, and a practicing artist, was named curator.

Born the year the Smithsonian was founded, Holmes claimed—only partly in jest—that he was predestined to devote his life to the institution. After graduating from a normal school for teachers in Hopedale, Ohio, he came to Washington to study art with Theodore Kauffman and Eliphalet Frazer Andrews, then director of the Corcoran School of Art. First hired by Smithsonian scientists to draw shells and birds, Holmes was appointed artist to the United States Geological Survey on the Hayden expedition of 1872. His drawings for this and subsequent surveys in the West earned for him a reputation as a topographical artist without peer, a draftsman and painter who could impose the vision of an artist upon that of a scientist. His studies in archaeology, anthropology, and ethnology brought national and international recognition. Throughout these activities and his administrative duties, he maintained practice as a painter in watercolors and oils. Trips abroad made him familiar with the collections of European museums, and he spent a season in Munich studying with Frank Duveneck. An active member of the art community, he exhibited at the Corcoran biennials, the American Watercolor Society in New York, and the National Academy of Design.[13]

The National Gallery's Advisory Board of five members (including Holmes) consisted entirely of artists: Frank D. Millet, of the American Academy at Rome, chairman; Frederick Crowninshield, president of the National Fine Arts Federation; Edwin H. Blashfield, president of the National Academy of Design; Herbert Adams, president of the National Sculpture Society. Their appointments as advisers implied that artists were to be considered as premier authorities in their own field and American art a priority. Librarian Cyrus Adler of the Smithsonian explained the rationale: "In the administration of the Gallery the same policy would be followed . . . as had been followed in scientific matters [in which scientists determined Smithsonian policies for science], namely, that the professional artist and the professional student of art only would be considered . . . [and] that the time has passed when the man of affairs and patrons of art were the people to administer a gallery of art." Adler also pointed out that though a national gallery is obliged to contain all the artworks owned by the nation, "it was fair to assume . . . that this Gallery would pay special attention to American art."[14]

Upon invitation of President Roosevelt, members of the advisory board met at the White House to discuss their goals with him. The president continued to take an extraordinary interest in programs of the gallery, especially in the promotion of the nation's own art.

Board members first considered the question of the collection's scope, whether it ought to include such objects as ceramics, glassware and textiles, Asian art, sculptures from the Pacific Islands, handcrafted works by indigenous peoples of North America—all already included in Smithsonian collections—or focus on European and American painting and sculpture. Art museums founded in the 1870s—the Metropolitan Museum of Art in New York, the Museum of Fine Arts in Boston, the Philadelphia Museum of Art, and the Chicago Art Institute—did acquire such items along with Western fine arts, and collections of the Louvre and other European institutions served as important precedents for an inclusive practice. Still, though not limiting future possibilities, the advisers determined that for the present, emphasis would be given to the "fine arts," especially to painting and sculpture. Considerations within the bureaucracy suggested the prudence of such a choice, for the institution had already defined areas of anthropology, ethnology, and industrial arts where extensive collections of other kinds of art objects were held. Limitations of space and budget, as well as the professional activity of board members, made their decision practical and predictable.

Publicity about the Johnston bequest and the name of "the National Gallery of Art" persuaded a major collector to give a choice selection of his American paintings to this prestigious setting in Washington: beginning with a gift of 50 paintings in 1907, William T. Evans's donation to the National Gallery comprised 150 works representing 106 American artists, all of whom were living or recently deceased. The collector's favored theme of landscape painting included George Inness's *Sundown* and Theodore Robinson's *Old Church at Giverny*; in a wide range of figure works, Thomas Dewing's ethereal female figures contrasted with the stalwart women in Winslow Homer's psychological confrontation, *Visit of the Old Mistress*.

Evans's public show of confidence in contemporary American art gave an encouraging boost to the art community. Grateful for his patronage and for bestowing their works on a national collection, artists sometimes offered him a discount or directed him to a particularly good piece for this purpose. Mary Cassatt wrote the collector that she considered it a great distinction to be included in his gift to the National Gallery of Art.[15]

Keeping abreast of developments at the gallery, the White House took pride in this show of support for American art. When Evans's first group of paintings was shown in Washington (at the Corcoran for want of gallery space at the Smithsonian), President Roosevelt wrote the collector of his appreciation—and took advantage of the opportunity to send a message to Congress:

> The White House, Washington, April 6, 1907
>
> My Dear Mr. Evans:
>
> I have just been over to see the fifty specially selected paintings by American artists which you have so generously given to the nation. I feel that action such as yours works in direct and practical fashion to encourage the development of American art and to foster its appreciation. I am particularly gratified at seeing such a gift come to Washington. You doubtless know that Mr. Freer's noteworthy collection of paintings has also been deeded to the nation. Your gift, taken together with what has already been done, will form the cornerstone for a national gallery of art in the nation's capital. In my judgment, a building to harbor this national gallery has become a necessity. In the case of the Freer collection the generosity of the donor provided for its housing, but it is impossible that this should be ordinarily the case. An adequate building must be provided so that there may be incentive for gifts such as that of the Harriet Lane Johnston collection and yours. I very earnestly hope that Congress will at

a very early date provide an adequate building for a national art gallery. With renewed thanks, believe me,

Sincerely yours,
Theodore Roosevelt.[16]

The goal of acquiring funds for a building specifically for the art gallery engaged the efforts of Charles Doolittle Walcott (figure 15), appointed in 1907 as secretary of the Smithsonian to succeed Langley. A geologist and paleontologist, Walcott was an immensely effective administrator. While at the helm of the institution he maintained scholarship in his own field and at the same time was active in the founding of several national scientific bodies. Though necessarily having to spend most of his time with the science divisions that constituted the much larger portion of the institution, he consistently promoted its art interests as well.

Secretary Walcott courted prospective donors Peter Arrell Brown Widener of Philadelphia in 1910 and John Gellatly of New York in 1924.[17] In 1925 through contact with Peter's son Joseph E. Widener, he again sought the possibility of luring the Widener collection into the Smithsonian fold. Convinced that failure to acquire important collections was due to the lack of a dedicated building, he became an active advocate for that goal, addressing a convention of the American Federation of Arts to press its urgency.[18]

In the meantime, with construction of a new National Museum Building (figure 16, subsequently called the National Museum of Natural History), officials had the opportunity of showing recent art acquisitions together as an entity identified by the new title. A hall dedicated to the National Gallery of Art (NGA) was rushed to completion and opened in 1910 before other parts of the building were ready, displaying within its assigned space the gallery's permanent collection and initiating an active exhibition program.

Accessions and Exhibitions of the first National Gallery of Art

"Nation's Art Show—National Gallery Opens Informally Next Thursday in New Museum Building," announced the *Sunday Star* in a two-page spread on March 13, 1910.[19] Three reproductions of paintings from the Evans collection with a photo of the building gave readers some idea of what to expect in the art gallery within this new structure on the mall. A central hall extended from the rotunda on the south to the north of the building fronting Constitution Avenue; it was divided by screens into a large area of 40 by 60 feet and six smaller galleries, each about 15 by 18 feet. Walls were covered with burlap, a dull green in some galleries and a warm gray in others; the floor was marble mosaic.[20] Here the public could view recent gifts of the Johnston and Evans collections supplemented by other works. Halls

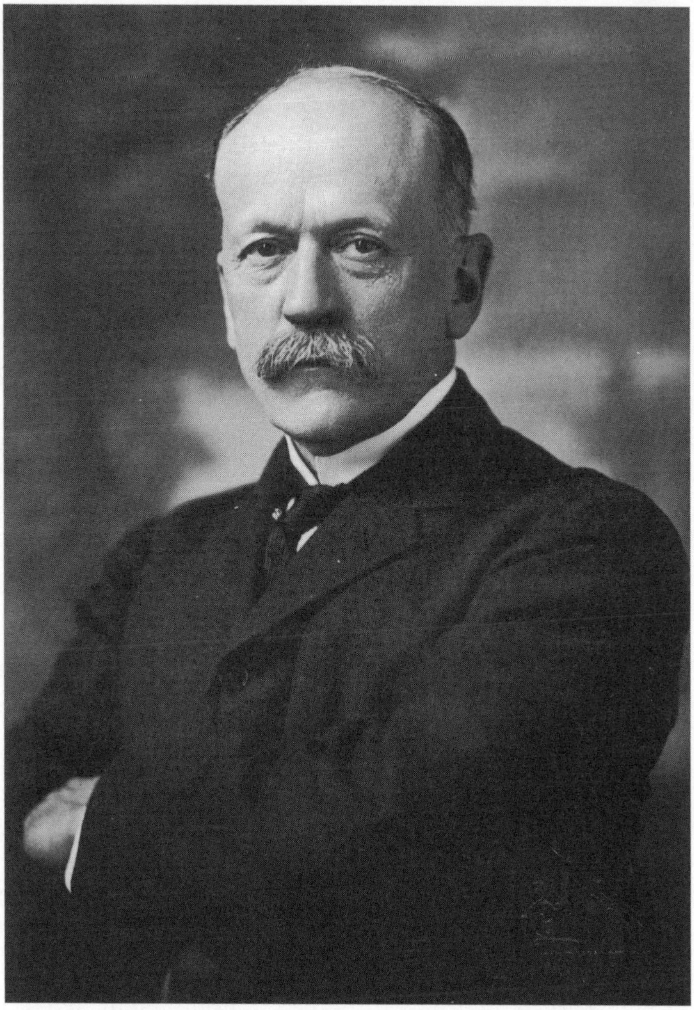

Figure 15. *Charles Doolittle Walcott.* Smithsonian Institution Archives, neg. no. 82-3142.

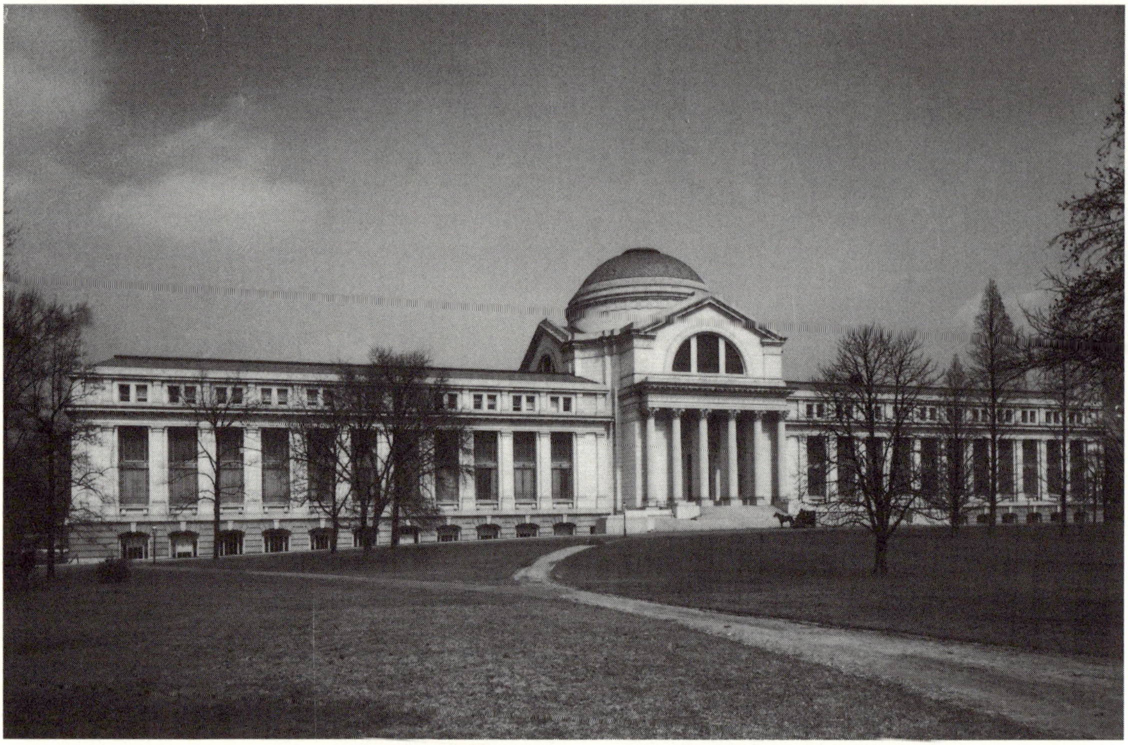

Figure 16. *The New National Museum Building* (National Museum of Natural History), ca. 1910. Smithsonian Institution Archives, neg. no. 26560.

of exhibits relating to anthropology and ethnology bordered the gallery, which administratively was situated in the Department of Anthropology. Several sculptures and casts were placed in the rotunda area (the elephant, familiar to visitors today, did not arrive until the 1950s). Paul Bartlett's equestrian *Marquis de Lafayette*, a life-size model in plaster of the bronze in Paris, stood impressively before a hall of nature specimens. (Bartlett's statue in Paris occupied its original site at the entrance to the Louvre from 1907 until 1984, when it was displaced by the glass pyramid of I. M. Pei and moved to the *Cour la Reine*.)

Without acquisition funds, the gallery was completely dependent upon donations from private individuals and transfers from the Capitol Building and other government agencies. Fortunately, the prominence resulting from the new title continued to bring works into the collection. Three notable gifts received during the three decades of the National Gallery era added to the holdings of both American and European paintings and other art objects.

First, the unusual conditions devised by Henry Ward Ranger, a landscape painter and close associate of William Evans, make his bequest still operative today. In 1914 he signed over his estate of $200,000 to the National Academy of Design in New York City for the purpose of distributing paintings by living American artists to public galleries and libraries throughout the country, works to be selected from the annual exhibitions of the academy by its council members. The National Gallery of Art could recall for its collection any of the works so placed within a period of five years after the death of the artist; otherwise, if not claimed, the work would become the permanent property of the gallery to which it had originally been assigned. Thus the Ranger Fund was designed to serve three important purposes: to patronize living artists, to disseminate American art throughout the nation, and to honor outstanding artists by placing their works in the National Gallery of Art in Washington. An early group of Ranger Fund paintings selected by the National Academy were exhibited at the NGA in 1930 (figure 17); Holmes is seated on the bench at the extreme left, and his assistant clerk, Glen J. Martin, stands looking at a painting. The first Ranger Fund acquisition for the permanent collection, *Cliffs of the Upper Colorado River, Wyoming Territory* by Thomas Moran (figure 18), was received in 1936.[21]

Second, the Ralph Cross Johnson donation of 1919 consisted of a choice group of 24 European paintings: Italian "primitives," Dutch and Flemish seventeenth-century works, Italian Renaissance and eighteenth-century paintings, and portraits and landscapes by British artists. As was true of Harriet Lane Johnston's European paintings, some works in the Johnson collection were open to questions of authenticity, but for the most part they proved to be genuine.[22]

In 1929 the collection of John Gellatly—first sought by Secretary Walcott five years earlier—was at last acquired by the Smithsonian. The largest group of works ever received by the gallery from a single donor, it consisted of 161 paintings (mostly American) and close to 1,500 other art objects (mostly foreign). Ranging widely through time and space, Gellatly's gatherings included ancient Egyptian and Greek glass, bronzes, and jewelry; Indian and Chinese paintings, sculpture, ceramics, glass, and bronzes; European medieval tapestries, enamels, furniture; Renaissance and Baroque ivories, jewels, and jewelry. In contrast to this breadth of world art, Gellatly concentrated narrowly on American paintings of his own time. Of 104 oil paintings by living or recently deceased American artists, 84 were by just five painters: Thomas Wilmer Dewing, Childe Hassam, Albert Pinkham Ryder, Abbott Handerson Thayer, and John Twachtman. The New York collector's acquisitions thus consisted of a sweep through European and Asian cultures of the past and a select group of American works from his own era.[23]

The Smithsonian's National Gallery of Art sponsored more than a hundred temporary exhibitions between 1906 and 1937, featuring arts and crafts of Asian, European, and South American countries, though more than half of the total events represented artists of the United States. Departments of the federal government

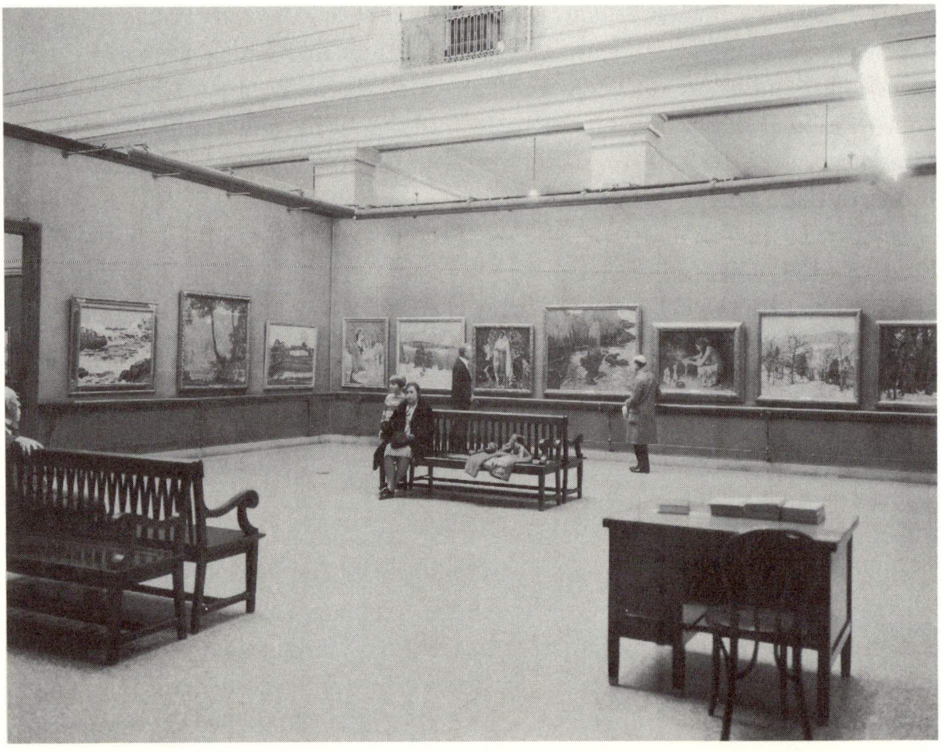

Figure 17. *Exhibition of Ranger Fund Paintings*, with Director Holmes (seated on bench at left), Assistant Clerk Glenn J. Martin (standing on the left), and visitors in the Gallery. Smithsonian Institution Archives, neg. no. 18052-C.

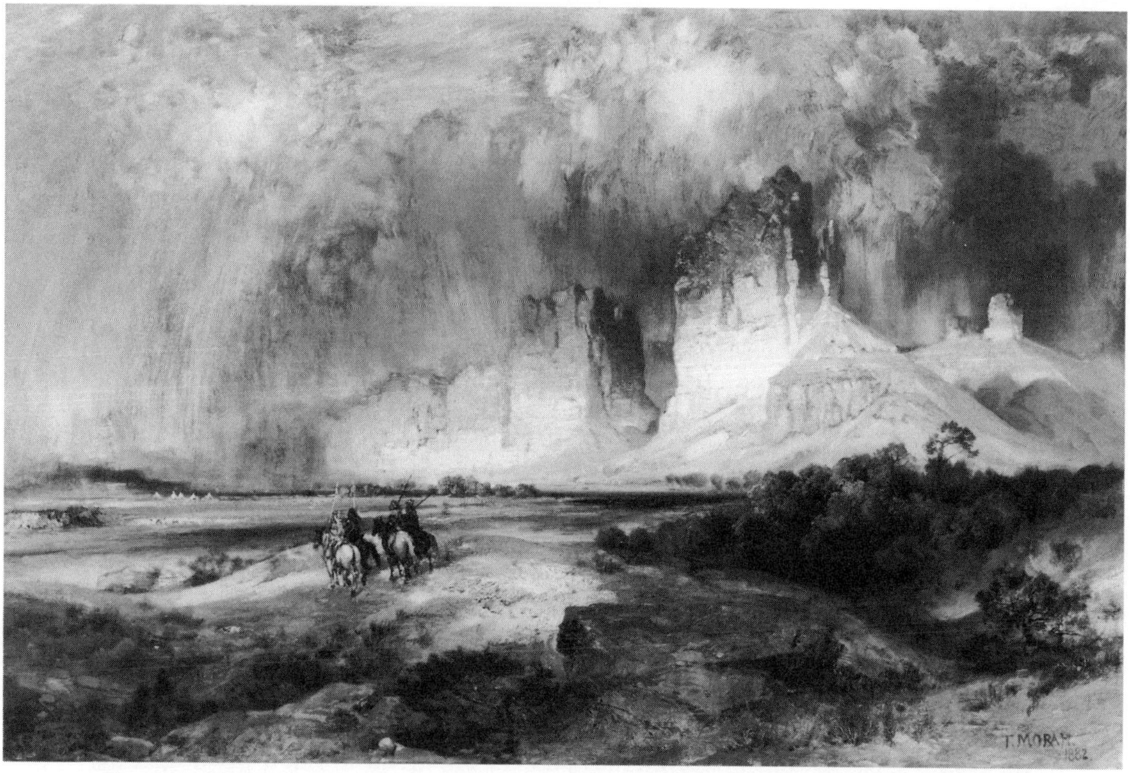

Figure 18. Thomas Moran, *Cliffs of the Upper Colorado River, Wyoming Territory*, 1882. Smithsonian American Art Museum, Bequest of Henry Ward Ranger through the National Academy of Design.

participated regularly as exhibitors. Drawings and models for the Lincoln Memorial by competing architects Henry Bacon and John Russell Pope, presented in 1911, were followed by other shows pertaining to proposed monuments in Washington and elsewhere in the nation. Forty-five paintings of scenes in national parks, canvases by Albert Bierstadt and Thomas Moran supplemented by oil studies and photographs, were placed on view by the National Park Service in 1917.[24]

Local and national art organizations served artists and craftspersons by presenting their works to NGA audiences. The American Federation of Arts, involved with promoting both American and foreign art, sponsored a variety of exhibits including a 1915 showing of work by contemporary artists of the United States and European nations previously shown at the Carnegie International in Pittsburgh. Ethnic groups and foreign embassies also displayed contemporary works; the Italy-America Society in 1916 presented almost 300 pieces of modern Italian crafts.

Reflecting on the significance of the Great War in Europe and the contribution of the United States to its conclusion, a group of patriotic citizens organized the National Art Committee for the purpose of commissioning portraits of the Allied leaders for the collection of the National Gallery. Painted by Cecilia Beaux, Joseph DeCamp, Edmund C. Tarbell, Douglas Volk, Irving Wiles, and other American artists, groups of these canvases were shown in 1921 and 1923.[25]

Two exhibitions of works by "American Negro Artists" were held in May 1929 and May–June 1930.[26] These events included paintings by Archibald Motley and William H. Johnson, recent winners of the annual William E. Harmon Awards "for distinguished achievement among negroes." Favorably reviewed in the press, the more than 60 paintings and several sculptures shown in 1929 attracted an enthusiastic audience, estimated at over 8,000 (the exhibit was on view for about two weeks), with some 75 to 90 percent of the crowd being "colored visitors." Significantly, the busiest days were the two Sundays of the exhibition, when close to 1,400 and 1,600 visitors were counted, as compared with weekdays, which averaged around 500, confirming that visitors were mostly of the working class. Except for the special case of this exhibition, it is difficult to determine the identity of the viewing public in the National Gallery of Art or even the numbers, for attendance statistics ordinarily related to the entire museum building.

Organized by the Harmon Foundation and arranged by the Committee on Race Relations of the Washington Federation of Churches, a local interracial group, the exhibit constituted an uncommon event at this time anywhere in the United States and especially in the nation's segregated capital. When Dr. Anson Phelps Stokes was seeking a Washington venue for the Harmon exhibit that had opened in New York City, Leila Mechlin, art critic for the *Washington Star*, encouraged him to contact William H. Holmes. "If shown at the National Museum under the auspices of the National Gallery," she pointed out, "it would have a certain dignity, and at the same time would be equally open for inspection to white and colored."[27] Mechlin was a shaker and mover on the Washington and national art scene. In addition to her position at the *Star*, she was editor of the *American Magazine of Art* (formerly *Art and Progress*) from 1909 to 1931, and secretary of the American Federation of Arts from 1912 to 1923.

Art and Artifact

Temporary showings were often mounted in hallways and foyers of the museum building while the permanent collection occupied the main gallery spaces—as many works as could be accommodated. Bordered by displays of ethnology and anthropology, these works could not be viewed except in conjunction with such things as totem poles and iconic paintings (figure 19), a juxtaposition that visually embodied a basic issue of early twentieth-century art: were the ethnic objects properly classified as ethnological "artifacts," or could they be called "art" and considered on the level of meaning imputed to Western art? And, a related question, how did the distorted images in certain works by contemporary European and North American artists—who were profoundly affected by the unfamiliar forms found in African and Polynesian sculpture and aboriginal American images—relate to their own Western tradition? As some critics asked, could their works be considered "art"?

The response of Gottfried Semper to the 1851 Crystal Palace Exposition still held true for those who considered handmade objects of non-Western peoples as artifacts, useful solely as evidence of cultural evolution and the study of beliefs and mores. Because these works originated in preindustrial societies, they were perceived as the beginning of a progressive development that culminated in the art of the West. Believers of this persuasion also tended to consider new forms of modern Western art as aberrant images outside the developmental evolutionary schema of art history and therefore of no lasting value for the future.

According to objective criteria held since the Renaissance, works of art were judged according to how well they conveyed the visual world in regard to correct anatomical proportions, the illusion of space through linear perspective or values and color, and the convincing effect of three-dimensional objects in space. Such works as the totem pole and the painting in the ethnology exhibit obviously did not meet any of these requirements and therefore could not be called art; even pre-Renaissance European paintings without those features had earned the appellation of "primitive." Modernist artists who deliberately rejected such qualities put their works in the same category.

New ways of looking at art and its origins provided possibilities for other conclusions. By applying concepts of biological theory to the creative processes of art and literature, French philosopher Hippolyte Taine established new criteria for the evaluation of works. A follower of Herbert Spencer and Darwin, Taine believed

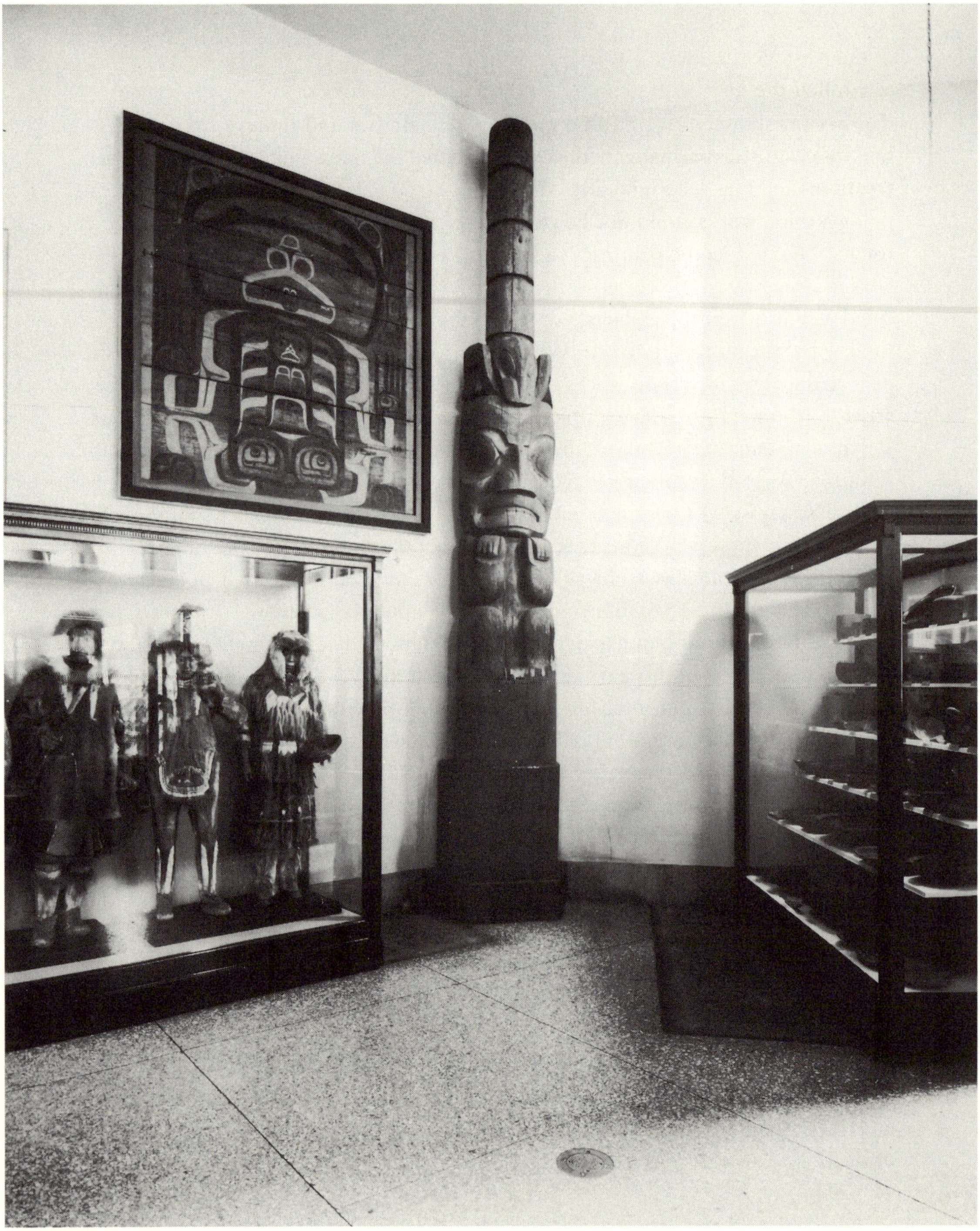

Figure 19. *"Artifacts."* A totem pole and iconic painting in Ethnology exhibit. Smithsonian Institution Archives, neg. no. 38121-A.

in the existence of natural laws that determined human activities as surely as they controlled the germination and growth of plant and animal life. In his *Lectures on Art*, first translated in the United States in 1865 by John Durand (a son of the artist Asher B. Durand), Taine described the analogy of natural products with human creations:

> We shall first study the innate and preliminary history which explains the outward and final history. I shall first show you the seed, that is to say the race, with its fundamental and indelible qualities, those that persist through all circumstances and in all climates; and next the plant, that is to say the people itself, with its original qualities expanded or contracted, in any case grafted and transformed by its surroundings and its history; and finally the flower, that is to say the art, and especially painting, in which this development culminates.[28]

According to Taine's principles, the totem pole with its distorted shapes of human and animal forms owed its appearance to the racial and historical lineage of its creator, its cultural environment, and the time of its making; it could therefore be judged according to how fully it embodied those aspects of its generative origin. (Taine's definition of "race" referred to groups of people living in a shared geographic and climatic environment rather than to physical characteristics, as the word is used today.)

Other voices continued to expand the definition of art in the early years of the twentieth century. In Paris, Henri Bergson stressed an intuitive response to works of art in place of an intellectual approach. He emphasized a need for "setting aside conceptual thought" and becoming aware of "a vision which is scarcely distinguishable from the object seen." Theories of this French philosopher were joined from Germany by Wilhelm Worringer, who countered the objective basis of Western art with the psychological theory of empathy, applied to both modern Western works and non-Western objects of preindustrial cultures. Writing in London, Roger Fry coined English phrases and rationale for the radical new forms in European art and African sculpture, and Russian artist Wassily Kandinsky verbally articulated ideas about art as conveying a nonmaterial reality which he visually expressed in his own abstractions. These sources and others offered new possibilities of responding to creations of human minds and hands, whether in preindustrial societies or the twentieth-century Western world.[29]

All the works by living or recently deceased American artists in the permanent collection of the National Gallery of Art represented conservative art derived from traditional Renaissance principles. Situated within the ethnic exhibits, they fostered the perception of the Western works as distinct from, and superior to, the handmade objects of non-Western cultures in the surrounding galleries. As visitors moved through the exhibits, the arrangement of the halls, side by side, implied this conclusion, a convincing message not only for visitors to the gallery but for also for institution officials who, for decades—into the 1960s—would permit only conservative art to enter the collection. Moreover, the administrative head of the gallery for three decades, William H. Holmes, was an anthropologist as well as an artist. At this time the Smithsonian Department of Anthropology promoted research that, through comparative studies of skulls and brains, placed Caucasians (males only) at the top of human physical and mental development, with all others below on various rungs of the evolutionary ladder. It followed that the cultural products made by those who were inferior by nature belonged to a category apart from the creations of the most elevated minds.

The sheer weight of natural history and anthropology at the Smithsonian operated as a factor in keeping the art collection and theories of art history grounded in nineteenth-century imagery and within certain concepts of cultural evolution. By the first decade of the twentieth century, when the title of "the National Gallery of Art" was bestowed on the collection, the physical sciences and psychological theory had already become significant sources for artists and writers. New conceptual approaches to interpreting the phenomena of nature and human experience went far beyond the possibilities of visual observation that still served as a basis for traditional artists. Yet the very things that helped to keep art at the Smithsonian conservative—ethnology collections of objects from the Americas, Africa, and the Pacific Islands—served as powerful catalysts for artists outside the mainstream in their break with tradition.

A hundred years after Western paintings were placed in proximity with totem poles in the NGA galleries, defining the terms of "art" versus "artifact" continues to be a lively issue for museum curators. No longer perceived as labels intrinsic to particular pieces, the categories today can be deftly manipulated through the manner of presentation. An object in a museum—almost any object—when isolated and spotlighted, for example, suggests uniqueness and preciousness, like a work of fine art, as opposed to showing the same item alongside similar pieces without distinguishing it in any way, as is common in arrangements of ethnology exhibits. Works of Western art, too—paintings, sculptures or photographs—can cross over the traditional line and through didactic and polemic labels become perceived primarily as artifacts that interpret cultural values rather than as aesthetic experiences. In the last decade, such presentations have become more common, particularly in exhibitions of American art.[30]

Planning for a Building

To promote the gallery and give it more visibility, Secretary Walcott separated the National Gallery of Art from the Anthropology Department in July 1920 and made it an independent bureau. He successfully sought a congressional appropriation of $15,000 to permit the hiring of staff members assigned exclusively to the gallery rather than requiring that it share employees with other departments.[31] Formerly appointed curator of the gallery and now named director, Holmes was freed from his administrative responsibilities with the Anthropology Department. At the same time, Walcott expanded the five-member NGA Advisory Board (which had served from 1906 to 1920) to a fifteen-member Board of Commissioners. It was to include five artists, as before but also five experts in the fine arts and five business or professional men interested in art—thus moving the group closer to the membership typical of trustees and boards in other art museums. First appointees to the newly constituted NGA Board of Commissioners were artists Herbert Adams, a sculptor, and Edwin H. Blashfield, a painter, both members of the original group; Daniel Chester French, a sculptor; Gari Melchers, a painter; and William H. Holmes, a painter, again representing the institution. The art experts consisted of John E. Lodge of the Museum of Fine Arts, Boston (who would be appointed first director of the Freer in 1923); Frank Jewett Mather Jr., art historian at Princeton; Charles A. Platt, an architect and painter; Edward Willis Redfield, a painter; James Earl Fraser, a sculptor. Appointed as public men interested in the fine arts were W. K. Bixby of St. Louis; Joseph H. Gest of Cincinnati; Charles Moore, Detroit; James Parmelee, Cleveland; and Herbert L. Pratt, New York City.

Walcott acted as ex officio member of the board. The secretary's crucial assistance in the areas of budget, staffing, and the appointment of a broader group of interested board members significantly advanced the National Gallery of Art toward the promise of expanded collections and programs in the future. His actions took place at a time of accelerated activity for museums in the United States: in the 1920s and early 1930s many new museums were established across the country, and the number of visitors significantly increased.[32]

At the urging of Secretary Walcott, Congress in 1923 set apart a site on the north side of the Mall facing Constitution Avenue between Seventh Street and the National Museum of Natural History (where the gallery was still located).[33] Smithsonian Regents privately raised $10,000 for an architectural study and commissioned Charles A. Platt, architect of the recently completed Freer Gallery, to prepare the plans. Platt submitted sketches of the proposed building to commission members in October 1924, and the following March the architect's concept was made public. Reminiscent of the Freer, the first-floor corridor framed "a court . . . [and] a lounge and tea room at the further end . . . with windows opening on the trees and grass. The court will make places for a certain number of pieces of sculpture," observed art critic Royal Cortissoz, "but in its broad character is intended to give the building a kind of friendly center."[34] A grand gallery for paintings on the uppermost floor was to be skylighted. The architect's "stated intention in the National Gallery was to design a functional and well-lighted art museum, not an ornate palace for the nation's treasures."[35]

The tangible reality of a design in process accelerated support efforts. Holmes sought public support through lectures, articles, and a radio address.[36] Through their widespread network the Federation of Women's Clubs appealed to Americans across the country for support of the gallery project. The American Federation of Arts, spurred by its secretary, Leila Mechlin, launched a nationwide drive to encourage members to write their senators and representatives in Congress on behalf of an appropriation. Support statements were solicited and received from national leaders who represented various aspects of the power structure in America: Samuel Gompers, president of the American Federation of Labor; General James G. Harbord, of the Radio Corporation of America; Arthur Page, of the publisher Doubleday, Page; Edward Robinson, director of the Metropolitan Museum of Art; and Charles M. Schwab, president of United States Steel.[37]

A legislative proposal was initiated in 1924 by Senator Henry Cabot Lodge authorizing $2.5 million to begin construction of a gallery building that was not to exceed $7 million in cost. It did not pass, but an upcoming proposal for an extensive public building program in Washington seemed promising, and supporters planned to amend that bill to make specific reference to the National Gallery. No sooner had hopes for success risen via the major building plan, however, when they were dashed: Reed Smoot, chairman of the Public Building Committee, announced that a building for the National Gallery would not be included in the proposed plan because of "fairly good prospects" that a private benefactor was going to give a gallery to the government.[38] A Republican senator from Utah, Smoot was also a Smithsonian Regent.

It had not been necessary for Senator Smoot to name the potential benefactor; he was understood to be Andrew W. Mellon (figure 20). Subsequent newspaper articles directly linked Mellon with the proposed building. "Now Secretary Mellon is to do for the nation what Congress has refused to do," announced the *Times*, and the *Washington Star* speculated that "the donor of this munificent gift to the people" must be Andrew W. Mellon, "who, it is known, has been keenly interested in the development of art in America and particularly in Washington. . . . With the National Gallery suitably housed, as now appears to be assured, Washington will indeed be an art center of importance."[39] Efforts toward support of the building campaign ceased, for Congress certainly would not provide a grant if a possibility existed that private money would finance the structure.

Mr. Mellon's Encounter with Dr. Abbot

One of the nation's great financiers, Andrew Mellon had come to Washington in 1921, appointed by President Warren G. Harding as secretary of the treasury. His acquisitions of art began in 1882 when he traveled in Europe with Henry Clay Frick. Attracted first to Barbizon landscapes, he afterward centered his collection on old master paintings.

When Charles Doolittle Walcott, one of the most effective secetaries in Smithsonian history, died in February 1927, he was succeeded by one of the weakest, Charles Greeley Abbot (figure 21). An astrophysicist, Abbot did not possess Walcott's efficiency as an administrator or his commitment to art at the institution. Mellon, who had initiated contact with the Smithsonian, must have soon realized that Abbot was pliable. Beginning late in 1929, the two men held conversations and exchanged memos that—at Mellon's request—were kept secret from National Gallery commissioners. In 1931 Mellon was appointed a member of the commission; he never attended a meeting, but Abbot kept him informed of the business that transpired.[40]

Within the National Gallery, exhibition space was not the only problem; leadership and direction had waned. Holmes had been an extraordinary individual in

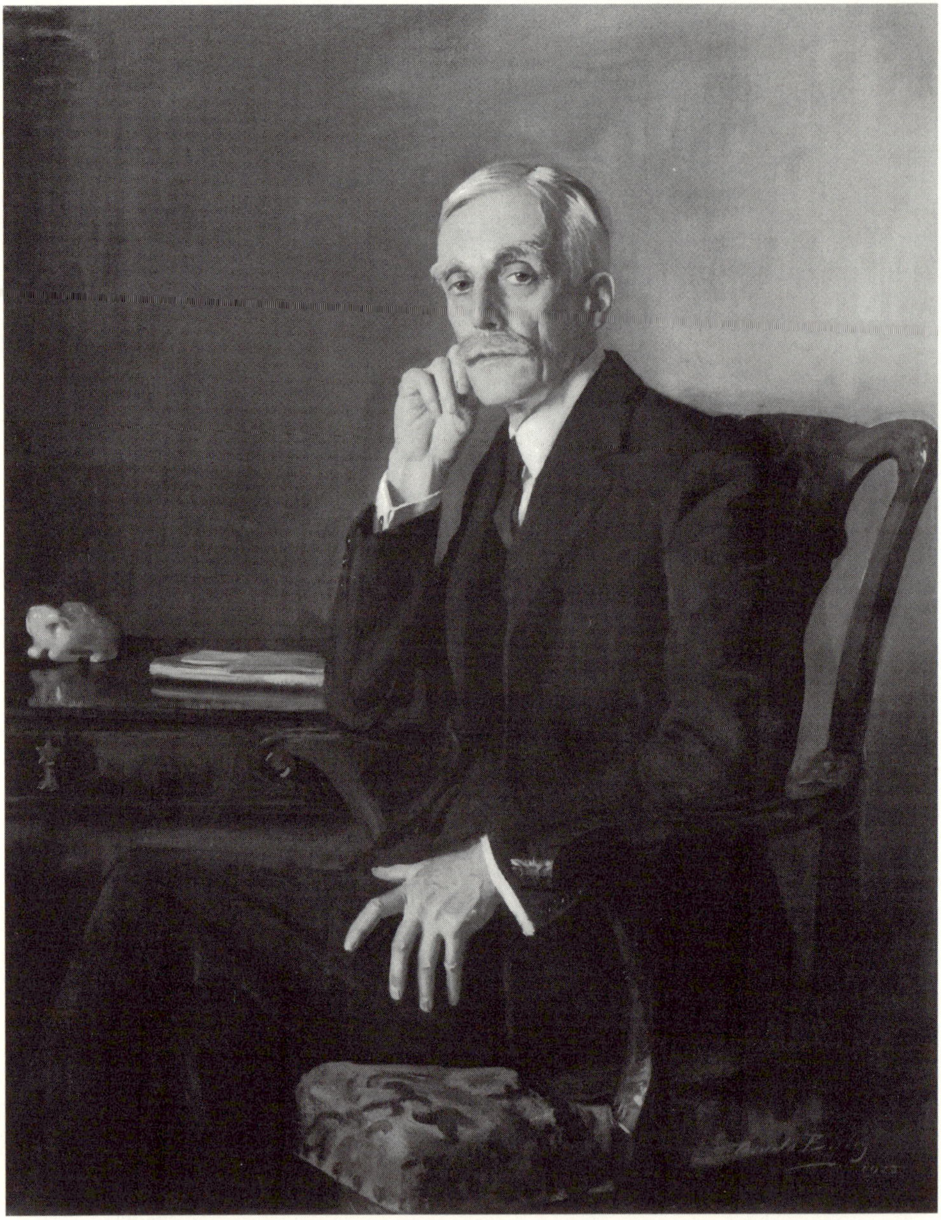

Figure 20. Sir Oswald Hornby Joseph Birley, *Andrew William Mellon*, 1923. National Portrait Gallery, gift of Paul Mellon.

his time, but he was now in his eighties and in poor health; in 1926 he underwent amputation of his left leg. His notice of retirement had been refused several times by Abbot, who insisted that he remain. When at last Holmes did leave the institution in 1932, the year before his death, Abbot made no effort to seek a new director, remaining unresponsive to requests of the commissioners to initiate a nationwide search for appropriate candidates. Their reaction to this frustrating state of affairs

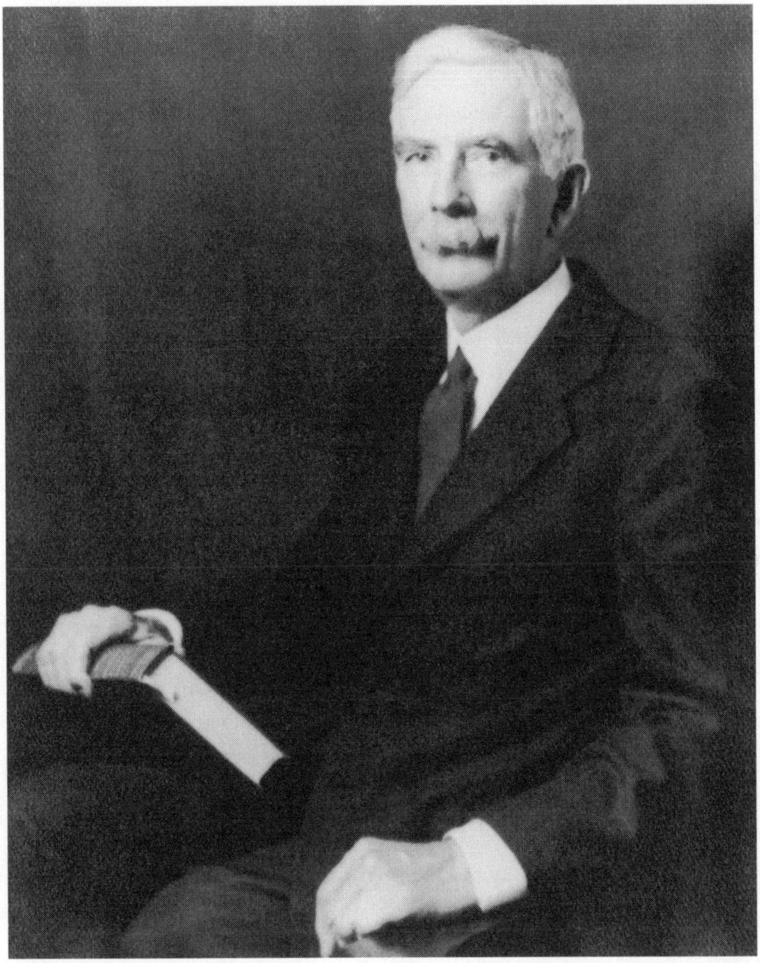

Figure 21. *Charles Greeley Abbot*. Smithsonian Institution Archives, neg. no. 42563.

ranged from agitated to outraged, for they were as enthusiastic and as committed to the gallery as ever and continued to offer ideas for its development. Frank Jewett Mather, for example, proposed that a membership drive be held to raise funds for the operation of the gallery. Abbot agreed to present Mather's idea to the Regents, but nothing came of it. The secretary's last reference to the pressing need for an art building had accompanied his announcement of the Gellatly bequest in 1929.

Abbot broke his silence in March 1934 in response to a letter from Joseph H. Gest, chairman of the commissioners. Gest got his attention by including a letter from Frederic Allen Whiting, president of the American Federation of Arts, in which Whiting questioned whether the Smithsonian was the proper custodian for a National Gallery of Art—and whether a scientist was capable of administering an institution with the scope of the Smithsonian.[41] Referring to the frustration of commission members over the past several years, Gest pointed out that "we are not making tangible progress in shaping the National Gallery of Art as we all desire."[42] "Speaking confidentially," Abbot replied,

> our great embarrassment is the fact that Mr. A. Mellon, while yet Secretary of the Treasury, requested me not to accept Dr. Holmes' resignation as Director. After Dr. Holmes' actual retirement, Mr. Mellon requested me not to appoint a successor because Mr. Mellon had definitely in mind a very large gift covering not only the erection of a building, but its sufficient endowment to enlarge it 50 years hence, so as to insure to the United States the leading national gallery in the whole world.
>
> You will see that while this prospect still hangs before me (I have the intimation from close to Mr. Mellon that he has it stabilized in his will), I am debarred from pushing any other plan. This makes our present administration of the Gallery look very badly to many, probably including Mr. Whiting. . . . You will also recognize, I am sure, that since the Smithsonian had been recognized by a legal decision as "*the* [double underline] National Gallery of Art," since it owns the Freer, the Gellatly, and some other collections, it would be a difficult legal problem to unscramble the eggs [in reference to Whiting's proposal that the NGA should be removed from the Smithsonian].

Abbot closed by giving Gest permission to use his letter in any way which in his judgment "would not be apt to lose us Mr. Mellon's favorable intentions."[43]

To Abbot's great distress, a journalist with the *Washington Post*, James Waldo Fawcett, reported in a March 19, 1935, radio program Mellon's intent to give the nation a building for an art gallery—adding that it was to be entirely separate from the Smithsonian's National Gallery of Art. Abbot immediately wrote to Mellon asking for clarification, congratulating the collector for his "glorious benefaction" before admitting his apprehensions:

> It was stated by Mr. Fawcett that your intention is to erect and endow a gallery of old master works, and that this is to be a separate thing from the National Gallery of Art. That you think the Congress should erect and maintain a National Gallery worthy of this nation.
>
> About six years ago, when your plans were still in formation, you requested the Smithsonian Institution to refrain from filling the vacancy of Director of the National Gallery of Art. I obtained an interview with you. At that time I got the impression that you intended to build and endow the National Gallery of Art, and you approved of my appointing Mr. Ruel P. Tolman as Acting Director pending further developments.
>
> For that reason we have taken no steps either to appoint a Director or to ask Congress for funds for a building.
>
> Now that your plan is announced, and as it does not contemplate your building or endowing the National Gallery, it seems to be the time for me to push forward on that program.
>
> I write to ask you to confirm definitely or correct my understanding as explained above, before I call together the Permanent Committee of our Board to act in the matter.
>
> Please be so good as to inform me at your earliest convenience.[44]

Mellon responded that neither Mr. Fawcett nor anyone else was authorized to speak for him, and since he was now in the midst of tax litigation, he could not turn his attention to plans "as to where the building will be erected and under what conditions it may be given."[45]

Actually, a brief notice had appeared in the *Washington Star* a month before the Fawcett radio address asserting, "Nothing is further from the wish of Andrew W. Mellon than any desire to hurt the National Gallery of Art project, first formulated many years ago and repeatedly urged by leading citizens in Washington and elsewhere throughout the country. . . . [H]e has stipulated that his gift is a separate and distinct institution—a collection of old masters, a building to shelter that collection and an endowment to enlarge it from time to time."[46] The straightforward decision reported by the *Star* was not conveyed by Mellon in response to Abbot's inquiry.

The litigation to which Mellon referred pitted the federal government against the former secretary of the treasury. In contention was the legality of a transfer of certain securities and the donation, as a tax deduction, of five paintings to the Mellon Educational and Charitable Trust.

As late as the December 1935 meeting of the NGA Commission, confusion still reigned as to Mellon's intention in regard to his potential gift and its relation to the Smithsonian National Gallery of Art. Commission members contemplated the possibility of the Mellon collection as a unit of the National Gallery of Art, located either as a wing of a very large building or as a separate structure among a group of related buildings. "It is understood that Mr. Andrew W. Mellon has in view the establishment of a gallery of works of art of the highest excellence at Washington in association with the National Gallery of Art. Thus far, however, his plan appears not to be finally shaped," they reported to the Regents.[47] The idea that the rumored building would house the Smithsonian's National Gallery with a wing for the Mellon collection was not at all inconceivable, for Mellon's collection was small, consisting of a little more than 100 paintings and some 20 sculptures, whereas the National Gallery's collection of paintings and sculptures, in addition to works on paper and objects in the Gellatly and other collections, numbered in the thousands of items.

The next month Abbot called on Mellon at his Washington home. He made extensive notes of their conversation (which he submitted to Mellon for corrections before referring them to the file). He again inquired "whether Mr. Mellon contemplated a general National Gallery or something devoted primarily to the Mellon works of art." Mellon stated that decisions for all such matters had been placed with the trustees of the A. W. Mellon Educational and Charitable Trust—such decisions being dependent also upon "the attitude of the Government towards the gift." The relation of the Freer Gallery to the Smithsonian was discussed, Abbot suggesting that it might serve as a model for the Mellon collection. "Mr. Mellon's idea, however, was that the gallery to be built by the Trust would be known as the National Gallery of Art to be held by the Smithsonian Institution for the National Government but to be managed and controlled by an independent Board of Trustees." Mellon brought up the possibility of a portrait gallery to be erected in connection with the gallery of the Mellon Trust. Abbot raised no objections to any point made by the financier, even the assertion that "it would be desirable to include in the new gallery some of the paintings in the present National Gallery but that a careful selection should be made, taking only those of the highest quality and importance."[48]

A year later, on January 3, 1937, a week after the Mellon gift to the nation was announced, Abbot sent a congratulatory telegram to the donor: "Gratefully delighted your princely gift, greatest in history stop Pledge all I can do to please you."[49] The nature of the relationship of the proposed gallery to the Smithsonian, however, was still unclear to Abbot; indeed, it would remain murky even after the drafting of the final bill.

The Mellon gallery was legally established as a bureau of the Smithsonian, for the 1846 founding act had stated that all objects of art in the city of Washington belonging to the government were to be under the jurisdiction of the Regents of the Smithsonian Institution. The building site, the building itself, and its contents were therefore appropriated to the Smithsonian, whereas complete control of the property and governance of the gallery were vested in a self-perpetuating Board of Trustees who were responsible only to themselves. This point, unsuccessfully challenged in Congress, resulted, wrote the attorney general, in "the anomaly . . . of government property being managed by a private group."[50] (Though the arrangement may have been unprecedented for the federal government, several art museums had forged a similar relation with municipal officials, following a pattern set by the Metropolitan Museum of Art in which the city of New York provides the land and the building while the museum corporation owns and administers the collections.)

The other point included in the final bill that directly affected the first National Gallery of Art was the transfer of its name to the Mellon project. At a preliminary discussion between government officials, the Smithsonian, and representatives of the Mellon Trust, Secretary Abbot made an unsuccessful last-ditch effort to retain that title for the institution.[51]

Justification for the appropriation of the title hinged "on the basis that the new gallery would be limited generally to paintings and sculptures, and that the Smithsonian gallery by that name, also contains porcelains, jewelry, etc.," explained Donald D. Shepard, one of the attorneys for the Mellon Trust. He continued:

> A study of the development of the great galleries of Europe has led the donor to the conclusion that the main gallery of this country's art collection should be reserved principally for paintings and sculptures, and therefore it seems appropriate, and he has suggested, that the name of the principal, and incidentally the most important national art gallery, should bear the designation of the National Gallery of Art. Therefore the bill provides, and it is understood that the Smithsonian Institution has no objection thereto, that the existing

> bureau of the Smithsonian Institution now designated as a National Gallery of Art shall hereafter be known as the "National Collection of Fine Art."[52]

Two years after completion in 1940 of the building for the new National Gallery of Art, the Mellon gallery acquired the Widener collection, which in the diversity of its objects compares with the Smithsonian's Gellatly collection. Eventually the new National Gallery of Art would include "Renaissance furniture; helmets; rock crystals; French eighteenth-century furniture and decorative arts; textiles and tapestries; and Asian decorative arts (primarily Chinese porcelains)."[53]

Andrew W. Mellon's manipulation of the Smithsonian secretary behind the screen of secrecy—with the full cooperation of Secretary Abbot—effectively diminished the visibility and effectiveness of the Smithsonian's art gallery for the years preceding the establishment of his gallery, so that the taking of its most valuable asset, the title of "the National Gallery of Art," appeared to be inconsequential to such an institution. Whether this was Mellon's intent from the beginning can only be speculated. Perhaps at one time he did consider a more viable connection to the primary museum power structure in Washington, but his associations with Abbot would have given him pause to wonder about leadership at the Smithsonian. A Walcott-Mellon relationship would have developed on very different terms. Mellon well understood the power of the name "the National Gallery of Art," its attraction to potential donors, the sense of authority and the illusion of exclusivity as a national art collection that it projected to the public, its justification for public funding, and its implicit association with quality and permanence as established by the National Gallery in London, a museum he much admired.

Reneging on his responsibility to the institution, Charles G. Abbot had handed over control of a Smithsonian bureau to an outside individual. Important questions about inner workings of the institution were properly raised by Mr. Whiting of the American Federation of Arts (in his letter to Commissioner Gest) as he observed the deterioration of the Smithsonian's National Gallery.

Approved by President Franklin Delano Roosevelt, a joint resolution was passed by Congress providing for the construction and maintenance of a National Gallery of Art on March 24, 1937. In a curious symmetry of history, a President Roosevelt again officiated as a "National Gallery of Art" was established. Once more the nation's chief executive expressed his personal cordial wishes for the new enterprise. No hint of the earlier acrimony on both sides marred the announcement of the Mellon gift.

If the Smithsonian Institution with its National Gallery of Art, the Freer Gallery and other collections, the Corcoran Gallery of Art, and the Phillips Collection had not existed, would Mellon have located his gallery in Washington? He was, of course, familiar with the capital city through his appointment to the president's cabinet, but Washington would have been a very different place without those institutions. In its relations with the Smithsonian, Congress had been associated for some years with museums and had an understanding of them as national entities. The Smithsonian formed a precedent and setting, historically, politically, and physically (in the location on the Mall) into which the Mellon gift could readily be situated.[54]

Defining "National" for a Gallery of Art, 1906 and 1937

Differing interpretations of purposes for a "national" gallery largely determined the visions that shaped each of the two institutions.

When that title was bestowed upon the Smithsonian's collection, a population spread out over a continent was settling into a self-conscious sense of nationality. In that first decade of the twentieth century the concept of "national" and the scope it implied pervaded the art world in the United States as never before, enabling individuals and institutions to perceive themselves as part of a larger entity, as "American" artists and patrons, recognized at home and abroad by their nationality. Participation by artists from every region of the nation in art exhibitions abroad had promoted this sense of identity, for those events made a point of emphasizing the national origin of each artist. At the great international expositions, artworks were presented in separate galleries assigned to each country; at the Paris Salons (annual exhibitions of contemporary art), catalogues stated the birthplace of each exhibitor, and art critics in their reviews described national stylistic traits.[55] The Carnegie Internationals in Pittsburgh from 1896 showed works by contemporary American artists in the company of their European peers, and in Washington the Corcoran Gallery's Contemporary American Oil Paintings, biennial exhibitions initiated in 1907, attracted artists from major urban centers throughout the country. All these shows, in Europe and the United States, were selected and judged by fellow artists.

Though a fervent national consciousness had inspired early nineteenth-century citizens such as Joel Barlow and Joel R. Poinsett and had motivated the founding of cultural organizations, the nationalist sentiment of that period had found expression mainly in rhetoric, for activities tended to be regional.[56] Exhibitions at the National

Academy of Design, for example, an artists' organization founded in 1825 in New York City, consisted almost exclusively of works by artists resident in that city. Difficulties in communication and transportation reinforced geographic limitations, but beyond those practical realities loomed an inability to acquire the overarching perspective necessary to sustain a truly national vision.

A broadened perception of the nation's art took place within the sharpened national consciousness that followed the Civil War. The carnage of the war with its goal to preserve the Union underscored the hope that such disunity would never be repeated; subsequent unprecedented ventures into international affairs, including war with Spain and the expansion of territory on the continent, in Hawaii, and in the Philippines, galvanized the image of a world-class nation. From across the Atlantic and the Pacific, streams of immigrants flowed into ports of entry, while African Americans within the nation, freed from slavery, sought jobs, homes, and education. European American citizens—not least of all those in the art world—felt a pressing need to define national values in order to acquaint these thousands of individuals from myriad cultures with what were perceived as traditional American beliefs and practices.[57] Ideals of acculturation aimed at the positive goal of acceptance, but the influx into urban areas of foreign languages, customs, dress, and styles of life posed a threat to established citizens and resulted in a backlash against the newcomers.

Issues related to these international and domestic affairs were debated and legislated in Washington, which was now unreservedly recognized as the center of national political power. Although New York City remained the country's unrivaled major center for art, and other communities of artists—especially in Philadelphia, Boston, Chicago, and Cincinnati—continued to thrive, more and more the "national" aspect of the arts pointed to the capital city.[58] The American Association of Museums, founded at a conference held at the Smithsonian in 1905, and the American Federation of the Arts, established in 1909 as a society representing eighty art organizations, chose Washington as the location for their headquarters and conferences. The American Institute of Architects, organized in 1857, and the Architectural League of America, founded in 1899, also had national offices there. By proximity to the seat of power, cultural organizations hoped to affect legislation and stimulate funding, goals that now seemed to be attainable.

Certainly, the legislative climate for the arts had never been more favorable. Efforts to remove the tariff on works of art, unsuccessful through several sessions of Congress, finally culminated in a revenue bill in 1909, the Payne-Aldrich Tariff Act, which exempted all art from import duty with the exception of recent works (paintings less than twenty years old and art objects less than one hundred). Four years later another change in tariff laws exempted all original works of art. In 1910 a bill was passed creating the Commission of Fine Arts, charged with overseeing the planning and erecting of national monuments in Washington. Significantly, appointed members included artists and architects as advisers, indicating their recognition as authorities for such projects.[59]

These developments toward national identity and the concentration of political power in Washington made the new title of the Smithsonian's collection extraordinarily timely for a focus on the nation's own art. At the institution's founding in 1846, programs of the art collection were directed toward living artists, and in 1906, exciting possibilities within the new status confirmed this emphasis. "Obviously a National Gallery should set forth the work of native painters," declared Leila Mechlin.[60] Acquisition of the Evans paintings accelerated the momentum toward contemporary American art. "They inaugurate the spirit that looks about to see what is being done here in America today, instead of ignoring what is close at hand and considering only what is foreign or old," wrote art editor Charles de Kay.[61]

Fervently nationalistic in his support of American artists, President Theodore Roosevelt believed that the greatest art was linked to nationality. "American work must smack of our own soil, mental and moral, no less than physical, or it will have little of permanent value. . . . [It] must in some degree express the distinctive characteristics of our own national soul," he declared.[62] Such a belief inspired similar sentiments in European countries also, where nationalistic political developments of the early nineteenth century received the affirmation of "scientific truth" as defined in the latter decades. "No art has hitherto become great that is not national—that is not stamped indelibly with the character of the race which produced it. To this rule there is no exception," remarked a British art critic in an article on German art.[63]

These commonly held ideas stemmed from several sources, including the enormous influence of Hippolyte Taine on the study of art and literature in the United States and abroad (introduced above in the discussion of art and artifact). Derived from what was commonly defined as "natural laws," his lectures and writings implied with unassailable conviction that the best art develops as distinctive products of a particular nation or race—as surely as vegetation is produced according to its seed, soil, sunshine, and rain. One of many critics and historians who accepted these principles, S. G. W. Benjamin in an essay on American art wrote of the "unswerving, determinate rigor of the laws which direct the development of the race, . . . laws from which we cannot escape if we would."[64]

The belief that human beings and their capabilities are largely determined by biology and environment served to justify prejudicial attitudes and actions in the United States as elsewhere in matters of race, gender, and immigration policy; within a generation it would be used for infamous purposes in Germany. Though a product of nineteenth-century evolutionary theory, it remains today as an all too familiar presence in national and world politics. Applied to defining a national art at the turn of the century, this concept produced division in the American art community when some maintained that a truly American art required birth and residency in the United States. Roosevelt's comment supported American artists in general, but he was particularly concerned with the kind of art whose subject and style "would smack" of the nation's distinctive life and thought. Artists who studied and worked abroad, particularly in Paris, became subject to a backlash against their works. "The American who lives in Paris till he is a mongrel Frenchman can never paint a great picture. . . . simply because the work of such men does not ring true. They must write and paint as they speak the language,—like mongrels, as they are, wrote critic Brooks Adams."[65]

In spite of such rhetoric, however, European-trained artists, secure in their international reputations and holding most of the positions of power in American art institutions, continued to be influential leaders in the art community at home. When President Roosevelt enthusiastically met with the newly appointed Advisory Board of the National Gallery of Art, each of the artists he talked with had studied and worked abroad, and their work (with the exception of Holmes's) typically did not depict American scenes. Factions within the art community argued over what determined authentic American art, but the overall goal favored support of the nation's own artists vis-à-vis European artists. The establishment of a National Gallery of Art in 1906 was perceived as an unprecedented opportunity to showcase paintings and sculptures by Americans.

The two national galleries differed in their relationship to the nation's citizens. As director of the Smithsonian's NGA, Holmes had sought public support for the Smithsonian's building campaign by targeting nationalistic sentiment. Describing the glories of the great art galleries in Europe, he wanted "to stir the pride of a people not accustomed to take a second or third place in any field worthy of their ambition."[66] As a member of the fin de siècle generation, Holmes believed that the fine arts represented the height of human achievement and identified the people's access to art as a foundation for the nation's progress—not only in art but also in spheres such as industry and economics. Through all his arguments he insisted that in a democracy, a national gallery of art ought to be supported by all the people rather than serve as the province of a few wealthy individuals. He repeatedly insisted that the gallery should be built "with a view not only to the place that American art holds today and must hold tomorrow but even to the far future, since art in its material forms is the most enduring, as well as the most precious, heritage of a people. A National Gallery is thus of necessity the property and responsibility of the people in the fullest sense."[67]

An echo from the past, this conviction had been held by Joel R. Poinsett, president of the National Institute for the Promotion of Science, and other leaders of pre-Smithsonian years who insisted that the arts in a democracy ought to be supported by public funds, in contrast to European patronage by royalty and private wealth. In the decade of the 1920s (when the Smithsonian's building campaign took place), as museums were becoming more oriented toward the public in its diversity of age, social class, and educational background, many voices joined in a populist view of appropriate museum support. "There is a great disadvantage to a museum in being given to the people by three or four interested persons. Where the money for creating the museum has been drawn directly from the people, it becomes a cosmopolitan and democratic institution. A conductor or a policeman, a carpenter or hodcarrier will know where it is, because he helped to pay for as well as to build it," insisted Frederic Allen Whiting, director of the Cleveland Museum of Art (and the outspoken critic of Abbot's handling of the Smithsonian National Gallery of Art, as reported above), at a 1923 discussion, "The Place an Art Museum Should Occupy in a Municipality."[68]

By 1937 this ideal had slipped into oblivion. Almost everyone, from Franklin Roosevelt to journalists to ordinary citizens, expressed profound gratitude for Andrew Mellon's collection and the building he gave to the nation, "the most munificent public gift of art in history," effused art critic Alfred M. Frankfurter in a typical response.[69] The gallery was to be supported by federal appropriations—that is, from taxes, which derive from the citizens—but Mellon's initial donation had made the project possible, and pledges of continued support guaranteed the growth of collections and programs. In the midst of the Depression, the wealth represented by the collection and the building plan evoked genuine appreciation for the donor's generosity. The procedure of beginning a project with private money and then turning to government funds to maintain it had early been established in Washington; it was the manner in which the Smithsonian itself was initiated and subsequently supported.

Mellon's choice selection of European masterpieces and his intention to continue gathering a collection of similar quality put the future potential of the Washington gallery on a level with impressive holdings in the great American and European museums. Crucial to the outpouring of national pride inspired by his project was its title as the National Gallery of Art and its location in Washington. Impressive gatherings of European works were already shown at the Art Institute in Chicago, the Museum of Fine Arts in Boston, and the Metropolitan Museum of Art in New York (which from its founding had cast itself in the role of a national institution), but they lacked those two essential attributes.[70] "Obviously Mr. Mellon envisions for Washington and the Nation a gallery as important as the National Gallery in London," observed Philip N. Youtz, president of the American Federation of Arts, and indeed, enhanced national prestige was a major goal of the founder.[71]

In common usage from the late nineteenth century, the term "masterpiece" was consistently identified with works in the Mellon collection. Originating with a practice in Renaissance guilds, in which a journeyman apprentice presented a well-crafted piece to qualify for the title of master, it came to denote a superior work by a particular artist. Its larger meaning required historical links from the past that led up to the "masterpiece"—which in itself provided the basis of inspiration for future works. For example, one of the most famous connoisseurs of this generation, Bernard Berenson, included in his history of Renaissance artists only those painters who "belong to a movement of constant progress."[72] This linear concept of art history moving toward the goal of producing masterpieces that subsequently inspire further creative innovations could not readily be applied to past or contemporary American art, further alienating the new National Gallery and its public from the nation's own art.

Upon learning of the Mellon gallery's policy to show only works by artists who had been dead at least twenty years, American artists turned livid. "A gallery devoted exclusively, or mainly, to the great works of the past, in no way represents or fosters the national culture," wrote Ralph M. Pearson of the Artists Congress to President Franklin D. Roosevelt. "Mr. Mellon's belief that the greatest social value lies in the chance to gaze in awe and reverence at a rare and costly masterpiece of other times and places, rather than in production and participation, is an illusion indicating his divorce from the art experience and his consequent fear and incapacity to deal with that experience for its living, constructive values."[73] Cantankerous Missouri painter Thomas Hart Benton made the same point:

> There is nothing national whatever in Mr. Mellon's museum. We are fortunate to have it, to be sure . . . [since] the collection . . . properly regarded . . . may provide immense stimulation for art in this country. But they [the Mellon paintings] are *not* our art and we cannot for a moment regard them as such. . . . If we don't want our culture to be a series of imitative gestures we must keep our educational procedures out of the hands of those who don't know or recognize anything else and who are so certain that art is an attribute of the dead that they put thirty years death clauses in their purchasing programs to keep out the vulgarity of Life.[74]

Both Benton and Pearson recognized the value of experiencing great art of the past; their objection was to the term "national" for a gallery—in the nation's capital—that would operate to feature European masters and virtually exclude works by the nation's own artists, particularly living artists. (The policy of excluding works by artists until twenty years after their death was nullified some years later, and the National Gallery of Art today maintains an active collection of modern art, much of it American.)

Had the Mellon gallery been founded a decade earlier, such objections would not have been so passionate. The second National Gallery of Art opened its doors in an era of great economic hardship, when federal programs offered subsistence relief to artists and hosts of other citizens in need. The wealth represented by paintings in Mellon's collection heightened a poignant contrast between patronage of the living and the dead.

Government subsidies for artists and art centers had set up a relationship with the federal bureaucracy and served as an overt assurance that the production of art mattered within the overall scheme of the nation's recovery from depression. Considering all that FDR had done for living American artists, art critic and writer Forbes Watson, a technical director of one of the New Deal art programs, was deeply disappointed by the president's unqualified acceptance of the Mellon gift: "It is provocative to think of him accepting for the people, among other valuable assets, works of the Renaissance which have been given to us by collectors who have concentrated on the past and ignored the present."[75]

In an attempt to reconcile these contrasting responses to the announced program of the Mellon gallery, an editorial in *Art Digest* observed: "There are some among us who buy and support the artists of our own age. We are called patrons. There are others, less the gambler but yet just as interested in developing the cultural life of

America, who buy the creations of artists long since dead. They are called collectors. Both are indispensable, if we are to become an art-minded nation."[76]

The thriving nationalistic fervor of a generation earlier had subsided; painters such as Benton tended to be identified as "regionalist" artists rather than with the more encompassing term "American." Federal art programs invigorated the arts within specific geographic sections throughout the breadth of the nation, contributing to a conception of American art as diverse, according to the distinctive history and culture of each area.

Another potent force working against a strong nationalistic spirit in American art in the late 1930s resulted from the control of artists in fascist countries, particularly Nazi Germany, where the promotion of a nationalist art was used for political and propagandistic purposes. Hitler's speech in Munich at the opening of the "Great Exhibition of German Art 1937" stated his intent to "clean house" in the field of art as he had done in the political arena, so that deviations from what he defined as true German art would be forcefully eliminated. The plight of artists in the Third Reich and elsewhere in Europe powerfully affected the course of art and art criticism in the United States, countermanding calls for nationalism in American art as had been sought in the generation of Teddy Roosevelt—and rendering much less conceivable the idea that a national gallery should primarily present the nation's own art.[77]

Defining "Art" for a National Gallery

Pearson and Benton and others who objected to the policy of not showing works by living artists in the new National Gallery defined the function of such an institution quite differently from the way its founder did. In the 1930s, interpretations of John Dewey's *Art as Experience* occupied teachers from grade school to university courses, putting phrases such as "participation" and "living values"—used by Pearson in his letter to FDR—into the art vocabulary. For Pearson and Benton, viewing a collection of masterpieces implied responses that could be merely passive instead of the experiential interaction of an active mind with a work of art, as Dewey advocated. Barriers were easily raised between the ordinary life of most viewers and images in paintings from the European past that represented, in Pearson's words, "other times and places."

These objections centered on the question of whether an art museum should appeal to an elite faction of the public, those whose educational background provided familiarity with famous works of art, or instead aim to attract all levels of society as a populist institution. American artists of the era, through the subject matter of their murals and easel paintings, had immersed their work in the history and daily life of ordinary Americans, and the establishment of community art centers throughout the country brought the experience of art to an untold number of citizens across different levels of society. Although masterpieces of the Old World did not relate directly to the vulgarities of contemporary existence, however, the philosophy of art that informed such collections, no less than the ideal of participation, asserted a relationship to the lives of viewers—though from another perspective.

Born in the 1850s, Mellon belonged to the earlier generation of connoisseurs that included Henry Clay Frick and John Pierpont Morgan. These men formed their ideas about art in the late nineteenth century when the search for biological and cultural origins preoccupied scientists and historians—and the study of history became a quest for identity. A fascination with the past amounted almost to an obsession during the late-century decades, particularly for art of the Italian Renaissance, aggrandized as the height of human achievements by the Swiss historian Jacob Burckhardt in his publication of 1860, *The Civilization of the Renaissance in Italy*. One of Henry James's characters expresses the reverent adoration inspired by Renaissance art, describing art in Florence as "the prime of art. . . . The sun stood high in heaven, and his broad and equal blaze made the darkest places bright and the dullest eyes clear."[78]

Both collectors and artists sought to bask in that blaze of glory. Collectors modeled their own philanthropic selves after the great patrons of the Renaissance; Frick and Morgan created architectural settings for themselves and their art objects that seemed to be transported from Renaissance villas (and parts actually were), buildings that still serve as galleries where their collections can be viewed. Architect of the building for the Mellon gallery, John Russell Pope designed a classic structure based on Beaux Arts architecture that looked back to antecedents in Italy as an appropriate staging for Mellon's choice selection of mostly Renaissance paintings and sculptures. Mellon conceived of his gallery as a means of conveying to the public the enlightened benefits that he found in great works of art: "There is a particular need for a great national gallery of art for the artistic education of our people and it is apparent that the reputation of such an institution is dependent upon the quality of art to be exhibited in such a gallery. . . . The national prestige which flows from the possession by a country of a great gallery of art is immeasurable."[79]

Smithsonian benefactor John Gellatly, on the other hand, like the Medici of fifteenth-century Florence, patronized artists of his own time. Still, by juxtaposing American paintings with decorative pieces and furnishings from Renaissance Italy, he sought aesthetic affinities that he believed enhanced the experience of the contemporary works. In Childe Hassam's colorful canvases he found "a permanence in beauty which will endure for as long a time as have the masterpieces of the 15th century." Such images as Abbott Handerson Thayer's *Virgin Enthroned*, with its deliberate recall of sixteenth-century Venetian madonnas, reached "well into the realms of the Renaissance," as the artist wrote Gellatly.[80] This phenomenon of creating a distinguished lineage for the nation's contemporary artists was not confined to the United States; in Paris, French critics found in their countrymen's art direct connections to the great Italian masters of the fifteenth and sixteenth centuries.

For Thayer, Gellatly, and their contemporaries—including the founder of the second National Gallery of Art—the past was not dead and irrelevant; instead, it represented the highest attainments of civilization and offered intellectual understanding and aesthetic beauty to enlighten the present. Whereas many Americans of the early nineteenth century had found revelations of the divine Creator in the awesome wonders of nature, their descendants in the latter decades were transfixed by the marvelous creations of man.

At the time of the founding of the Mellon gallery, however, a historical imagination that could relate within the same museum the art of living American artists to masterworks of the past was rare in the United States—though some private collectors, such as Gellatly, made a practice of exhibiting Renaissance decorative pieces together with contemporary American paintings. When the Louvre first opened to the public as an art museum in 1793, on the same day an exhibition of works by living artists was shown in a prominent gallery. The practice of showing current paintings and sculptures in proximity to great works of the past continued at the Louvre for decades. In the United States such a possibility was hindered by an endemic ambiguity toward the European past—fostered by the pride of independence and a disquieting sense of cultural inferiority.

A negative attitude toward living American artists erected a more insurmountable barrier against promoting contemporary art along with works of acknowledged masters of the past. In France, living painters and sculptors, considered to be essential to the identity and economy of the country, enjoyed a celebrity status similar to that of movie stars or athletes in the United States today. Artists in this country at best were perceived as marginal to the serious business of the nation. Moreover, the art world itself lacked a sense of historical continuity with its own heritage. Late-century artists who had rejected their immediate forebears, the midcentury landscape and genre painters, finding their paintings parochial with no connection to their own works, were in turn dismissed by artists, art critics, and historians of the twentieth century as expatriates whose productions were outside the "truly American" tradition.

Major changes in the art world and the nation took place in the thirty years that separated the founding of the two national galleries in 1906 and 1937. The new National Gallery heralded exciting opportunities for seeing great art in Washington—but diminished interest and support for American art. During the next three decades the optimistic ideals that had accompanied establishment of the first National Gallery—now called the National Collection of Fine Arts—for all practical purposes would disappear, whereas the high expectations held for the second would be attained.

4

Rejecting Modern Art for Washington, 1930s–1960s

On March 15, 1937—in the same month that Congress accepted the Mellon gift—a resolution was introduced in the House by Representative Kent E. Keller, a Democrat from Illinois, to provide for construction of the long-awaited housing for the Smithsonian's art gallery. The possibility of a building—at last—for the nation's first art collection as it began its history under the title National Collection of Fine Arts (NCFA) renewed hope for its mission to promote past and current American art in all its modes. Stating the name of the proposed structure as the "Smithsonian Gallery of Art," the bill reserved a site on the Mall fronting Constitution Avenue between Twelfth and Fourteenth Streets (today the location of the National Museum of American History). The name given to the proposed building was probably meant to distinguish it from the Mellon Gallery of Art. Three types of collections, designated as appropriate contents for the gallery, described the NCFA's holdings: "paintings, sculptures . . . and other types of art"; "portraits of eminent American men and women"; and "the works of contemporary artists deserving of recognition." (Based on a practice of the Luxembourg and Louvre museums, a relationship, never carried out, was proposed between the Smithsonian and Mellon collections: the former would acquire contemporary works, the best of which, after a period of time that allowed for evaluation, would become part of the latter.) The sum of $4.8 million authorized for construction, however, proved to be a stumbling block, and the Bureau of the Budget reported that President Roosevelt "was reluctantly obliged to postpone action on the project for the time being."[1]

A little more than a year later, a revised version of the proposal was passed by Congress and approved May 17, 1938, by the president.[2] Possibilities for the site were expanded to "the Mall . . . between Fourth and Fourteenth Streets and Constitution Avenue and Independence Avenue." In place of an appropriation, Smithsonian Regents were "authorized to solicit and receive subscriptions of funds from private sources . . . to meet the cost of the construction of the building, including furnishings and equipment thereof." The new resolution did provide a grant of $40,000 for expenditures of the Smithsonian Gallery of Art Commission, a group authorized to obtain a suitable plan for the building, including compensation for awards in case an architectural competition were held.

Plans for a Dynamic Gallery

Charged with the responsibility of securing an appropriate architectural design, "by competition or otherwise, preferably by competition," the newly appointed commission consisted of Frederic A. Delano (the president's uncle), chairman of the National Capital Park and Planning Commission, who also served as chairman of this group; Edward Bruce, director of the Treasury Section of Painting and Sculpture, part of New Deal art projects; Gilmore D. Clarke, chairman of the Commission of Fine Arts; Senator Alben W. Barkley, chairman of the Joint Committee on the Library; Representative Kent E. Keller, chairman of the Committee on the Library of the House; Charles G. Abbot, secretary of the Smithsonian; and Charles L. Borie, architect and chairman of the Smithsonian Art Commission (the new title of the former National Gallery of Art Commission—and a name confusingly similar to that of this committee, the Smithsonian Gallery of Art Commission, charged solely with the architectural competition). An eighth member was to be named by the Regents, but Delano, who also sat on that board, persuaded fellow Regents to delay the appointment until a major donor for the building appeared, so that as an appointed member of the group the donor could participate in molding plans for the gallery. In the continuing absence of such a benefactor, the Regents failed to appoint an additional member to the commission. (Retired from a business association with railroads, Delano, now in his mid-seventies, served with enormous energy the several boards he sat on in Washington. In addition to those mentioned above, he was a member of the Federal Reserve Board.)

Other provisions essentially repeated the 1937 draft of the unsuccessful bill—plus an item that added unusual scope to programs for contemporary art: "In order to encourage the development of contemporary art and to effect the widest distribution and cultivation in matters of such art, the Regents are hereby authorized to solicit and receive funds from private sources, to acquire (by purchase or otherwise) and sell contemporary works of art or copies thereof, to employ artists and other personnel, award scholarships, conduct exhibitions, and generally to do such things and have such other powers as will effectuate the purposes of this subsection." This bold emphasis on contemporary art very likely originated with two members of the new commission, Delano and Bruce. Before the legislation was formulated, they had discussed together the need of a gallery for works by living artists, and Delano subsequently infected Roosevelt with his enthusiasm for such a goal. His and Bruce's efforts reflected the attempts to perpetuate official ties between artists and the federal government which had begun in the 1880s and gathered momentum in the New Deal era.[3]

At the first meeting of the Smithsonian Gallery of Art Commission, Chairman Delano stated as his preference for a building site the two-block area between Fourth and Seventh Streets on the south side of the Mall, opposite the site for the new National Gallery of Art. Stressing the need for economy in construction, he proposed adapting a type of structure used at the 1916 World's Fair in San Francisco and the 1933 World's Columbian Exposition in Chicago: windowless walls formed by lightweight partitions to extend the exhibition space. He further showed advanced thinking about museum practices by insisting that visitors who were disabled or elderly be given special conveniences, as had been done at the temporary expositions. Commission members agreed with his thoughts on the construction of the building and approved the suggested site.

Within eight months of their first meeting, in January 1939 the commission announced a nationwide architectural competition to design the Smithsonian Gallery of Art. It was to take place in two stages: the first for all contestants; the second restricted to those whose designs were judged the ten best. Offering $7,500 as first prize, $3,500 for second, and $1,000 each for the next eight, the contest was open to all architects who were United States citizens. In addition to the award, the first-place winner was to received a fee of $18,000 to design the building. Distinguished architects John A. Holabird of Chicago, Henry R. Shepley of Boston, George Howe of Philadelphia, and Walter Gropius of Cambridge, Massachusetts were named jurors, together with the ubiquitous Delano; Professor Joseph Hudnet of the Department of Architecture at Harvard University acted as professional adviser, and Thomas Mabry, an administrator at New York's Museum of Modern Art, as technical adviser.

Designating the site on the south side of the Mall, competition details specified the area of initial construction as 1.5 million cubic feet, and the completed building as 3 million cubic feet, said to be approximately the same size as planned for the Mellon Gallery. Architects were asked to consider providing natural side light for 30 percent of the exhibition area and natural top light for 20 percent. Other stated requirements included an auditorium for about 1,000 persons and a lecture hall for 100, a reference library and a national lending library, in addition to administration and work areas, exhibition and storage spaces.

In the announcement of the competition, members of the commission not only stated technical requirements to prospective architects but also established priorities for programs of the gallery. "The importance of the new museum will arise from the potentialities of a unique service in the cause of American art that are inherent in its program of activities rather than from the value of the present Smithsonian collections, important though they are," began the statement of goals. Indicating that the building had to meet the twofold need of displaying the present collection and providing "an expanding program of services to the country at large," they placed far more emphasis upon the second requirement.

> The new Gallery is conceived as a dynamic rather than static museum of art. Reconstituted as an active, influencing agency, it will use its present collection and encourage further gifts in an effort to stimulate the creation of works of art of distinction and to elevate and sustain the public appreciation of those works throughout the country. . . . The works of art in its possession will become available through traveling exhibitions to people throughout the United States. . . . It will not only circulate large exhibitions to other museums but it is hoped to also furnish schools, community groups, and local "centers" with a wide variety of material in connection with contemporary painting, sculpture, architecture, graphic arts, photography, and industrial arts. . . . The Gallery is conceived as a national clearing house for the visual arts. In this capacity it must achieve maximum flexibility and freedom of extension if it is to fulfill the objectives of its program.[4]

The plan of reaching out to the public with exhibitions and other educational programs expressed the intensified concern in the 1930s for populist goals. Museums founded in the 1870s had included education as a major aim, but now such activities moved to the head of institutional agendas as a means of economic survival. The director of the Metropolitan Museum of Art, Francis Henry Taylor, wrote of "interpreting our resources in the light of their potential usefulness to society, and by reconciling the layman and the scholar—therein lies our only hope for survival in the modern world."[5]

The weakness of these broad programs and idealistic objectives proposed for the Smithsonian gallery lay in their proclamation by individuals who would have absolutely no responsibility for carrying them out, for their authors were members of a commission that was to be terminated upon submission to the Regents of an acceptable architectural design. In the absence of leadership from within the Smithsonian, the commission with great gusto had set forth goals of the institution's art program. To be sure, representatives from the Smithsonian, Secretary Abbot and Charles L. Borie, were members of the group, but most likely they had nothing to do with this mission statement; it carries the imprint of Edward Bruce.[6]

A lawyer, businessman, and a painter, Bruce was emboldened by his sense of power within the federal bureaucracy and set out to mold the Smithsonian Gallery of Art into his idea of the kind of art institution needed in Washington. Though mandated for the economic relief of artists, the Works Progress Administration's Federal Art Project and other New Deal art programs became vehicles throughout the country for experiments in the active relationship of art and artists to "the people." Holger Cahill, national director of the Federal Art Project, defined connections between art and society as important goals to be attained by artists' participating in "the life and thought and movement of their own time."[7] Imbued with tenets of John Dewey's philosophy, as were Bruce's assertions, Cahill's statement was published in 1936, two years before the guidelines for the legislative and architectural programs.

Emphasis upon contemporary American art was conceived partly as a complement to the Mellon gallery, defined as a collection of masterpieces of European art of the past. A focus on American art and the encouragement of living American artists also continued policies that went back to the Regents 1846 definition of art at the institution. Indeed, the legislation of May 17, 1938, and the published architectural program that followed put into official form nascent programs that had first been stated at the founding, strengthened by major acquisitions of contemporary American art in the Evans and Gellatly collections and renewed by William H.

Holmes's efforts to relate the Smithsonian's art programs to the nation's artists. By no means did the basic principles of Bruce's program conflict with the goals originally defined at the institution's founding or subsequently planned in 1906, when the title of the National Gallery of Art was conferred.

There was one significant difference between the mandate for the new building and previously stated Smithsonian goals: a relative lack of regard for the permanent collection—the most important reason for the necessity of a building as voiced by earlier spokespersons inside and outside the institution. In testimony before Congress promoting the 1938 legislation, some speakers had mentioned proper housing and display of the collections exclusively. Leila Mechlin testified that "a number of valuable art collections given to the National Gallery of Art [that is, the former National Gallery of Art] . . . constitute a moral obligation on the part of the Government to see that such a gallery is established." This was also the sole point made by Secretary Abbot in his appearance before the congressional committee.[8] Before the bill was drafted, however, Bruce conferred with Roosevelt, reinforcing Delano's advocacy of the same issue with the president, with the resulting emphasis upon active programs for living American artists.

No one questioned any of the statements in the resolution or the building program—in public. At their December gathering in the Castle, members of the Smithsonian Art Commission would set their own priorities for the proposed building, but before that meeting took place, conservative attitudes toward art in the capital city would prove a pitfall for gallery plans.

The ten architectural designs selected from 408 entries for the final stage of the competition were submitted by Paul Philippe Cret of Philadelphia; Albert Frey, Philip L. Goodwin, and Louis C. Jaeger, New York; Percival Goodman, New York; Robert W. Kennedy and Eliot F. Noyes, Cambridge; Harry F. Manning, Chicago; G. Holmes Perkins, Boston; Marc Peter Jr. and Hugh Stubbins, Boston; Dahlen K. Ritchey and James A. Mitchell, Pittsburgh; Eero Saarinen, Eliel Saarinen, and J. Robert F. Swanson, Cranbrook Academy, Bloomfield Hills, Michigan; and Edward D. Stone, New York. On June 28, 1939, jurors announced that they had arrived at a unanimous decision, awarding first prize to the design of the Saarinens and Swanson (figure 22) and second prize to Percival Goodman. "Both offer simple, direct solutions in which all facilities are adequately provided for and in which the relation of part to part is correct," the jurors explained in a letter to the Smithsonian Gallery of Art Commission. They elaborated: "The design submitted by

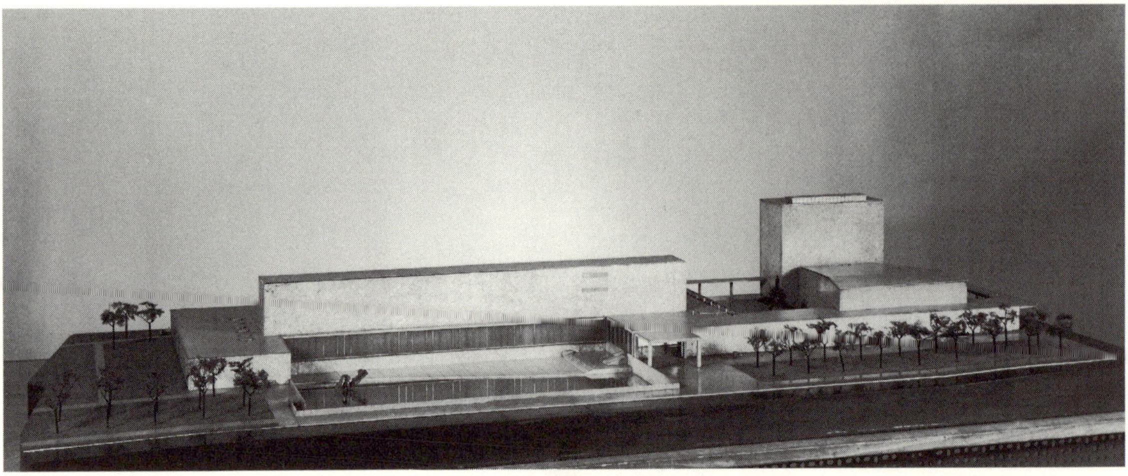

Figure 22. Eliel Saarinen, Eero Saarinen, and J. Robert F. Swanson, *Model of Smithsonian Gallery of Art*. Smithsonian American Art Museum, Gift of Eero Saarinen.

Eliel Saarinen is considered especially appropriate in relation to the site. It offers a remarkable clarity of composition in mass and a restraint and dignity in expression which appears to the majority of the jury especially suitable for a building to be built on the Washington Mall." Jurors also liked the possibilities for expansion offered by the design—one of the conditions of the competition—and in this respect they felt it edged ahead of the second-place winner. The other eight final contestants were each awarded third prize.[9] The following day the Smithsonian Gallery of Art Commission met and, in accord with the competition guidelines, adopted the recommendations of the Jury of Award and moved to submit their report to the Smithsonian Board of Regents.

The jurors' selection of the Saarinen design, granting recognition in Washington to the modern idiom, was hailed as a victory in current architectural wars that set traditionalists in opposition to modernists. A writer in *Architectural Forum* reflected on the implications:

> The significance of this competition, however, overshadows the importance of the building or the success of the method. That an impeccable jury should have chosen—for Washington—a building without the usual Roman draperies is not only a tribute to their courage and honesty, but gives, at long last,

> some hope that the Capital may show three-dimensional evidence of its existence in the twentieth century.
>
> This triumph for the modern approach by no means implies a flaunting of all that Washington stands for, but rather a step towards its fulfillment. . . . The great virtue of the winning design, aside from the technical excellence of its solution, is that it shows beyond the possibility of denial that the monumental tradition of Washington can be given appropriate expression, and new vitality, within the framework of modern architecture.[10]

"It is asserted Saarinen's design is perfectly suited for a factory," countered a journalist expressing opinions of the other side. "Critics declare that, set on the Mall across from the Greco-Roman Mellon Gallery, in the long and pillared perspective of Constitution Avenue, the Smithsonian structure will be not a decorative accent in the city beautiful, but an eyesore extraordinary."[11] Professional and public controversies notwithstanding, the jurors' selection was accepted by the Smithsonian Gallery of Art Commission.

Two other official bodies also had to agree to the design, however: the Commission of Fine Arts, authorized to evaluate proposed construction in Washington, and the Smithsonian Regents. The Commission of Fine Arts steadfastly represented the traditionalists. To each commissioner Chairman Clarke sent a copy of the letter he had received from Charles Moore, who had chaired the Commission from 1915 to 1937 as a staunch advocate for the classical style:

> I have just been setting down on paper the records of the early architects, Thornton, Hoban and Latrobe, Bulfinch, Robert Mills and Walter—seventy years of uninterrupted classicism from Washington to Lincoln. Then the pseudo-classicism of Mullet in the State, War, and Navy [today called the Executive Office Building], the travesty of the Pension Office [the National Building Museum], the Richardsonianism of the Post Office, and the screaming golden dome of the Congressional Library. And finally the return to dignity, good proportions and elegance of the plans of 1901 and their development.
>
> And now come the plans you are wrestling with for a Smithsonian Art Gallery which threaten to foist on Washington a building architecturally far inferior to the Pension Office and for sheer ugliness more assertive than the State, War and Navy—an epitome of the chaos of the Nazi art of today. I trust that Congress will refuse to make appropriations for a building so abhorrent to the history and architecture of the city.[12]

Comparing the Saarinen design with Nazi art was sheer nonsense: Albert Speer, chief architect for the Third Reich, was firmly committed to the classic tradition. In that regard, he and Moore had much in common.

Clarke proposed to Abbot a recommendation to the Regents that the Saarinens and their colleague Swanson be considered simply as winners of the competition—who would be asked "in due time" to make a suitable design for the location on the Mall.

When the Smithsonian Art Commission (NCFA's board) met in December 1939, their representatives to the selection committee, Abbot and Borie, reported on details of the rules, the result of the competition, and the "suitability of the prize winning design." After "a very full discussion" Professor Mather proposed a resolution agreed upon by all: "The primary purpose of the Smithsonian Gallery of Art is worthily to house, classify, and exhibit such art collections as the Smithsonian Institution now has or shall have. The secondary purpose is to make an educational use of such art collections through direct instruction at Washington or through loan exhibitions in the United States or elsewhere."[13] Thus—somewhat tardily—the commissioners reversed the priorities as set forth in the competition program. They recorded no statement about the first-place design—which in itself serves as a comment. Commissioners present at this meeting, besides Abbot and Borie, were Louis Ayres, an architect; David E. Finley, director of the National Gallery of Art; John E. Lodge, director of the Freer Gallery; Paul Manship, sculptor; Frank Jewett Mather, Jr., art historian at Princeton University; George B. McClellan (son of the Civil War general), former mayor of New York and retired Princeton professor of economic history; Edward Willis Redfield, painter; and Mahonri M. Young, painter and sculptor.[14]

Moore had no need to worry that Congress might fund the Saarinen project, for the resolution providing for the gallery specified that funds were to be raised privately. During congressional hearings on the bill, both Delano and Bruce stated that they knew of persons and organizations who would furnish funds for the construction. Bruce claimed that the Mellon trustees "convinced him they will contribute substantially toward the building." He also asserted that the Guggenheim Foundation was considering "an important contribution."[15] But in November 1939, five months after the announcement of the winning design, Delano wrote to Borie, "Mr. Bruce, I, and others, have as yet had no luck in getting private funds." Realizing that support was unlikely for a building disapproved by the Commission of Fine Arts,

Delano believed that the commission had "exceeded its authority . . . overlooking the fact that the purpose of the competition was not to get a *final design*, but to *select an architect*."[16]

All hope for the Saarinen plan—or even of the first-place winners named as architects of the proposed gallery—disappeared, at least for the time being. And time was running out. Within a couple of years the urgent priorities of a global war would take precedence over the architectural project of an art museum.

Subsistence Survival—While Two Directors Make Lemonade

From the moment of its publication the Saarinen design for the Smithsonian Gallery of Art engaged architectural historians as an exemplary study in the controversy between traditional and modern styles, all the more significant because of connections to official Washington. In real life at the National Collection of Fine Arts, the effect of the building competition was entirely negative. Acceptance of the design by the architectural committee and its subsequent rejection by the Fine Arts Commission and Smithsonian Regents resulted in failure once again to provide a proper building for the institution's art collections and programs.

Following Abbot's retirement, the Regents in January 1945 appointed as chief officer of the institution Alexander Wetmore, an ornithologist. Like his predecessor, Wetmore considered the establishment of the Mellon gallery as a fulfillment of the Smithsonian's mandate for art. "In addition to its scientific activities, the Smithsonian is charged in its act of foundation with responsibility for national art treasures," he noted in his second annual report. "The art feature has culminated recently in the National Gallery of Art, given to the Nation by Andrew W. Mellon." Wetmore regularly reported first on National Gallery of Art activities, proudly relating such items as numbers of visitors and new accessions and publications, before turning his attention to the National Collection of Fine Arts. While offering NCFA occasional verbal sympathy for its unfulfilled needs, he offered no assistance in promoting its programs through budgetary or other assertive actions. In his centennial report of 1946, a list of new buildings proposed for the institution included a museum of history, a building for industrial and aviation collections, and additional facilities at the zoo—without a hint of a building for the art collection.[17] After architect John Russell Pope's monumental marble building rose on the Mall, the National Collection of Fine Arts was overshadowed by its glamorous and wealthy sibling institution while being maintained as a "second-rate affair," as Acting Director Ruel Tolman had predicted.

Funding barely provided subsistence survival. In 1938, the first full year under its new name, NCFA received $33,525, of which $16,542 was required for the maintenance of the Freer Gallery (considered a unit of NCFA), leaving just under $17,000 to cover the National Collection's salaries, supplies, and other necessary expenses. By 1952 the appropriation had been increased to $47,265, including the apportionment for the Freer. In that year funding for the entire Smithsonian totaled $2,553,200, and the federal appropriation for the National Gallery of Art was $1,240,000.[18] Whereas both the Freer and the Mellon galleries had access to private funds for certain professional and administrative salaries and other expenses, NCFA was totally dependent upon its federal appropriation (with the exception of the Catherine Walden Myer Fund, which provided about $600 annually for the purchase of miniatures).

These deprivations were to remain virtually unchanged until the mid-1960s. For the intervening twenty-five years, two directors, Ruel Pardee Tolman (figure 23) and his successor in 1948, Thomas Montague Beggs (figure 24), together with a staff that varied from three to eight persons, continued to acquire works, care for the collection, and mount exhibitions for a Smithsonian museum that was effectively ignored by the institution.

Following the old adage about what to do if you are handed a lemon, Tolman made lemonade; he pushed NCFA toward excellence in one particular area. His education had included several institutions in California—the Los Angeles School of Art and Design and the University of California, among others—and in Washington he had studied and taught at the Corcoran School of Art. Tolman began his career at the Smithsonian in the Division of Graphic Arts. A printmaker and painter, particularly of miniatures (as was his wife, Nelly Summerel McKenzie), Tolman concentrated on acquiring miniature paintings as a means of dealing with limited storage space and funding. The subjects of these diminutive works that measure less than a couple of inches are usually portraits. They are painted in water color on porcelain, paper, or parchement, though most commonly on ivory; more rarely, the painting medium is oil on copperplate. Through the earlier gift of the Catherine Walden Myer Fund, Tolman made choice purchases, and because of his expertise in the field he was able to attract important donations. NCFA thus developed one of the finest collections of miniatures in the country. Tolman's acquisitions include ivories by the most famous

American painters of miniatures: Henry Benbridge, John Henry Brown, Edward Greene Malbone, and James Peale.

Educational outreach became the special focus of Beggs, initially through a bequest received shortly after he became director. A graduate of the Yale School of Fine Arts, he had also studied in France at the Fontainebleau School, established after the war for members of the American Expeditionary Forces, and had done

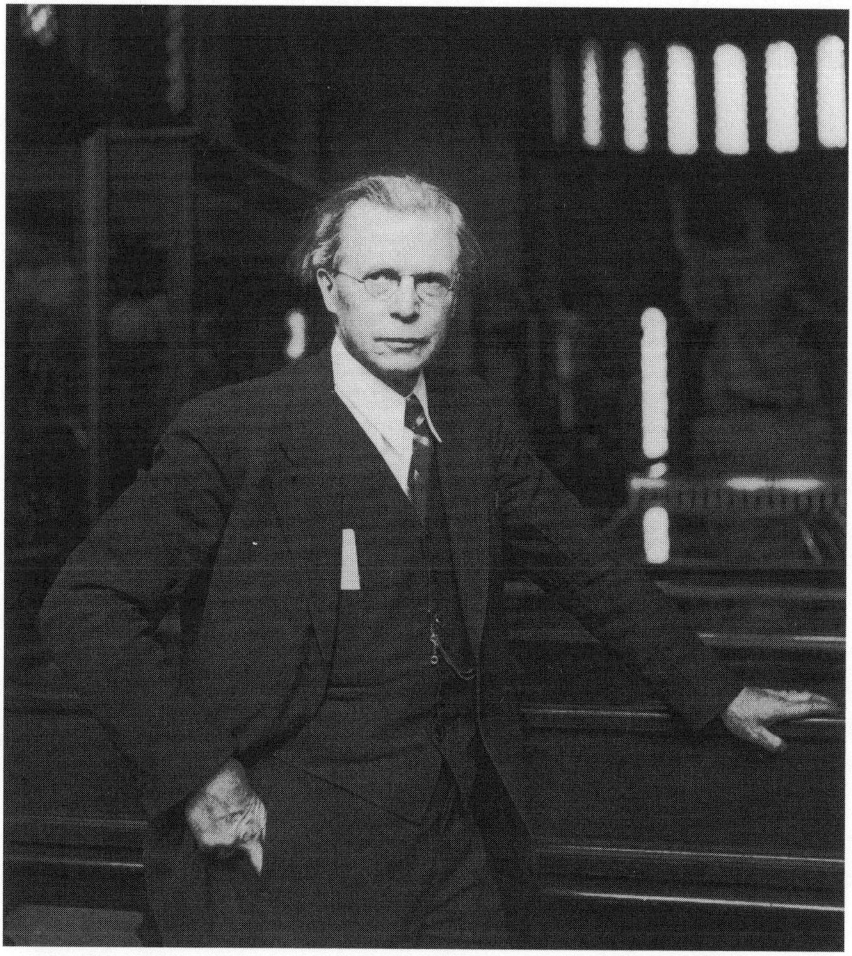

Figure 23. *Ruel Pardee Tolman*. Smithsonian Institution Archives, neg. no. 95-20516.

graduate work at Harvard University.[19] Like his predecessor, Beggs was a painter and teacher, and while on the faculty at Pomona College he had admired pastels by Alice Pike Barney in the school's collection. Upon learning that a Smithsonian department had received donations from the Barney family, he sought a gift to NCFA.[20] In 1951 the artist's daughters, Laura Dreyfus Barney and Natalie Clifford Barney, in memory of their mother presented a collection of her paintings and pastels, works by her contemporaries, and a number of sculptures and other objects

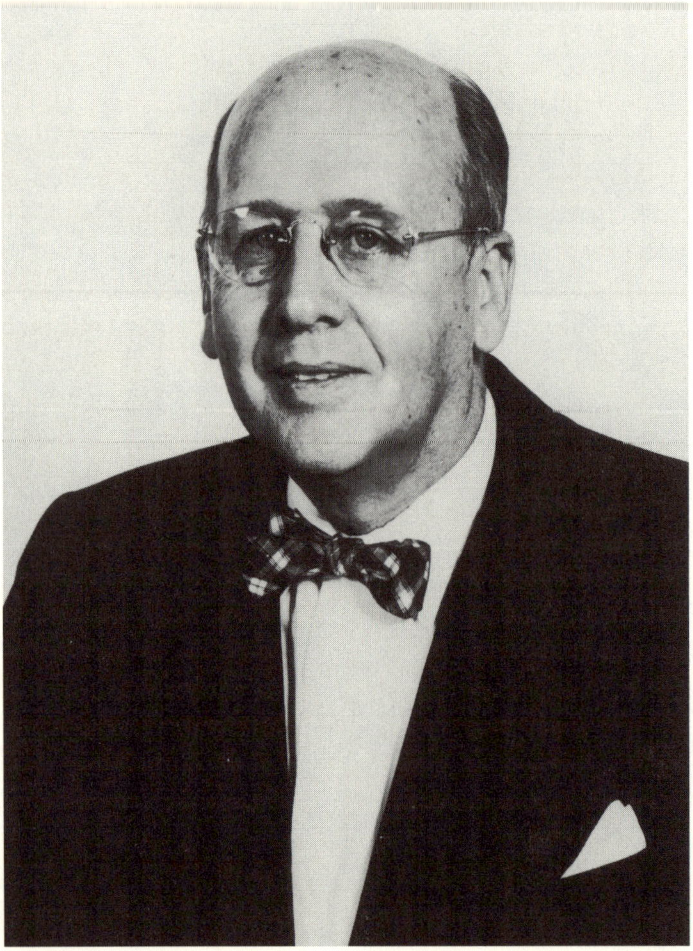

Figure 24. *Thomas Montague Beggs*. Smithsonian Institution Archives, neg. no. 91-5759.

of art with the intent that they be part of a loan collection to further Mrs. Barney's mission of extending the experience of art to a wide audience. In 1960 Laura Barney presented Barney Studio House on Sheridan Circle in Washington and subsequently gave the contents of the house and other furnishings. The Barney donation further enriched NCFA's impressive group of works by fin de siècle American artists and provided the basis for an active lending program to agencies in Washington and educational institutions and art centers throughout the country.[21] Beggs rightly felt that his greatest contributions to NCFA were the Barney acquisitions and the programs they made possible.

With support from the Barney Memorial Fund and a grant from the Department of State, the Smithsonian Institution Traveling Exhibition Service (SITES) was initiated at NCFA in September 1951. Directed by Annemarie H. Pope, widow of the architect of the National Gallery of Art, the service became self-supporting by 1957. Exhibits in fine arts, crafts, history, and science were organized by museums in the United States and abroad, then circulated by the service. From 32 exhibitions sent out in the first year, the volume swelled in ten years to 135 sent to more than 300 participating museums. Because the terms of the Barney Fund precluded sending exhibits out of the country, a grant from the State Department was needed to expand the service in that direction.

SITES was one of only three major exhibition services at this time. The American Federation of Arts circulated shows within the states and sent exhibits overseas under the auspices of the State Department's United States Information Agency (USIA); the Museum of Modern Art also organized exhibits for showing outside the country. The SITES program specialized in obtaining exhibitions from abroad to show in U.S. museums. The practice of circulating exhibits of art, if not uniquely American, certainly developed here with energy and a distinctive sense of mission, encouraged by the geographic breadth of the country and distance from European institutions. As early as the first decade of the twentieth century the American Federation of Art had initiated its program with the purpose of making the experience of art accessible to more citizens.

A Maverick among the Commissioners

More accessions came into the NCFA lending collection than to the permanent collection during the 1950s, for lack of proper gallery and storage space continued to cause the loss of major donations. There was another reason too—the continuing aesthetic and political conservatism of NCFA's director and members of the commission.

After the founding of the second National Gallery of Art, although NCFA's commissioners changed their name from the National Gallery of Art Commission to the Smithsonian Art Commission, the board remained otherwise as it had been reorganized in 1920 with membership of five artists, five experts in fine arts, and five business or professional men. Appointed by the Regents upon recommendation of the commissioners, members served a term of four years, but because they were regularly reelected, in reality they had lifelong tenure. Made a member in 1931, Paul Manship in 1944 was elected chairman of the commission and continued in that role for the next twenty years. Appointed to the commission in 1938, David Finley was elected chairman of the executive committee in 1944 and—since members of the executive committee also experienced recurring reelection—held that office for more than a decade. The agenda for the annual meeting in December typically involved the reelection of members whose four-year terms were concluding, reelection of the executive committee, the occasional replacement of members who had died, and the examination of artworks presented for consideration as accessions.

A static, conservative board might well have served the needs of an art museum dedicated to art of the past, but NCFA had inherited a special concern for American art and, through the 1938 legislation, was specifically directed toward programs and collections in contemporary American art. Dealing with the National Collection's problems and potential required an awareness of American art of the past and present, a knowledge of American art institutions, and a willingness to participate in the political process on the national level. In 1947 the one individual in the nation who best incorporated these qualities was elected to the commission, Lloyd Goodrich.

Associate director of the Whitney Museum of American Art and pioneer historian of American art, Lloyd Goodrich had committed his career to the art and artists of the United States. In the 1930s he had charge of the New York Regional Committee for the federal art programs, an early experience with the government's involvement with art; the relation of government to art remained a focus of his concerns. In a 1948 article for *Magazine of Art* he wrote of the governmental neglect suffered by "our national collections of art." Referring to the gifts of William T. Evans and John Gellatly, he pointed out that NCFA "has a collection of nineteenth-century

American art equal to those of many leading museums, including seventeen Ryders . . . but although many attempts have been made to secure funds from Congress, the collection is still crowded into a few galleries in the Natural History Museum, surrounded by scientific collections, with the pictures hung two deep, and practically unknown to the public."[22]

Experiences with federal patronage during the New Deal era had raised expectations in the art community for the government's potential role in the nation's art. A proposal of late 1948 and early 1949 by the American Federation of Art (composed of twelve national art organizations representing artists, museums, educational groups, architects, designers, decorators, and other art vocations) formed the Committee on Government and Art under the chairmanship of Goodrich. Members drafted a resolution requesting President Harry S. Truman to appoint a commission "to consider the whole question of the Government's relation to art, to study existing governmental agencies and methods, and to submit recommendations for their improvement." Their statement contained an item written with NCFA in mind: "We believe that collections of art donated to the Nation by public-spirited citizens but without donation of funds to house and maintain them, deserve adequate maintenance and exhibition by the Government."[23]

President Truman authorized the Commission of Fine Arts under the chairmanship of David Finley to undertake such a task, a move that distressed Goodrich and other committee members, who had proposed a larger study group more broadly representative of the art world. They also objected to allowing the Commission of Fine Arts in effect to investigate its own responsibilities. As a result, after Finley's group submitted its report to President Eisenhower in 1953,[24] Goodrich's committee published its own statement the following year, emphasizing the conviction that "the primary purpose of governmental art activities should be, not subsidizing the art world nor supporting artists, but the use by the Government of art for public purposes. . . . [Such activities are] important because of their public nature, the scale of the audience they reach, their broad social purpose, their widespread influence on public appreciation and understanding, and their vital role in our cultural relations with other nations." It specified "the maintenance and exhibition of collections of art belonging to the Nation" as one of the activities "which can be carried on only by the Federal Government."[25]

Members of the Commission of Fine Arts in their report referred to NCFA by essentially repeating statements from the 1938 legislation. They called for an expansion of NCFA's activities in programs of art education throughout the nation and in the cultural exchange programs sponsored by the State Department. Though basically agreeing with those recommendations, Goodrich's committee went into more specifics, stressing that NCFA was "inadequately financed and maintained." But the points that raised the hackles of NCFA's commissioners were criticisms of the Smithsonian Art Commission—their own group—for being "a self-perpetuating body, whose members serve until retirement," and their incompetency to guide activities relating to contemporary American art. The report went on to make recommendations for broadening representation on the commission and other agencies to include art museum professionals, art historians, and members of other national art organizations in order to give "the art world a voice in nominating the members of bodies that determine governmental art policies."[26] Goodrich's committee, for the same reasons, also proposed that appointments to the Commission of Fine Arts be broadened maintaining that here too members of the larger art community should be involved in naming members.

Even before submitting his report, Goodrich had freely expressed these points as his personal opinions to Thomas Beggs and certain congressmen.[27] Completely open in stating his criticisms—even to those he censured—Goodrich brought a refreshing sense of integrity and honesty to Washington politics, but he must have begun to wonder if the Smithsonian Art Commission would vote to continue his membership within their group (he mentioned his doubts to Beggs). In 1955, the year after his committee's report to the president was published, he was eligible for reelection. Members of the NCFA commissioners executive committee at their November meeting considered the pros and cons of having such a maverick in their midst. "I think that if we were organized according to Mr. Goodrich there would be a predominance of radical artists and the equivalent to a lobby for artists," asserted Thomas Beggs, but on the point of keeping him within the commission, NCFA's director believed that "it is better to have him with us than working against us. . . . His presence is stimulating if we can get him to think in the correct way." "He may be safer here than on the outside," agreed Gilmore D. Clarke, adding, "I think you need someone who thinks the other way." "Personally like Lloyd," admitted David Finley, "but don't go along with his ideas. Will be happy to have him reelected." Finally all agreed to endorse Lloyd Goodrich for reelection to the Smithsonian Art Commission.[28]

Tension continued to be generated by Goodrich, who did not learn "to think in the correct way." He was convinced that among commission members only he and

Charles Sawyer, former director of the Worcester Art Museum, Bartlett H. Hayes Jr., director of the Addison Gallery of American Art, and possibly the artist Andrew Wyeth were competent to judge in matters relating to contemporary American art.

Art as a Threat to the Nation

Beggs's fear of "radical artists" infiltrating the commission or gaining representation in the collection loomed in his mind as a double menace of leftist politics and modernist art, inseparable Siamese twins of subversion bent on destroying American traditions. The specter of international communism had motivated the federal government in 1947 to institute a loyalty oath for government employees, thus officially initiating the suspicion and fear that soon enveloped the nation. Under attacks by Wisconsin Republican Senator Joseph McCarthy, chairman of the Committee on Government Operations and its Subcommittee on Investigations, the populace was ostensibly divided into two camps, those loyal to the United States and those committed to the nation's overthrow.

George A. Dondero, a Republican congressman from Michigan, carved out his own niche in a defamation campaign by concentrating on artists, their works, and art organizations. On the floor of the House in 1949 he began accusing specific artists and art organizations of being communist dominated. Even a prestigious honorific organization such as the National Institute of Arts and Letters came under condemnation. It was a perverse promotion of sorts for the status of American artists, considering that congressmen had formerly tended to look upon them as marginal to the nation's interests, but now, along with writers, movie stars, and theatrical performers, they were perceived as having power to subvert the nation. The situation could have been appreciated for its irony except for its devastating effect upon the careers of individual artists and the entire climate for art in the nation. In a blast at a Washington institution, Dondero called the Corcoran Gallery, along with the Virginia Museum of Fine Arts at Richmond, a victim of a "cultural Fifth column" and warned against "a chain of Red instigated artists' organizations designed to control art and artists in the United States."[29]

Thomas Beggs was a true believer in Dondero's pronouncements. Highly critical of Goodrich's Committee on Government and Art—and fearing that its members might be placed on NCFA's commission—he informed Smithsonian Secretary Leonard Carmichael that certain organizations represented in that group had been cited by Dondero as communist affiliated or dominated, notably the Arts Equity Association and the National Institute of Arts and Letters. He looked upon Dondero—who referred to particular artists as "germ-carrying art vermin" and "human art termites"—as a watchdog against legislation that would provide for misguided changes. Beggs also suggested, in the draft of an essay on radical communism and art, that the possibility of communist-leaning artists within the Treasury Section of Painting and Sculpture (of which Bruce was the director) who "were prominent among the supporters of the Smithsonian Gallery of Art Act . . . made many skeptical of the value of developing a NCFA program."[30] No documentation supports this claim as a reason why the Saarinen building project was not implemented. What was certain—and damaging for the course of American art in the 1950s—was the association of modern art with political subversion.

The Michigan congressman exploited the ambiguity conveyed by new forms of art, which appeared impenetrable to many who were schooled in representational depictions of the visible world. Claiming that "modern art [was] shackled to communism," Dondero in a 1956 speech charged that the American Federation of Art (AFA) through its exhibitions tried "to force acceptance of its monopoly of radical culturalists at the expense of the American taxpayer." He was indignant that AFA had selected Jacob Lawrence's work to send abroad and characterized Stuart Davis, Philip Evergood, Jack Levine, Ben Shahn, and Max Weber among other artists as "unfit to represent American culture. . . . The priceless heritage of our art and culture," he proclaimed on the floor of the House of Representatives, "must be protected for future generations and not be ruthlessly destroyed by so-called art manifestations that have been consciously designed to disintegrate cultural standards and have proven to have been an effective means of destruction."[31] The word "communist," wrote Ben Shahn, one of the accused, "is used to mask a variety of purposes. It is used by the philistine to vilify art or music or literature that is foreign to his understanding."[32]

Dondero's rantings cannot be reduced to a simplistic interpretation of the government imposing its power over the arts. By going beyond accusations that linked individuals and organizations with radical politics to attacks on works of art, Dondero honed a message that many artists wanted to hear. Conservative painters and sculptors and their organizations, notably the National Sculpture Society and the National Academy of Design, abetted his efforts by supplying him with material for his whetstone. They had a lot at stake professionally if the expressionist and abstract styles won out over their own traditional modes—a loss of prestige and income and the potential immortality of artists whose fame endures beyond their lifetimes.

Infighting within the American art community—artists bent on destroying artists—emerged once again. In the mid-nineteenth century a group of painters had protested to the federal government about Italian-born artists working at the Capitol; during fin de siécle decades, expatriate American artists who had studied and resided for a time in Europe found themselves unwelcome upon their return; and now, in the mid-twentieth century, painters and sculptors working in modernist styles were tagged "un-American" and tainted besides with the suspicion that they harbored the aim to overthrow the government. The definition of what constituted "American" art remained foremost in these controversies, not in determining a relationship to the nation but in creating boundaries within the art community for exclusionary purposes.

The idea that new art forms were destroying cultural standards must surely have seemed convincing to NCFA's director Thomas Beggs, trained a generation earlier as an artist in the figurative tradition; to the commission chairman, Paul Manship, a past president of the National Sculpture Society; and to David Finley, director of the National Gallery of Art, where the collection was synonomous with European art from the past. To Manship's credit, even though he deplored the new idioms, he together with certain fellow members of the National Sculpture Society disavowed his organization's condemnation of a 1951 show of modern sculpture at the Metropolitan Museum.[33]

Many of the "new" artists and "art manifestations" were hardly new by this time. Since the early 1930s the Whitney Museum of American Art, under Goodrich's influence, had been presenting unjuried biennial exhibitions that included works by such artists as Oscar Bluemner, Stuart Davis, Arthur Dove, Yasuo Kuniyoshi, Theodore Roszak, and Max Weber; recent exhibitions had included paintings by Milton Avery, Adolph Gottlieb, Balcom Greene, Jack Levine, Joan Mitchell, George L. K. Morris, Robert Motherwell, Jackson Pollock, and Ben Shahn, among others. In Washington, Duncan Phillips's collection, opened to the public in 1922, was built around European and American modernists.

Senator McCarthy's power eroded with the Army-McCarthy hearings, and in December 1954 he was censured by the Senate. At a crucial moment when the National Collection of Fine Arts could have supported American artists under attack, however, officials had joined the bandwagon of suspicion that was to persist into the 1960s.

David Winfield Scott, who succeeded Thomas Beggs as director of NCFA, observed that when he arrived in Washington in 1963 there was still a palpable sense of fear surviving from the McCarthy era. When making one of his first public statements about future programs at NCFA, Scott remarked, "We're out to convince people that the Government will give support and encouragement to American art with no intention of interfering."[34] The conservative taste of museum administrators and commissioners within a suppressive political climate had impeded NCFA's development toward modern art, while any potential for acquisitions and programs was all but snuffed out by an indifferent Smithsonian bureaucracy.

"Next Door to Dinosaur Bones and Totem Poles"

Goodrich, his fellow art commissioners, and Beggs could agree on one issue: NCFA desperately needed a building; it was impossible to regard the scatterings of art in the Natural History Building as a national collection of art. The commissioners now believed that construction of a building would require an appropriation by Congress in addition to donations from private sources, the exclusive means of funding cited in the 1938 bill. Secretary Leonard Carmichael, a psychologist appointed in 1953 to succeed Wetmore, remarked in an annual report on the need to move NCFA away from its incongruous setting "next door to dinosaur bones and totem poles."[35]

Still a viable possibility for the proposed building, the Saarinen museum project, created more than a decade earlier, looked as if it had just left the drawing board. In May 1953 at the invitation of Representative Charles R. Howell, a New Jersey Democrat, Eero Saarinen came to Washington to discuss reviving interest in the award-winning design. (Eliel Saarinen had died, and J. Robert F. Swanson was no longer connected with the project.) The meeting included Howell, Saarinen, Arne Randall of the Health, Education, and Welfare agency, John L. Keddy, Assistant Secretary of the Smithsonian, Thomas Beggs, and J. George Frain, research assistant to Howell. In the same year a model of the plan by the Cranbrook architects was displayed in the Natural History Building and also featured in an exhibit in Washington sponsored by the American Institute of Architects.

Renewed publicity about the proposed gallery reopened a flood of responses that read almost exactly like the comments of 1939: on the one hand, "it is beautiful, functional and reflects the time we live in"; on the other, a "bare, boxlike building," a "squatty, 'modern' nightmare some lunatic has proposed for the Smithsonian," and so on, ran critiques of the Saarinen building during the era when styles of domestic architecture were popularly known as "ticky-tacky."[36] Beggs still considered the design too modern for the Mall, but he did not actively oppose it. The intervening years, however, had brought a change in taste—and membership—to the Commission of Fine Arts, which now endorsed this gem of modern architectural design. Current members included David Finley, chairman; Pietro Belluschi, an architect and sculptor; George Biddle, a muralist, sculptor, and central figure in the creation of the Federal Arts Programs; Joseph Hudnut, an architect and professor of architecture who had acted as adviser to the 1939 competition jury; Edward F. Neild, an architect; Elbert Peets, a landscape architect; and Felix de Welden, sculptor of the Iwo Jima Marine Memorial.

Congressman Howell introduced a bill to fund the Smithsonian Gallery of Art as part of a plan to establish a National War Memorial Arts Commission, an agency that would concern itself with building a new theater and opera house in Washington (an initial effort that eventually resulted in the John F. Kennedy Center for the Performing Arts). Realizing the difficulties such proposals would raise, he characterized discussions of the bill as between those who believed "that the arts are living and must be encouraged with every resource at hand, and those who regard the arts basically as the product of a past age, which must be preserved rather than encouraged."[37] Acceptance of the Saarinen plan for purposes of the arts memorial would require increasing the size of the auditorium from a seating capacity of 1,200 to 3,000 or 3,600, which Saarinen, still enthusiastic about the project, believed to be possible.[38] As other sites were under consideration for the theater and opera house, perhaps that change would not be necessary. An enlarged version of Howell's bill dealt with additional controversial issues that threatened its acceptance.[39] But the death blow to the Saarinen gallery came from an entirely different direction.

The Patent Office Building, vacated twenty-five years earlier by the agency for which it had been built, had since been occupied by the Civil Service Commission. That department now planned to move elsewhere, and the Government Services Administration proposed demolishing the building to provide space for a parking garage. In March 1955 the architect Wallace K. Harrison asked Representative Frank Thompson Jr., a New Jersey Democrat, to help him save the structure from destruction, thus initiating endeavors on the part of the House, the Commission of Fine Arts, and President Dwight D. Eisenhower to preserve one of the oldest and most beautiful federal buildings in the capital.[40] It is not clear who first had the idea, but these efforts became combined with a proposal to transfer the building to the Smithsonian for the use of the National Collection of Fine Arts. Presumably, proponents thought that identifying a function for the building would aid in saving it, and to many of those involved, that possibilty seemed an ideal solution to two problems.

Within the Smithsonian, Secretary Carmichael endorsed the possibility of the transfer, although responses of the Smithsonian Art Commission ranged from tepid interest to outright rejection. The big question was how acceptance of the Patent Office would affect the site on the Mall earlier designated for the Smithsonian Gallery of Art? David Finley and Lloyd Goodrich found themselves on the same side of the issue. Finley urged retention of the site for construction because he and other members of the Commission of Fine Arts envisioned the use of the former Patent Office exclusively for a portrait gallery, their preferred project, asserting that eventually NCFA with its contemporary works would have to move elsewhere because the portrait gallery would require the entire building.[41] Goodrich questioned the adaptation of a nineteenth-century structure for purposes of a modern art museum, expressing doubt over estimates claiming that renovation of the old structure would be far less costly than a new structure. Moreover, the transfer of the building for the use of NCFA still had to go through the uncertainities of congressional debate, so that, he warned, if the right to the site on the Mall were given up, "it looks as if we may fall between two stools." NCFA commissioners passed a resolution favoring the construction of a building on the Mall for NCFA, in agreement with the Commission of Fine Arts, which also advised the federal government that the Mall site opposite the National Gallery of Art should be retained for art purposes only.

The secretary had another agenda: the site on the Mall reserved for the Smithsonian's gallery of art was now coveted for an air museum. Even as the commissioners discussed the question of the Mall location at their December 1957 meeting, the decision to withdraw the site from the use of NCFA was virtually sealed. "We have the world's greatest collection of aircraft, instruments, and related materials," Carmichael told the art commissioners to emphasize the importance of "a central location where our visitors can see them."[42] The Regents felt they could get support in Congress by combining the request to transfer the Patent Office for use as an art museum with a proposal to build the air museum. In any event, they believed that funds to build a gallery on the Mall could not be requested at this time because as recently as 1955, Congress had appropriated $36 million for a Museum of History and Technology and committed funds to add wings to the Museum of Natural History. Moreover, construction for the air museum, wherever it might be located, would be very costly (a 1965 bill authorized $42 million for its construction).

Though an earlier supporter of a building on the Mall for NCFA, Congressman Thompson now favored the transfer of the Patent Office Building and introduced legislation to that end on August 6, 1957. He waxed enthusastic over the possibility of housing the National Collection of Fine Arts and the proposed portrait gallery "in a structure so charged with history." From a practical standpoint, he believed that renovation efforts would be much cheaper than a new construction and therefore easier to obtain through legislation. Still not convinced by that argument, Goodrich corresponded with Thompson as late as July 1958, and while agreeing that conversion of the Patent Office Building was politically most attainable at this point, he stressed that it was "far from an ideal or final solution." Goodrich reviewed past events and envisioned a tantalizing opportunity for the future—about to be lost:

> Almost every civilized nation in the world has in its national capital a museum devoted to the art of the nation. The new Smithsonian Gallery of Art, situated on the Mall opposite the National Gallery of Art, would have been an outstanding demonstration to our people of the value and importance of the creative art of our country.
>
> I still believe that this is an ideal which should not be forgotten; and that none of us interested in American art should support the relinquishing of the Mall site until it is apparent that the fight is hopeless.[43]

But it was hopeless. The National Collection of Fine Arts, waiting in line within the Smithsonian for more than fifty years for its turn at proper housing, was elbowed out again by other interests of the institution.

The marginality of American art and its austere climate of neglect at the Smithsonian reflected its current status in the nation at large during the decade of the 1950s. Rarely taught in universities, art of the United States was considered déclassé, of little interest aesthetically or historically—though special kinds of achievement, such as the folk art celebrated at Williamsburg, Virginia, were found worthy of notice. When the contemporary scene became revitalized with the energy of abstract expressionism, that phenomenon served to diminish further the value of works by the previous generation, now judged as inconsequential because, in the prevailing linear theory of art history, they had failed to lead up to new masterpieces. Major art museums deaccessioned turn-of-the-century American paintings, sometimes selling for a few hundred dollars canvases that today might bring a price in five or six digits. Public monumental sculpture, enjoying a resurgence in the nation, was perceived by some as having begun in the 1950s; equestrian figures and historic monuments of a former time seemingly had become invisible. Scholars who wrote about mural art of the 1930s rarely made a connection between those works and the earlier great mural programs at the Capitol, the Library of Congress, state capitols, and libraries as if the painting of public murals were a new development.

Adding to the reasons for indifference was the dominance of science and technology following World War II. During the war years, Smithsonian scientists had provided invaluable aid to the War Department; one important service, for example, was conveying crucial information about the terrain, flora, and fauna on little-known Pacific islands. Advanced technology on the sea and in the air was decisive in concluding the conflict. How could a gallery of art compete with a new building to house the institution's technology collections, or the addition of wings on the Natural History Museum, or a structure to memorialize America's air superiority, from the invention of the airplane to the present?

An act to transfer the Patent Office Building to the Smithsonian Regents was passed by the 85th Congress and signed by President Eisenhower March 28, 1958, virtually ending any claim to the Mall site. The modernity of a building based on the Saarinen design and the possibility of a museum of the nation's own art located opposite the National Gallery of Art had vanished. On the Fourth of July in 1976 the Air and Space Museum would open on the site, instantaneously becoming the most popular museum at the Smithsonian and, reportedly, in the world.

And yet the vision of the Cranbrook Academy architects for a Washington art gallery was not to disappear entirely. Shortly after the Air and Space Museum opened, the spirit of the Saarinen building appeared on the Mall: "I. M. Pei's National Gallery East Building, completed in 1978, is the spiritual child of the Saarinens' design," observed *Washington Post* architectural writer Benjamin Forgey.[44]

Coming Full Circle

The art collections were to return to one of the most beautiful neoclassic structures in the United States, built at a time "when neo-classicism had a vitality it has never had since," Goodrich declared, in spite of his disappointment over losing the Mall site. "Its gray stone masses, its severe Doric colonnades, have a simplicity and power that make later neo-classic edifices look like stage settings."[45]

Legislation authorizing the transfer of the Patent Office Building came exactly one century after the national collections of history, science, and art had left the spacious exhibition hall on the top floor for the Smithsonian Castle on the Mall. During the intervening years, besides housing the patent records and models that documented native ingenuity, the stately building had served unanticipated and often contrary purposes. The classic beauty of its marble columns and vaulted ceilings became a setting in Civil War years to billet the First Rhode Island Militia and serve as a hospital for casualties of the battles of Second Bull Run, Antietam, and Fredericksburg. The wounded and the dying bedded in the galleries were visited by President Lincoln and comforted by Walt Whitman and Clara Barton (then a Patent Office copyist). In March 1865 the gaslit halls hosted a gala celebration for Lincoln's second inauguration. "I could not help thinking what a different scene they presented to my view a while since," mused Whitman on that occasion, "filled with a crowded mass of the worst wounded of the war. . . . Tonight, beautiful women, perfumes, the violins' sweetness, the polka and the waltz; then the amputation, the blue face, the groan, the glassy eye of the dying . . . and many a mother's son amid strangers, passing away untended there."[46]

On September 24, 1877, fire had destroyed the west and north wings of the building: that is, the sections on Ninth Street (where the fire originated) and G Street. Those units had been constructed with steel girders before the need to fireproof steel was understood. That the masonry vaults in the older sections survived in good condition was especially fortunate, as the original draft of the Declaration of Independence was among the historic documents and memorabilia still displayed there.[47]

The Patent Office had occupied the building from 1840 to 1932, sharing space with the National Institute for the Promotion of Science until 1862, and the Department of the Interior from 1849 to 1917. Divided into a warren of office cubicles from 1932 to 1963, the vaulted halls had echoed with the clattering typewriters of the Civil Service Commission (figure 25). Government administrators, bereft of common sense as well as taste, had covered marble pillars in the east wing (today called the Lincoln Gallery) with layers of green paint, which now had to be removed by a tedious and expensive process in a $6 million renovation (the estimated cost of the Saarinen building in 1939). True to the familiar congressional practice of economy in the short run, the refurbishing fund was shortchanged, resulting in compromises of lighting and floor treatment characterized by one architectural critic as "barbaric crudeness."[48] Nevertheless, NCFA found the prospect of escaping from *Triceratops* and the biggest elephant ever shot too exhilarating to be diminished by disappointments over light fixtures (figure 26 shows the collection's "temporary" quarters for fifty-seven years).

As planning began for NCFA's transfer, other Smithsonian collections were reshuffled in preparation for the opening in January 1964 of the new Museum of History and Technology (today called the Museum of American History). Two types of collections under consideration for that building affected the nature of NCFA's rebirth on G Street. Ceramics had been located in three separate areas of the institution: the exhibit halls of NCFA, the Department of Ethnology, and the

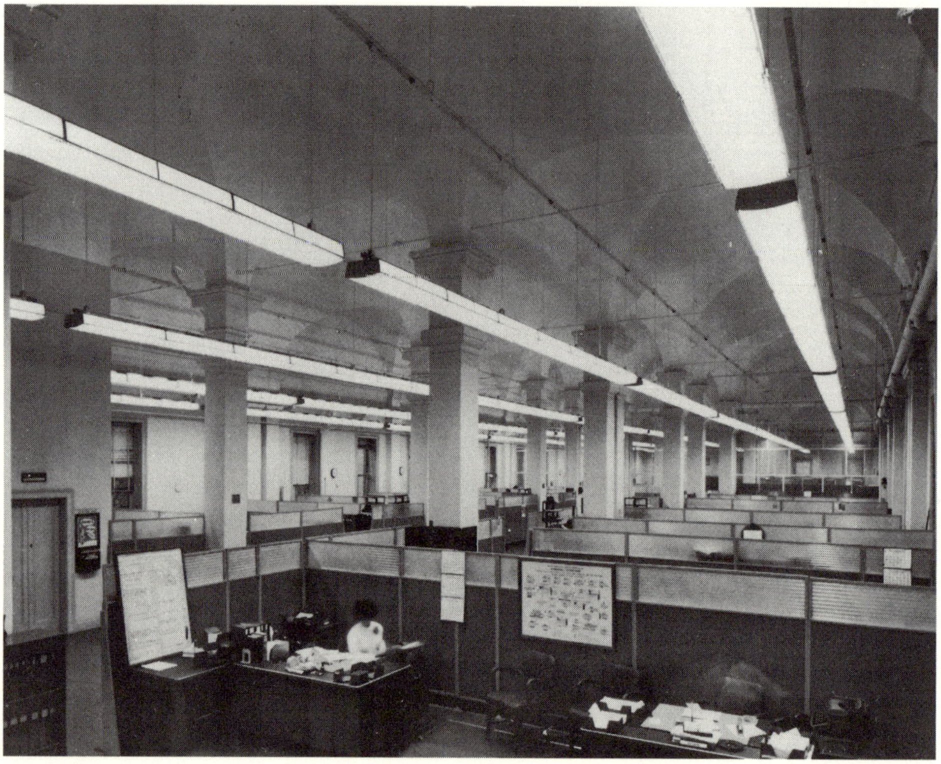

Figure 25. *East Wing of Patent Office Building during occupancy by Civil Service Commission.* Smithsonian Institution Archives, neg. no. 92-1795.

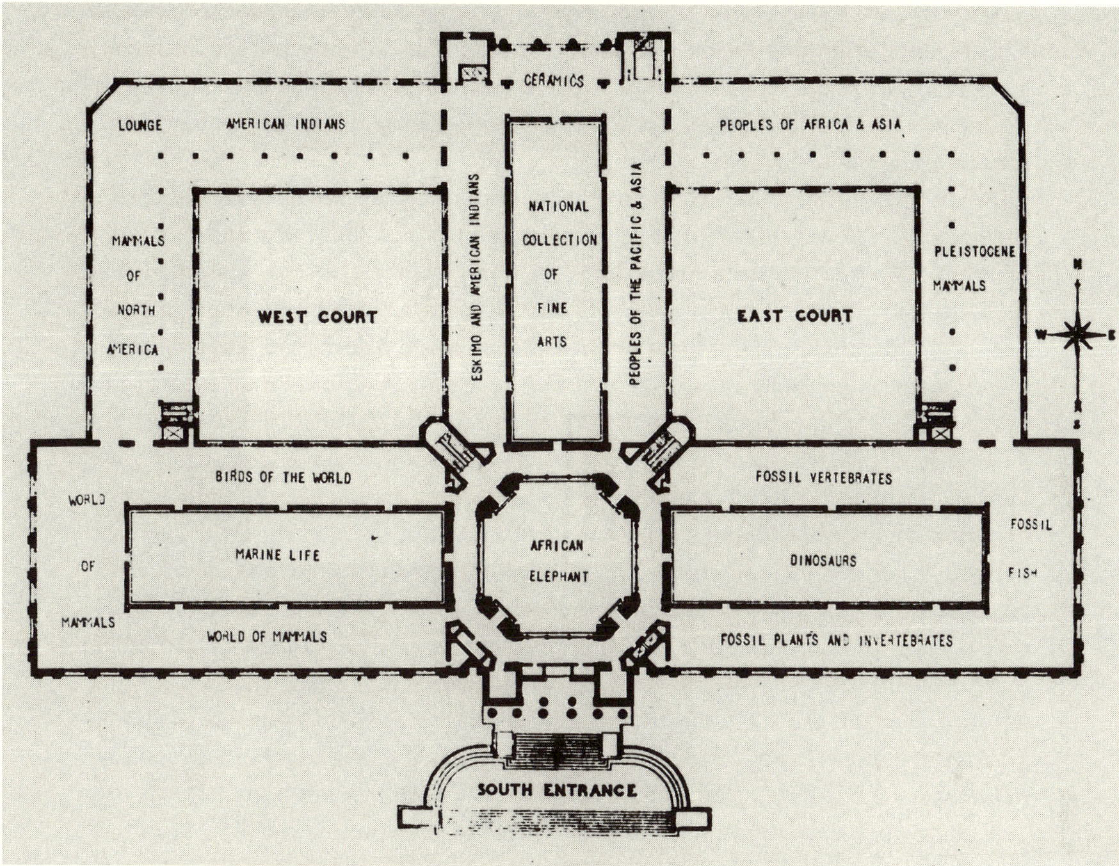

Figure 26. *Plan for Museum of Natural History Building*, before 1967. Smithsonian Institution Archives, neg. no. 77-10933.

Arts and Industries Building. These objects were now brought together for a ceramics hall to be situated within the History and Technology Building. Gifts that had included ceramic pieces along with paintings, such as the Gellatly collection, would remain intact within NCFA.

Following Goode's reorganization of the collections in the 1880s under the curatorial hand of Sylvester Koehler, prints had been exhibited primarily for the educational value of illustrating technical processes rather than for their aesthetic quality. This historic rationale determined the placement of graphic arts in the Museum of History and Technology. As with ceramic pieces, NCFA would retain prints it had acquired through gifts and purchases. An extensive collection of photographs, assembled within the former Division of Graphic Arts primarily as historical documents, was not an issue because NCFA, like most art museums at this time, was not yet collecting photographs as works of art.

Envisioned since the days of the early republic, a nascent portrait gallery had existed from the origin of the art collection, beginning with sculptures and paintings inherited from the National Institute and continuing with gifts presented through the years by individuals and organizations. The collecting and exhibiting of portraits of distinguished individuals was highly valued as a historical record of national achievement. Secretary Walcott had considered the 1923 exhibition of portraits of World War I leaders the institution's first visible step toward establishing a national portrait gallery. At times, plans had called for portraits to remain within the major art collection, as when the 1924 Platt museum design was proposed to house both art and history holdings. Finally, the confluence of plans within the Smithsonian, together with efforts of certain congressmen to provide proper housing for the institution's art collections, and the availability of the Patent Office Building enabled officials to establish the National Portrait Gallery in 1962 as an independent Smithsonian bureau. Charles Nagel as the first director would complete preparatory plans for the installation of the gallery in the architectural setting to be shared with the National Collection of Fine Arts and preside over the opening of the National Portrait Gallery in October 1968. Marvin Sadik would take over as director in July 1969.[49]

Plans for the momentous move of the National Collection of Fine Arts began to take place under David Winfield Scott, who succeeded Thomas Beggs as director in 1964. After many years of struggle, hopes and plans for a vigorous program and a representative collection of American art were to break out of the Sisyphean pattern that had characterized so much of NCFA's history. Just before this new era began, in December 1963 members of the commission paused for a photograph (figure 27).

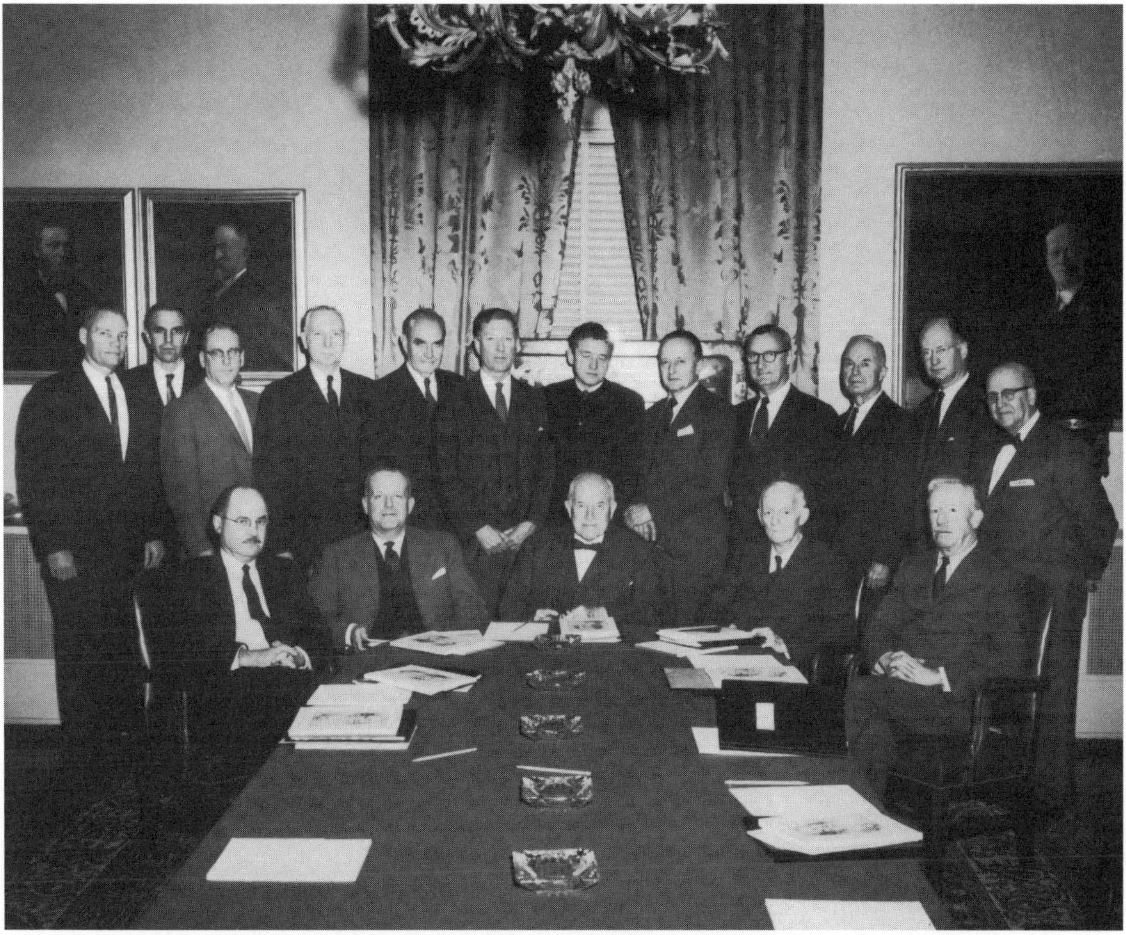

Figure 27. *NCFA Commissioners*, December 1963. Seated, left to right: Edgar P. Richardson, Henry P. McIlhenny, Paul Manship (chairman), David E. Finley, Lloyd Goodrich. Standing: Theodore W. Taylor (assistant to the secretary), David Scott (NCFA assistant director), James C. Bradley (assistant secretary), Leonard Carmichael (secretary), Gilmore D. Clarke, Barlett H. Hayes Jr., Andrew Wyeth, Ogden M. Pleissner, Paul Mellon, Walker Hancock, Charles H. Sawyer, Thomas M. Beggs (NCFA director). Smithsonian Institution Archives, neg. no. 94-4414.

5

Opening a New Era for Art at the Smithsonian, 1960s–1980

In spite of the battery of shocks delivered by events of the 1960s—a divisive war in an unknown land, riots and confrontations at home, accelerated struggles for civil rights, political assassinations, earthlings in space with the incredible goal of landing on the moon—those years were propitious for the rebirth of the National Collection of Fine Arts. Through the agitation and ferment a renewing quest emerged: an examination of national values, new perspectives on the nation's history, curiosity and interest in the nation's art. At this favorable moment for NCFA, giant strides forward took place with the help of moral encouragement and essential monetary support from leaders at both institutional and national levels.

The election of John F. Kennedy in 1961 and the presence of Jacqueline Kennedy in the White House promoted a more favorable reception in Washington to endeavors of the art world than had been true in the 1950s. "I see little of more importance to the future of our country and our civilization than full recognition of the place of the artist," the president declared.[1] In spite of the brevity of his term in office, Kennedy initiated a national interest in the arts and art institutions. August Heckscher's 1963 report on the condition of the arts in the United States, made at Kennedy's request, helped to bridge a continuity of concern into the next administration.[2]

At a time when students and other groups were challenging traditional policies of universities and museums, revolutionary changes at the Smithsonian were initiated from within. S. Dillon Ripley (figure 28), an ornithologist, succeeded Leonard Carmichael as secretary of the Smithsonian on February 1, 1964. A window to an expanded world opened at the institution with his appointment—and nowhere

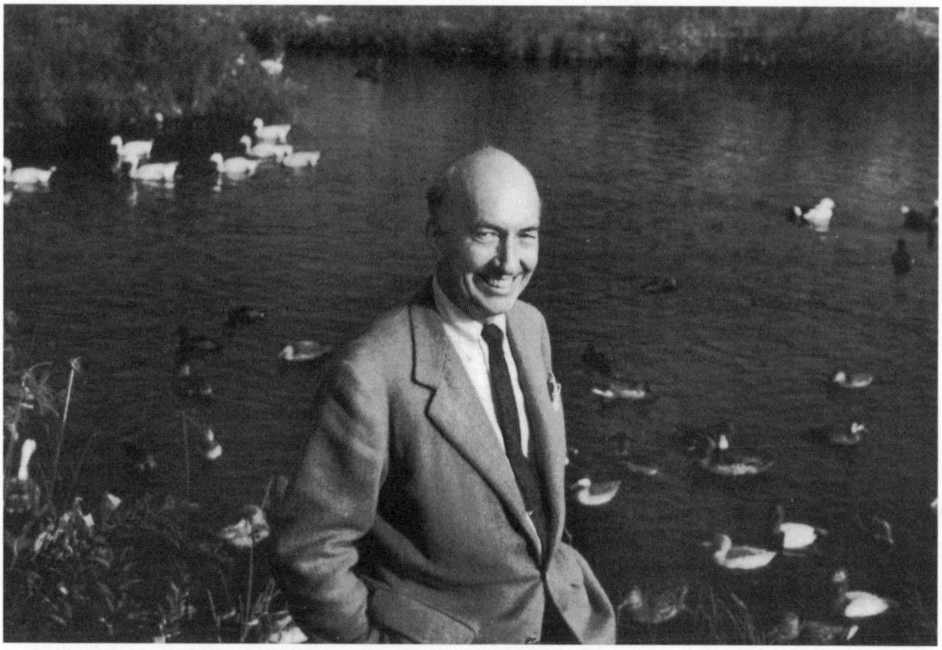

Figure 28. *S. Dillon Ripley*. Smithsonian Institution Archives, neg. no. 57272.

was the fresh air more invigorating than at NCFA. In June of that year Ripley appointed David Winfield Scott as acting director and subsequently as director. Named Special Assistant to the Secretary for Fine Arts, Thomas Beggs retired two years later. Acquainted with Scott from his years at Pomona College, Beggs had suggested him for the new position of assistant director that brought Scott to Washington in July 1963.

An art historian and a painter, Scott earned a B.A. at Harvard, M.A. and M.F.A. at the Claremont Graduate School, and Ph.D. at the University of California, Berkeley. During World War II he served in the Mediterranean theater and North Africa, terminating his military duty with the rank of captain. Prior to coming to the Smithsonian, he taught at Scripps College and the Claremont Graduate School, and served as director of the Florence Rand Land Art Gallery of Scripps College. His scholarly interests ranged from medieval art to contemporary Mexican painting. Like all the former directors—Holmes, Tolman, and Beggs—Scott was a practicing artist, having studied at the Art Students League in New York with John Sloan and others, and abroad, in Spain. As a watercolorist, he had exhibited widely.

Immediately, the new director began to gather a professional staff, individuals with academic degrees and museum experience: art historians Richard Wunder and William Truettner as curators of painting and sculpture; Jacob Kainen, a painter and printmaker who transferred from the Smithsonian Division of Graphic Arts, as curator of prints and drawings; Harry Lowe, a designer of national repute, as curator of exhibits; Adelyn Dohme Breeskin, formerly director of the Baltimore Museum of Art and president of the Washington Museum of Contemporary Art, as consultant. From a total of eight members in July 1964, within a year the staff numbered twenty-two, supported by an increased budget totaling $143,252. By 1967, the year of the move to the Patent Office Building, the staff stood at forty-eight and the budget allotment at $739,000.

From the moment of taking office, David Scott considered the documents of 1938 as legal and historic authorizations for current programs. "The wide expansion of the Collection's activities," he explained, were "inspired and guided by the farsighted legislation of May 17, 1938, and the [architectural] competition program which followed . . . for a gallery of modern and American art."[3] Dramatic changes at the National Collection thus represented a continuity, not a break, from earlier policies. Scott's passionate belief in art as a sustaining humanistic and spiritual resource arose from his education and his participation in a global war against fascist powers that had threatened those values. Communicated to staff members and translated into programs, his convictions gave direction and purpose to this time of renewal for the collection.

NCFA's director eagerly responded to the phrase in the building program of thirty years earlier that defined the Smithsonian gallery as a catalyst across the nation "to restore to American art a healthy relationship to the life of the community." He could find additional support for extending programs beyond Washington in the Heckscher Report, which advised that in order to make the National Collection "a truly representative museum of American art, a greatly expanded program of travelling exhibitions, catalogues and publications and reproductions should be initiated."[4]

To reach a national audience, Scott proposed to establish an Office of Community Exhibits that would provide exhibitions and materials for wide use in schools, libraries, and other community centers. Though similar to operations of the Smithsonian Institution Traveling Exhibition Service (SITES), the new office would differ in offering programs at low cost to the user. He also recommended sending art exhibitions to small towns by means of specially fitted trucks or "artmobiles" as mentioned in the Heckscher Report and then in use by several museums.[5]

Developing the Collection

Released from responsibility for collecting ceramics and European graphic arts with the establishment of those programs at the new Museum of History and Technology and—with the advent of the Portrait Gallery—no longer needing to acquire and maintain portraits for another agency, NCFA could now concentrate on its primary mission as a collection of American painting, sculpture, drawings, and prints. A much delayed foray into modern art began when Harry Lowe and Adelyn Breeskin returned from a buying trip to New York with a John Marin watercolor, *The Sea, Maine* (figure 29). Dated 1921, this painting was hardly shocking to anyone's sensibilities, but some staff members, recalling tirades against "modernists" in the not very distant past, wondered if the work might be too bold for NCFA commissioners. The acceptance of Marin's abstraction of a tossing sea symbolized a sea change at NCFA toward an entirely different mentality about art of the twentieth century.[6] Belatedly, NCFA was entering a phase more common to art museums early in their development, when identification with a building centers attention on the collection, and efforts to acquire works become a priority.

Scott and his staff made lists of artists inadequately represented in the collection and approached artists and collectors for contributions. The legislative moment favored their efforts, for at the time the tax law permitted artists to contribute their works to nonprofit institutions and claim deductions for the fair market value. (After 1969 they were able to deduct only the cost of materials used, leading to a decline in such gifts.)

The holdings could not be built up overnight, but it did not seem much longer before hundreds of new works arrived. The S. C. Johnson and Sons, Inc., collection of 102 paintings that had toured the country as "Art: USA" represented living artists of the period when the collection was formed, 1931–1962. More than 200 watercolors came from the Ford Motor Company; 1,100 works by William H. Johnson from the Harmon Foundation; a cache of works by Hiram Powers included the original plaster model for *The Greek Slave*; 100 sketches and studies of murals produced for New Deal projects came from the General Services Administration; 200 works were

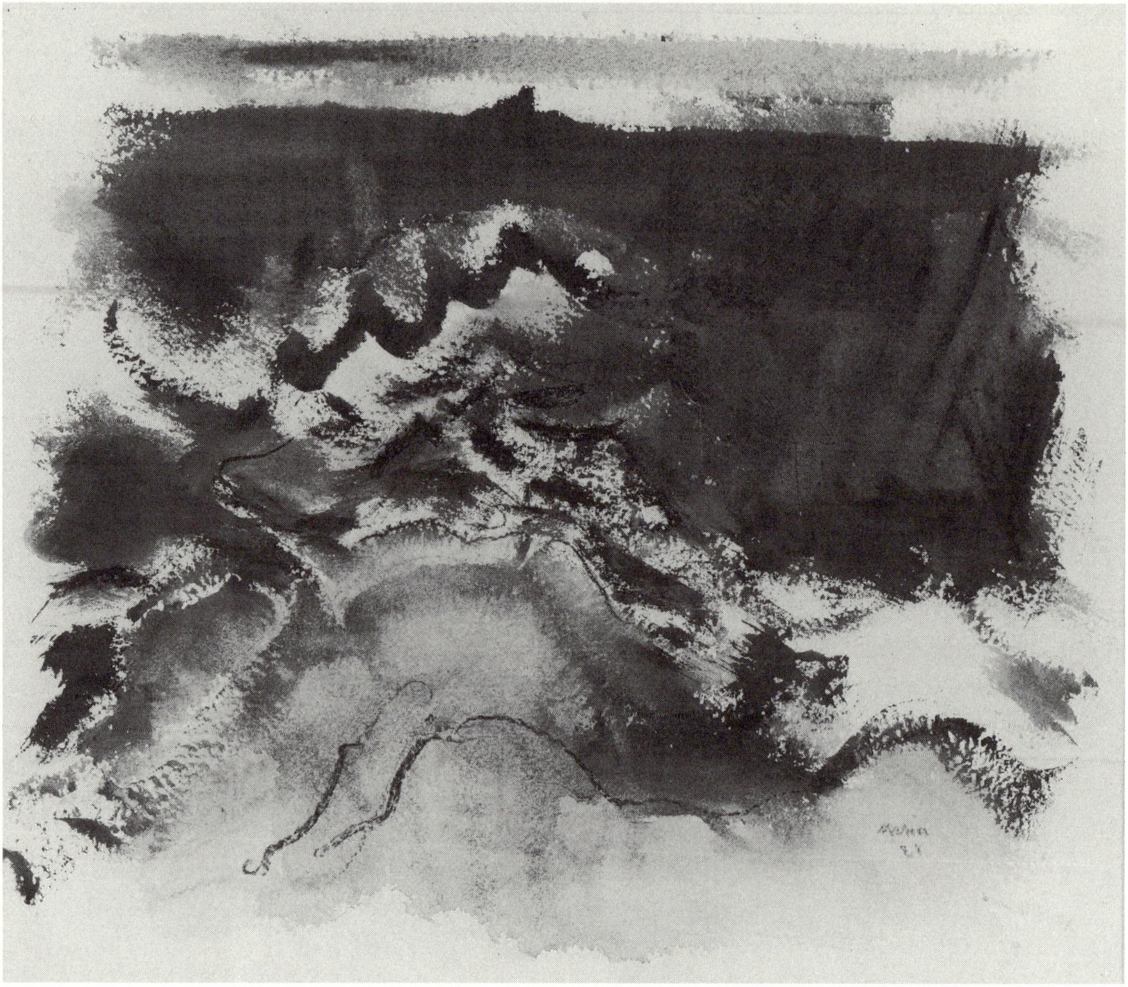

Figure 29. John Marin, *The Sea, Maine,* 1921. Smithsonian American Art Museum.

transferred from the Labor Department and 103 from the Department of the Interior Park Service. Sculptor Paul Manship, a former commissioner of the museum, gave 43 important pieces in 1965, the year before his death, and left a bequest to NCFA for half the contents of his two studios. The Johnson collection, gift of Irene and Herbert F. Johnson, was received in 1967. Among smaller but choice gifts were *Melons and Morning Glories* by Raphaelle Peale, Mary Cassatt's *Spanish Dancer*, and twenty paintings by Henry Lyman Sayen. Curator Jacob Kainen began systematically to develop the neglected area of graphic arts, acquiring 800 prints by prominent artists within a year after he joined the staff. All these acquisitions and many more were made in three years' time, before the transfer to the new quarters.

A concentration on acquisitions brought public and congressional attention to NCFA—through notoriety. Contents of the Hiram Powers studio in Florence, virtually intact since the sculptor's death in 1872, were purchased in 1968 through the efforts of Curator Richard Wunder. Because the transaction was partly funded from the sale of European paintings in the Ralph Cross Johnson collection—two paintings by Francesco Guardi and a landscape by Richard Wilson—it brought critical response from the press. In addition to the purchase of the Powers studio, the sale of the Johnson paintings provided for a pair of portraits by Gustavus Hesselius and a second pair attributed to his son, John Hesselius. In June 1969 a painting attributed to Jan Massy was exchanged for one by Benjamin West, *Helen Brought to Paris*. At this time, since guidelines had not yet been defined by the Regents for the sale of works in Smithsonian collections, criticism of NCFA's actions eventually, in July 1970, led to a congressional investigation. The end result was the establishment of procedures for deaccessioning that involved NCFA's commissioners, the Regents, and the General Counsel's Office, in addition to the curators and director, for any such actions in the future. Assistant Secretary Charles Blitzer felt that the sale and the exchange did not need to be defended: "It seems clear to me that the NCFA, under Dr. Scott and Mr. Davis [Assistant Director], has used its resources admirably and prudently."[7]

Redesigning Exhibitions

Secretary Ripley authorized generous additional funding for exhibitions in the art gallery at the Natural History Building to bring visibility to NCFA before its unveiling at the Patent Office, and the staff organized a series of groundbreaking shows featuring American contemporary art. A memorial show of Stuart Davis paintings opened in May 1965 as a turning point for exhibits, even as the Marin watercolor had changed directions for acquisitions. In December 1965 an exhibition of paintings and sculptures featured 41 American artists, among them, Alexander Archipenko, Oscar Bluemner, Stuart Davis, Charles Demuth, Arthur Dove, Lyonel Feininger, John Marin, Stanton Macdonald-Wright, Morgan Russell, Charles Sheeler, Joseph

Stella, John Storrs, and Max Weber. In October of the next year a group of drawings by Jasper Johns was mounted, followed in May 1967 by a retrospective exhibition of works by Stanton Macdonald-Wright.

The cast of artists represented in these exhibitions would constitute an outstanding program in any museum, but to be shown at NCFA—a public museum in Washington where just a few years earlier such names had been vilified—marks these events as astonishing achievements. Scott planned to present annual one-person shows of works by one or two outstanding American artists over the age of seventy.[8] Highlighting nineteenth-century art, paintings by George Catlin and Frederic Edwin Church were presented in 1965 and 1966. Annual shows by local artist groups, presented at NCFA for some years, were replaced by this active exhibition program. The staff of the National Collection now initiated most of the exhibitions and accompanied the majority of them with catalogues published by NCFA.[9]

These shows not only signaled the viable rebirth of the National Collection; they also displayed creative ways of presenting exhibitions. A major problem for curators of art, how to array works in a gallery so that viewers can see each object for its uniqueness as well as within a meaningful relationship, was created at the same moment as the public gallery. The definition of an art museum as a place "where every separate object kills every other and all of them together the visitor"[10] can be appreciated by gallery audiences of today as in the past. Typical arrangements at this time featured a large painting hung in the center of a wall, with a symmetrical arrangement of evenly spaced works on each side (see again figure 17). This manner of display presents works of art as predictable, suggestive of a serene, balanced experience that is complete in itself without requiring anything from the viewer. Allowing space between pictures, curators aimed to lessen the confusion of earlier hanging schemes where paintings had been placed solidly across a wall and vertically in three tiers, their frames touching.

To encourage the involvement of viewers, Harry Lowe as exhibitions designer went beyond conventional models. He painted the walls specifically for each event and added appropriate context—standard approaches today, but in the 1960s never before used in museums in Washington. In a doorway of the Macdonald-Wright exhibit a billowing sheer curtain added visual excitement and engendered a sense of curiosity about what lay beyond (figure 30). Irregular spacing of the works—and the shapes and colors of the paintings themselves—further served to engage museum visitors personally. For the Church exhibition, Lowe installed an ogival arch at the

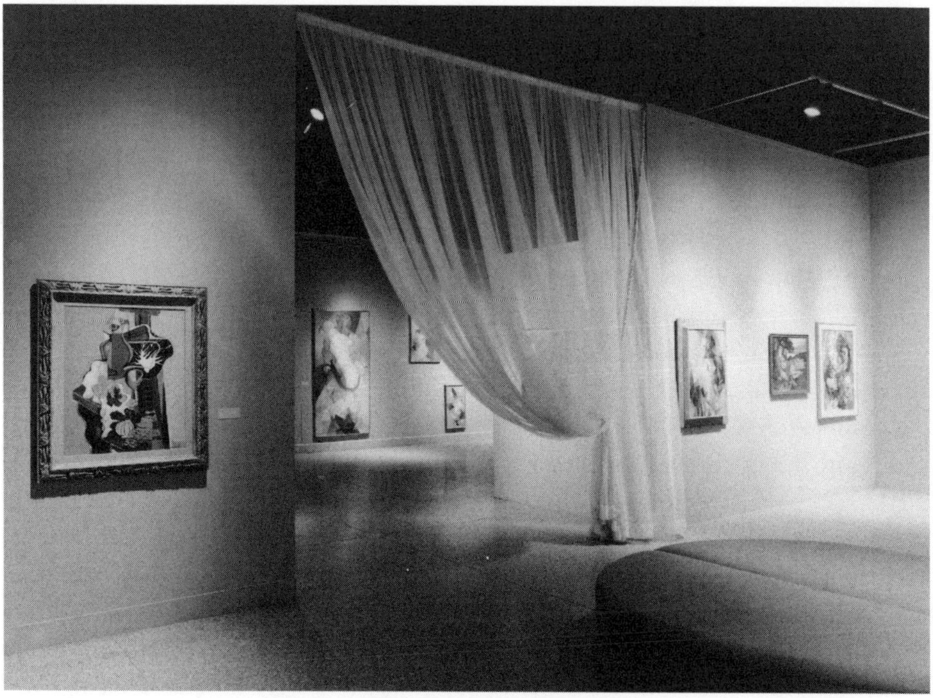

Figure 30. Installation: *The Art of Stanton MacDonald-Wright*, 1967. Smithsonian American Art Museum, Slide and Photo Archives.

entrance with decorative objects brought from Olana, the artist's studio home. The NCFA events brought the public new possibilities of responding to works of art by taking the viewing of an exhibit beyond expectations of the familiar to experiences of discovery. These presentations in NCFA galleries joined other creative approaches to exhibit design that began to appear in this decade of the 1960s, as "exhibition installation [became] the new pretender to originality. . . . [It was] in and of itself a *form of modern work*."[11]

Exporting American Culture

The 1938 legislation that mandated programs for NCFA had underscored the mission of sending American art throughout the United States. That document made no mention of sites outside the country, but such ventures were to become prominent in NCFA operations in the late 1960s and into the 1970s. The development of this activity can be better understood by reviewing briefly the museum's earlier involvement with international exhibitions, begun in the 1940s in response to wartime policies of the federal government.

Although many cultural activities were curtailed after Pearl Harbor, federal and Smithsonian officials considered ties with other nations in the American hemisphere to be "of vital importance not only for better relations between neighboring countries in the present time of emergency, but also as a permanent program after the war."[12] To help assure solidarity in the Western hemisphere, the State Department supported a cultural information and exchange program. Contact with scientific institutions in Latin America became one of the priorities for Smithsonian science departments, and NCFA regularly mounted exhibits of work from Mexico, Central and South America, and the Caribbean. Most of these events featured contemporary art and occasionally consisted of paintings or drawings of scenes in the "Good Neighbor" countries by artists of the United States. Sponsored by the ambassadors of participating nations and the Pan American Union, this intrahemisphere exchange continued through the late 1940s, amounting to at least two exhibits every year.[13]

After the war the State Department began to expand a cultural role outside the country through traveling art exhibits. Almost immediately it became involved in controversies that would mark its sponsorship of art exhibitions into the 1960s. First, modern American paintings purchased by the department for showing abroad were acclaimed while on a European tour that began in October 1946, but upon their return to their native land the canvases were denounced as works by leftist, radical artists, devoid of a commitment to American values. Intended to emphasize experimental trends in contemporary painting in the United States, the exhibit presented significant artists of the 1940s: Milton Avery, William Baziotes, Stuart Davis, Arthur Dove, Philip Evergood, Adolph Gottlieb, William Gropper, O. Louis Guglielmi, Philip Guston, Marsden Hartley, Walt Kuhn, Yasuo Kuniyoshi, Jack Levine, John Marin, George L. K. Morris, Georgia O'Keeffe, Ben Shahn, Charles Sheeler, Max Weber, Karl Zerbe. "Advancing American Art"—the exhibition title that became a misnomer—had to be withdrawn in response to critical voices from politicians and the public.[14] The political attacks on American artists and government-sponsored programs would continue for more than a decade, intensified by apprehensions of the cold war and the fear of communism that led into the McCarthy era.

Although also involved with sending American art abroad, the Smithsonian Institution Traveling Exhibition Services, unlike the USIA, did not arouse controversy. Apparently, an official imprimatur of government sponsorship heightened protests of events as showcases for radical art and artists with alleged communist connections. As a kind of culmination of dealing with accusations and innuendos, the besieged information agency announced in 1956 that future exhibits would exclude American paintings dated after 1917 (the date of the Bolshevik coup d'état), disclosing how ridiculous—and how threatening—the situation had become.[15]

President Dwight D. Eisenhower, however, warmly endorsed showing American art abroad, among other sorts of cultural exchange. Having gone through the horrors of a global war, he wanted to believe that such efforts toward knowledge and understanding could lead nations to live together in peace. The postwar power rivalry of the United States with the Soviet Union gave urgency to this ideal, so that entry into the culture arena became more assertive and openly propagandistic. The president's State of the Union message of January 1955 stressed the importance of the arts to the nation: "In the advancement of the various activities which will make our civilization endure and flourish, the Federal Government should do more to give official recognition to the importance of the arts and other cultural activities."[16]

Eisenhower followed up on this statement by establishing his "people to people" program of cultural exchange. Forty-one committees, representing as many fields of activity, were organized to implement the program; NGA director David Finley was appointed chairman of the Fine Arts Committee with Smithsonian Secretary Leonard Carmichael as vice chairman. "The story of American achievements in the fine arts soon will be told abroad," reported a *Washington Post* journalist in an article that implied competition and cultural superiority rather than friendly exchange.[17] Initially involving trade fairs, sponsorship was extended to performance artists, sports groups, and art exhibitions under the administration of the USIA, the Department of State, and the Department of Commerce (which concentrated on the trade fairs). Support for overseas programs would be continued by President Kennedy, who concurred with the idea of using art exhibits abroad to support American foreign policy, although this proved untenable during the Vietnam War.[18]

More trouble loomed ahead—this time drawing NCFA into the maelstrom of international politics. The Venice Biennale, begun in 1895, and the São Paulo Bienal, initiated in 1951, had through the years attracted various sponsors for the American section. Early in the century the Venice events were organized by the commercial

Grand Central Gallery in New York City, and from 1954 to 1962 by the Museum of Modern Art. Subsequent sponsorship by USIA brought criticisms that resulted in the government agency's withdrawal from the 1966 Venice Biennale. The Smithsonian was tapped to take over what had become a political hot potato, and Secretary Ripley assigned this responsibility to NCFA. A protest was raised before NCFA's program got started. Frank Getlein in the *New Republic* questioned whether international exhibitions properly related to the stated missions of NCFA, "since representation of art abroad can hardly be called either research or the instruction of American citizens."[19] David Scott, however, enthusiastically defined this major new endeavor as a fulfillment of the mandate to promote contemporary American art.

Formerly with the international section of USIA, Lois Bingham transferred to the National Collection of Fine Arts to direct the newly established International Art Program. Exhibits were proposed and selected by officials of other institutions, with NCFA handling organizational and administrative details. To encourage a diversity of viewpoints, commissioners for the exhibits were appointed from a variety of art museums; Henry Geldzahler of the Metropolitan Museum of Art was appointed commissioner for the 1966 Venice show, which featured paintings by Helen Frankenthaler, Ellsworth Kelly, Roy Lichtenstein, and Jules Olitski. In the catalogue for that event, Secretary Ripley related NCFA's involvement to Smithsonian tradition. "Beginning more than a century ago," he wrote, "the Smithsonian Institution pioneered in the international exchange of scientific and scholarly information. This XXXIII International Biennial focuses on the Smithsonian's National Collection of Fine Arts and its interest in the international exchange of ideas in contemporary art."[20] The 1967 São Paulo Bienal, "Environment U.S.A.: 1957–1967," was selected by William C. Seitz of the Rose Art Museum at Brandeis University. To call attention to the sponsorship of NCFA and discuss problems of the biennials, the National Collection in December 1966 presented a symposium to a standing-room-only audience: "How Should American Art be Presented Abroad?" featuring Grace Borgenicht, Clement Greenberg, Hilton Kramer, Abram Lerner, and Kenneth Noland as panelists.

Transferral of sponsorship to the Smithsonian aimed to disconnect politics from presentation of the exhibits—an overly optimistic goal for the 1960s, as would be confirmed at the tenth São Paulo Bienal, due to open in September 1969. Earlier that year, artists of Brazil began to withdraw from the event to protest the repressive military regime of their country, and they tried to persuade other nationals to do the same, particularly the Americans. Gyorgy Kepes of the Massachusetts Institute of Technology, organizer of the American section, having lost nine of twenty-three participants, concluded in July that he had to cancel the presentation. Unable to find a substitute in such a short time, in August the Smithsonian informed the Brazilian Embassy and the Department of State that no American representation would be sent. The exhibition developed by Kepes, centering on the relationship between art and technology, was shown the next year at NCFA and MIT.[21] But political reverberations affecting the biennials continued to involve NCFA into the 1970s.

Though the biennials were the most publicized exhibits sent abroad, each year NCFA's International Art Program also organized a dozen or more shows of American contemporary art, nineteenth-century art, and folk art. Of particular interest among these, an exhibition of painting and sculpture by contemporary African American artists was sent in 1966 to the First World Festival of Negro Arts at the Palais de Justice, Dakar, Senegal. With a foreword by Hale Woodruff, the catalogue (printed in French and English) featured Barbara Chase, Emilio Cruz, Sam Gilliam, Richard Hunt, Jacob Lawrence, William Majors, Norma Morgan, Robert Reid, Charles White, and Todd Williams.[22]

Relating to Institutions at Home

Energy generated in the mid-1960s by NCFA's rising star joined a new constellation at the Smithsonian. Within a few years the arts and humanities—the non-sciences—attracted more attention from the institution than had been true in more than a hundred years of previous history. In 1962 the National Portrait Gallery was founded; the new National Museum of History and Technology (now the National Museum of American History) open in 1964; in the same year the National Cultural Center, established as a bureau of the Smithsonian, was renamed the John F. Kennedy Center for the Performing Arts; the Anacostia Neighborhood Museum (most original of Secretary Ripley's projects, with collections and programs centered on its African American community) opened in 1967; in 1968 the Cooper-Hewitt Museum of Design in New York City was transferred to the Smithsonian; in 1969 ground was broken to construct the Joseph H. Hirshhorn Museum and Sculpture Garden; and plans for the Renwick Gallery of NCFA were under way from the late 1960s.

When the Hirshhorn collection was first offered to the Smithsonian in 1966, Ripley suggested that it become part of NCFA—before he realized its magnitude. Although it contained some works of nineteenth-century American art, the bulk of objects were European modern art with a concentration in sculpture. The two art museums thus had distinctive types of collections and program possibilities, with only some overlap. Conflicts arose over NCFA's new activity in mounting exhibitions of modern art, however. Scott suggested to Ripley that a discussion be held to consider limitations upon accessions and programs of the Hirshhorn and NCFA so that each might operate within its own territory, but the first director of the Hirshhorn, Abram Lerner, reportedly, did not consider this necessary, preferring that the Hirshhorn have complete independence to follow its own course. This situation marked one of the most serious ruptures in deteriorating relations between Scott and Ripley.[23]

Meanwhile, administrators at the Corcoran Gallery, where shows of contemporary American art had been mounted regularly for more than half a century, began to wonder if NCFA were an awakened giant that would tread on its territory. "The N.C.F.A. has carefully avoided activities of the sort the Corcoran has developed," Scott wrote in response to the inquiry of Dorothy Phillips, curator at the Corcoran. "We will, of course, continue to survey American Art, both in our changing exhibits and our permanent collections. This is a basic responsibility that derives from our legislative mandate."

Addressing questions from Richard A. Madigan, assistant director of the Corcoran, Scott wrote more specifically, "Basically, our concerns are three: (1) preservation and display of art belonging to the government; (2) promotion of the appreciation of art (for the nation); (3) encouragement of art (for the nation)." He related all three issues to directives in the 1938 legislation. Corcoran officials may well have recalled that only a few years earlier in resolutions before the House, Smithsonian Regents had been requested to "develop and present to the Congress on or before Jan. 30, 1962, a comprehensive plan to make the Corcoran Gallery of Art and its great collections of American art in the District of Columbia a part of the National Collection of Fine Arts, and for other purposes." Corcoran trustees had reported no interest in such a development—adding that most likely such a plan would not be possible under the act incorporating the gallery. Smithsonian officials therefore recommended that no further action be taken on the bills.[24]

Another question of potential conflict with Washington's oldest private art institution arose with NCFA's development of plans for a gallery of crafts in the Renwick building on Pennsylvania Avenue (built as the original Corcoran Gallery and transferred not long before to the Smithsonian). Now it was the Corcoran's turn to reassure the Smithsonian that it had no collection of American crafts and decorative arts, thus eliminating the possibility of competing programs.

Moving to New Opportunities

Exhibition activity proceeded in the hall of the Natural History Building along with the transfer of objects and offices to the new location in the Patent Office Building. One of the last exhibits in Natural History—the "temporary" quarters of the art collection for almost six decades—closed January 7, 1968. It featured "The Graphic Art of Mary Cassatt," a collection of the artist's etchings and lithographs accompanied by a definitive catalogue.[25]

Serving as an appropriate transition to NCFA's impressive new architectural setting, photographs of the Patent Office Building by New York photographer Peter Fink were shown in the foyer gallery of the Museum of Natural History, the final appearance of NCFA among "dinosaur bones and totem poles." The photograph *David Scott in Lincoln Gallery* (figure 31) suggests the beauty of spatial design and architectural details that would soon showcase the National Collection of Fine Arts and its new sibling, the National Portrait Gallery.

The task of moving some 11,000 items to their new home (figure 32) inspired an exciting sense of participating in a momentous beginning—even as it required a great deal of planning and an enormous amount of work. While others may exult in the visual arts as expressions of the human spirit, museum staffs can never forget that art works are physical objects of weight and dimension that must be—carefully, one at a time—packed, transported, and unpacked, examined, and then put in place again.

Renovation within the building proceeded with blueprints, architectural drawings, and gallery spaces continually checked against plans for the first installation in the Patent Office Building. An inaugural arrangement of more than 500 paintings, sculptures, and prints were mounted in nine spacious galleries. The third floor hall on the east side, now named the Lincoln Gallery in reference to the ball held there for President Lincoln's second inauguration, featured a historical survey of American art, and in the Granite Gallery on the ground floor, works on the walls formed a setting for small sculptures. A catalogue prepared for the opening reviewed NCFA's history and suggested the broad scope of American art represented by a range of donors—private collectors, artists, corporations—and transfers from federal government holdings.[26]

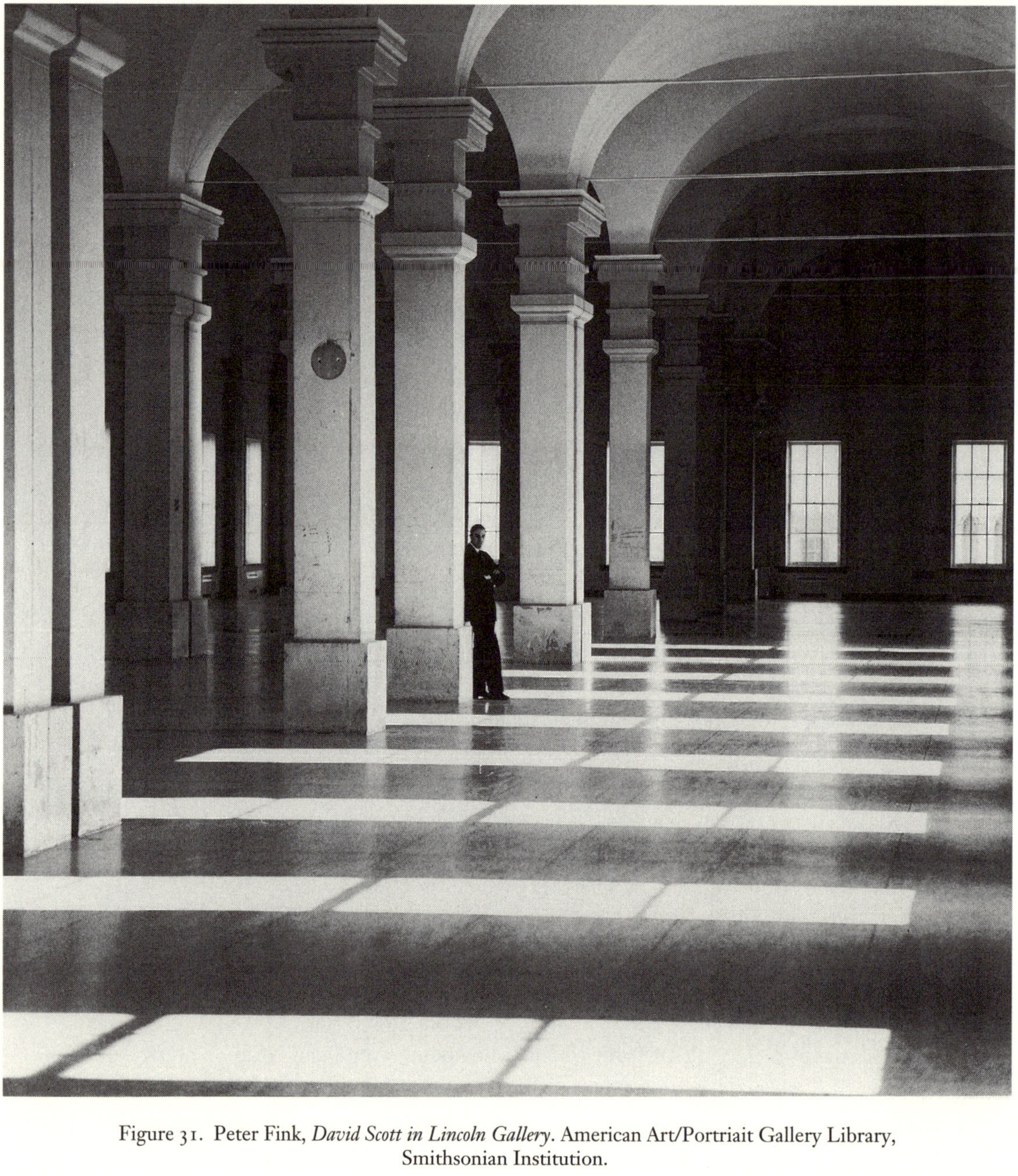

Figure 31. Peter Fink, *David Scott in Lincoln Gallery*. American Art/Portriait Gallery Library, Smithsonian Institution.

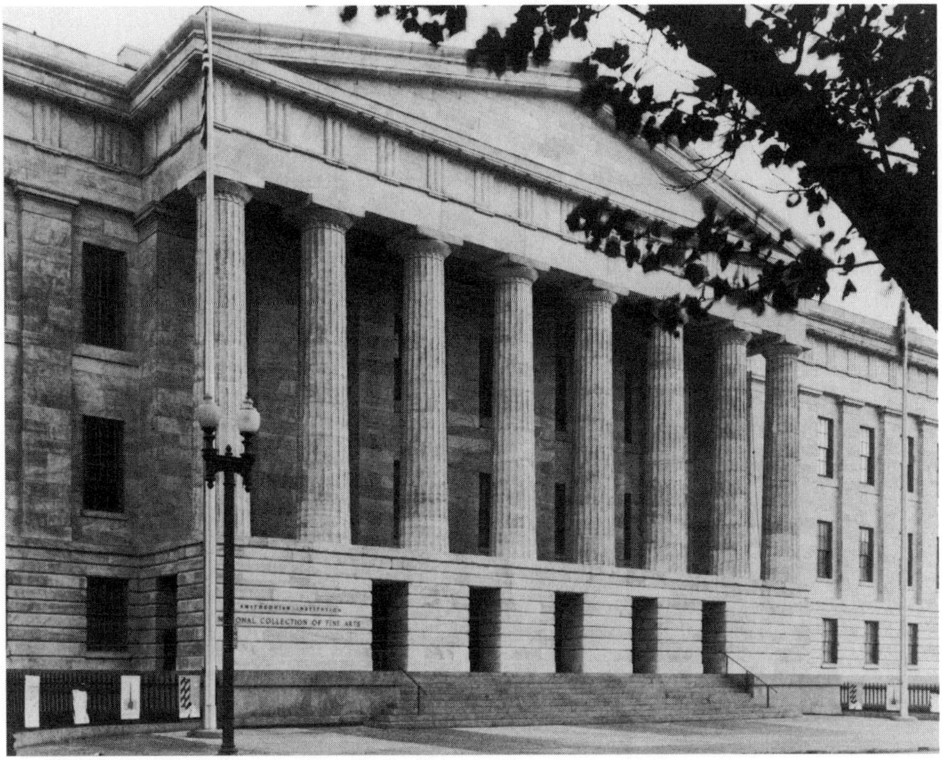

Figure 32. *NCFA Facade, Patent Office Building* 1968. Posters on the fence were commissioned for the opening by NCFA and funded by Mrs. Albert List of New York City. Artists are Allen D'Archangelo, Sam Francis, Lee Bontecue, Chrysa, Claes Oldenburg, and Larry Rivers. Smithsonian Institution Archives, neg. no. 53376.

Reflecting on the significance of this moment in NCFA's history, Director Scott wrote:

> The arts record the spiritual voyage of our nation and tell us whence we have come and what values and beliefs have guided and sustained us, in short—who we are. As a major, continuing repository for significant American Art, the National Collection is thus a vitally important resource.
>
> And the Collection is a force. In the terms of today's activists, it represents the march of the American spirit. It reflects our inquiry and our energy, our doubt and our affirmation. Enormous strength, courage, and faith emanate from the monumental building, from the paintings in its halls, from

> the sculpture in its court. Here we see process and creativity, discipline and imagination, the bridging from the past and from the present toward the future, the formulation of change, the confrontation with and embracing of the new.[27]

At last, the anticipation of many years became a reality. Emerging from unexpected turns and reversals of a meandering journey that had started before the founding of the Smithsonian, works of the nation's oldest art collection began their new life with a celebration in the courtyard of the Patent Office Building. Dressed in evening apparel, staff members, government and Smithsonian officials, art patrons, citizens of Washington, national and international guests gathered Friday evening, May 3, 1968, for opening ceremonies. President Lyndon B. Johnson was scheduled to speak, and, though it was rumored that he would not be able to attend, he did arrive, with Lady Bird and daughter Lynda Robb. Shortly after 9:30 he stepped to the podium (figure 33):

> This is a proud moment. I wanted to say that dedicating the new home of this National Collection makes me feel like a proud father, but . . . Mrs. Johnson said that would sound boastful. . . . So tonight, my friends, I am authorized to tell all of you that I do feel very much like a proud uncle of the National Collection. I think you know how an uncle is. He doesn't visit very often, but he likes his relations to do well and it is good to see that the National Collection is doing well. If I will never be remembered as a patron of the arts, I should be delighted to be known as an uncle of the arts.
>
> Truly, this is a historic night for all of us. Until now, the United States was the only great country which had no national museum devoted to its own art.

Beneath his obvious delight in NCFA's opening and his own part in it, however, the president was much distracted by another event—which could not have been far from the mind of anyone in the audience. He continued,

> This is a day we shall remember for another reason. It was 1 o'clock this morning that I was awakened and informed that Hanoi was prepared to meet us in Paris, to talk about peace. [Here he was interrupted by thunderous applause.] We often think about peace as an absence of war. But, in fact, peace is a struggle; an achievement; an endless effort to convert hostility into negotiation; bloody violence into politics; hate into reconciliation.

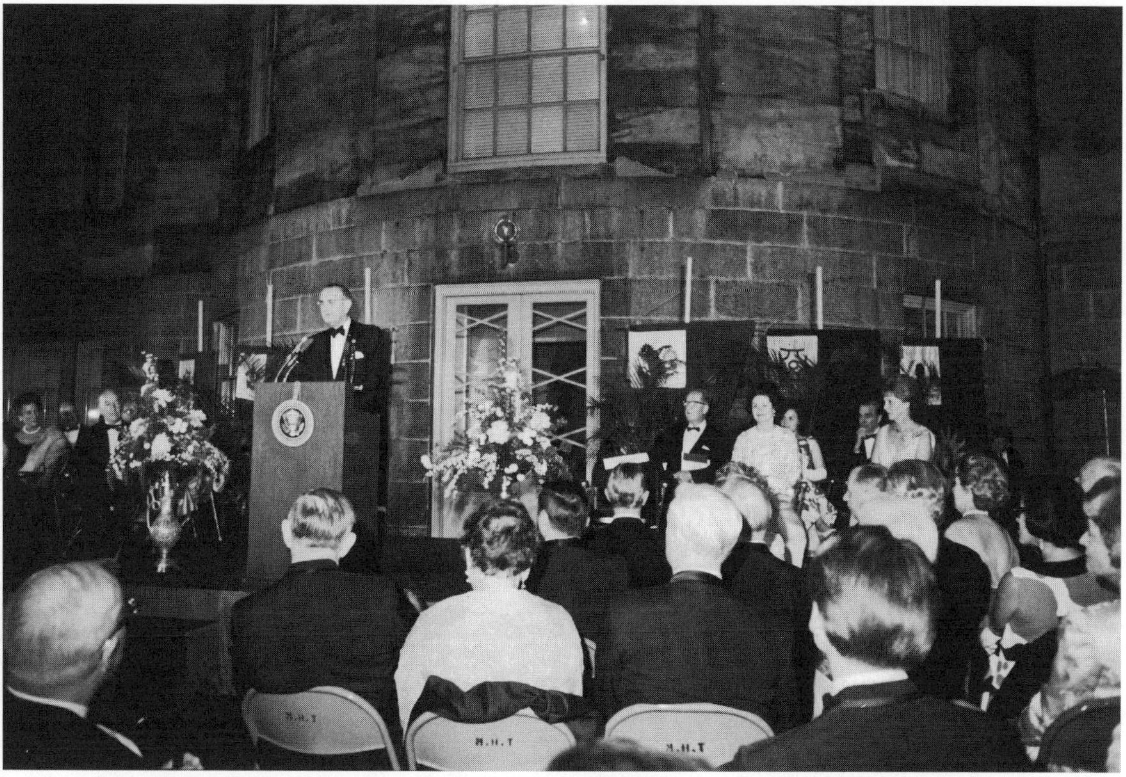

Figure 33. Jack Kightlinger, *President Lyndon B. Johnson at Opening Ceremony for NCFA in the Patent Office Building Courtyard, May 3, 1968.* Courtesy of Lyndon Baines Johnson Library, Austin, Texas.

> I have sought this moment for more days and nights than you will ever credit and in enough places for historians to judge that we were fully credible when we said "any time, anywhere."[28]

President Johnson's dedication of galleries in the Patent Office Building symbolized a watershed between past and present for the National Collection of Fine Arts, just as the years of this decade marked a continental divide in the history of the nation. Unfortunately, his good wishes for the future of NCFA were more solidly based than was the hope for an immediate end of the Vietnam War. Hostility and violence raged much closer to home than Southeast Asia. Students at Columbia,

Princeton, and Northwestern had recently joined campus protests that all but closed some universities, and Martin Luther King's assassination in the previous month precipitated the Poor People's March, on its way at that moment from Alabama to Washington. Destructive riots threatened life and property in major cities, including the nation's capital. Even as Johnson spoke to his elegantly dressed audience within the calm security of the Patent Office courtyard, incendiary fires were errupting on nearby Seventh Street and in the Fourteenth Street corridor, while marauding gangs vandalized shops and other commercial establishments.

Escorted by Secretary Ripley, President and Mrs. Johnson viewed works in the galleries (figure 34) and listened to chamber music played by the New England String Quartet. The next day's festivities turned to lectures and discussions on the mission of the museum in its latest reincarnation. In a symposium titled "Directions for the National Collection of Fine Arts," held in the library that was to serve both

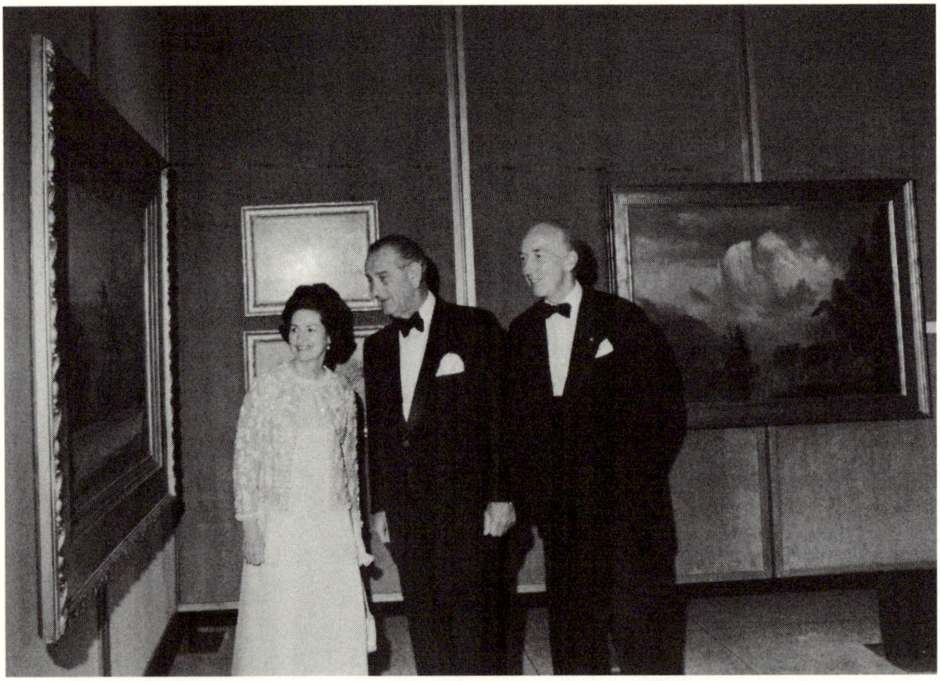

Figure 34. Jack Kightlinger, *President and Mrs. Johnson with Secretary Ripley*. Courtesy of Lyndon Baines Johnson Library, Austin, Texas.

the NCFA and the National Portrait Gallery, Edgar P. Richardson, a commissioner and one of the panelists, focused on the importance of the room in which they were meeting—the library. Much more study and documentation exists for European art than for American, he pointed out, and much of our own cultural history still remains to be researched. Richardson predicted that "the establishment in Washington of a national museum of American art with a great research library will inevitably bring with it the responsibility to be a center of information for the country. . . . [The library] will be an active and encouraging force in the intellectual and artistic life of this country, . . . a center for the increase and diffusion of knowledge," he concluded, linking this new potential to the phrase that founded the Smithsonian and set its basic agenda.[29] Other special events in celebration of the opening were aimed at particular groups, art professionals, teachers, artists, Smithsonian Associates, Smithsonian personnel, and the newly organized NCFA docents.

In response to the opening, Frank Getlein, art critic for the *Star*, reminisced on the past of NCFA—and how far it had come to reach this day:

> [The NCFA] has been ignored, shoved aside, burned out, given away and hidden behind the north end of a southbound elephant. A generation ago it even had its name stolen, which is about the worst thing that can happen to man or institution. . . . [T]he horrible things that have happened to the NCFA prior to its present happy arrival in snug harbor accurately reflect the changing regard and lack of regard in which art has been held by the American people, by their elected representatives in Congress and by the scientists who have run—and still do—the Smithsonian.[30]

Initiating New Programs—and an Unexpected Departure

During Johnson's presidency the first of a series of exhibitions of modern American paintings and prints was hung in the White House under the supervision of the director of NCFA, and both David Scott and Adelyn Breeskin served as advisers to the first White House Festival of the Arts in June 1965. Scott also took charge of the Changing Exhibitions Program, which involved placing works of art in the White House and the Executive Office Building every six to eight months on a rotating basis. Thus, a very positive relationship already existed between the National Collection and the current administration when Johnson lent an official presence to the opening ceremonies at the Patent Office Building.

Changes in the art world contributed to expansive opportunities for NCFA. New York City had usurped the role of Paris as the premier center for Western art, and artists of the United States were now in the front ranks of international contemporary art. It was indeed a favorable moment for the renewal of an institution committed to the nation's art. Most important to NCFA's renaissance, however, was S. Dillon Ripley, the most creative secretary the Smithsonian had ever known, whose crucial support made it possible for the National Collection of Fine Arts to move forward.

Ripley pushed the Smithsonian toward involvement with a broad potential public, tapping both "populist" and "elite" elements. A merry-go-round appeared on the mall—not far from the solemn bronze image of the first secretary, Joseph Henry. To promote scholarship, Ripley established the Department of Academic Affairs, which offered fellowships in all the fields represented by Smithsonian collections.

Another new venture aimed to use college students as "Guard-Guides" in exhibition areas, with the expectation that they could keep an eye on the security of objects while answering visitors' questions about the exhibited works. The NCFA at the Patent Office was selected as the site for this Ripley project, and Patricia Chieffo, with a professional background in education and art, designed a program. In place when the building opened, the Guard-Guides, initially twelve college students in red, white, and blue uniforms, eagerly greeted visitors in the galleries. Eventually their function as security guards was eliminated, and as "Museum Assistants" they continued to give information to the public, to research topics related to works on view, and to learn about museum vocational opportunities.

David Scott took a serious interest in public education programs and promoted them through staff members who were officially part of the Smithsonian's central Office of Education, assigned to the National Collection. Susan Sollins, a specialist in children's education, developed tours for children based on "confluent learning," whereby young visitors were taught to observe paintings and sculptures and kinesthetically act out shapes and movements in those works. Enthusiastic response from the children captured the attention of other education specialists, inspiring articles and television coverage that publicized the program at NCFA.

A year after the opening an editorial in the *Sunday Star* celebrated NCFA's first anniversary in the Patent Office Building, describing its reincarnation as a "remarkable phoenix-like achievement. . . . [U]nder the forceful leadership of director David W. Scott, the NCFA came out from behind the stuffed elephant and has become an extraordinary center of art in Washington." It concluded, "May the extraordinarily productive year now ending be the first of many for the NCFA and Dr. Scott."[31]

In that same week, Scott announced to his staff that he would leave the Smithsonian as of May 31. He gave no reason for his resignation, but behind the scenes, disagreements—big and small—beween Scott and Ripley had developed into an irreconcilable relationship between two strong personalities. Fervently immersed within the momentum of their first year's activities at the Patent Office Building, staff members were devastated. On June 1, 1969, Robert Tyler Davis, assistant director since September 1968, was appointed acting director. With an A.B. and M.A. from Harvard, Davis had previously served as director of the Portland, Oregon, Art Museum and Art School and the Montreal Museum of Fine Arts. David Scott was subsequently named consultant to the National Gallery of Art for the construction of its east wing. Acting Director Davis presided over a demoralized group of individuals trying to adjust to the abrupt departure of their leader. Meeting with the NCFA staff, Secretary Ripley reviewed the history of the museum, expressed concern for its continued progress, and gave his assurance that the process of selecting a new director was underway.

The search soon identified a promising candidate, a university professor without professional museum experience but with a coherent philosophy about museums and an overarching vision for a museum of American art. Joshua C. Taylor became the fifth director of the nation's first collection of art in January 1970. Educated at Reed College and Princeton, where he earned a Ph.D. in art history, he had taught for twenty-one years at the University of Chicago. The tradition of directors as practicing artists was maintained, for his degrees included an M.F.A., and at the begining of his career he had designed stage sets for the theater and the San Francisco Opera Ballet. In World War II he served with the infantry in the North African and Italian theaters, concluding his military career as a major.

Formed by education in the humanities and training in studio arts, in addition to participation in the Second World War, like his predecessor Taylor had a passionate commitment to the significance of the arts in the history of the nation and in the lives of individuals. Also like Scott, Taylor was a very decisive person, with little patience for the pecking order and procedures of a bureaucracy. He was to find himself often in sharp disagreement with the secretary, but in spite of frustrating differences, he and Ripley developed a great deal of respect for each other.

Directors of art museums in the 1970s can be characterized as individuals who were identified with their institutions and the distinctive style of programs they developed. Scott had attained such a reputation, as Taylor would do during his tenure. Beginning in the 1980s the role of museum directors, like that of presidents of universities, began to resemble CEOs in the corporate world, and scholars with backgrounds in the humanities found themselves in positions where success was measured by how much private money they could raise.

Taylor came to Washington as a scholar of international reputation for studies in American art, nineteenth- and twentieth-century Italian art, the arts of Mexico, and theories of nineteenth- and twentieth-century art. Besides teaching graduate students in the Department of Art History at Chicago, he was William Rainey Harper Professor of Humanities in the College. It was in these roles, as a scholar and master teacher, that he was to impress his mark upon NCFA.

A Policy of Elitism

A common criticism about art museums as public institutions is the accusation of elitism, the claim that through either deliberate intent or thoughtlessness, they tend to be exclusionary, directing exhibitions and every facet of operation to a knowledgeable inner circle—to those who can understand what they see in a gallery—instead of attempting to reach a broader and more diverse audience whose lack of specialized education or experience may be keeping them from an appreciation of works of art.[32]

NCFA's new director openly supported elitism as a policy—in the sense that everyone should be made part of the "elite" who enjoy and understand works of art. He traced the origin of his aim—and the conviction that it could be done—to his observations of the opera and museums in Italy, where all levels of Italian society attend performances and visit galleries with obvious understanding and enjoyment of what they hear and see.

Widely known for a primer on how to respond to art, *Learning to Look*—first published in 1957 and still in print—Taylor was a scholar who took a serious interest in making art understandable to a broad audience. He had no patience with the verbal jargon of art historians addressed to a closed circle of cognoscenti. So insistent was he that writing on art ought to be clear and understandable, and so opposed to any kind of categorical thinking that in his nineteenth-century art courses at Chicago, students were not allowed to use any word that ended in "ism." Defining the basic response to art as an encounter between a work of art and an individual viewer, he saw the museum as the natural place where such an experience could occur. In the spirit of John Dewey, he believed such encounters should not be passive but required active involvement with the memory, mind, and emotions. Philosophical roots in Benedetto Croce and Henri Bergson insisted on the primacy of intuitive response and understanding over verbal knowledge, with an awareness of the sensuous nature of the arts. Under his leadership all aspects of the museum were ultimately based on providing access to works of art for individuals at every level—the young child, the adult with no background, the developing student, the mature scholar.

One of Taylor's metaphors for this basic function of access in a museum was a bridge, "a bridge that should be well-traveled. Most people think of a museum as a kind of beachhead with no life of its own."[33] Upon this bridge the professional staff provides the means of approach to the works: "Instead of thinking of a museum as first of all a collection, or even a place to give 'shows,' it might be useful to think of it as a group of people, well informed about and devoted to the study of art, who carry a responsibility both to the larger world of art and to their immediate public. These are not communications people; they should be historians and critics who have something to say, both to their learned colleagues and to the community."[34]

Perhaps the most unusual characteristic of Joshua Taylor as the director of a major art museum was that he did not think of his institution as being in competition with others. Within the Smithsonian he had to compete for funds and space with other bureaus, of course, but in defining the collection and presenting exhibitions, his vision was founded on the uniqueness of NCFA as a Smithsonian museum and a national museum, dedicated to the nation's art. As he wrote Secretary Ripley:

> Much museum thinking is based on material possessiveness, but it seems to me that it is a unique aspect of the Smithsonian collections that they are based less on a pride of owning than on a pride of knowing. We build collections in order to know rather than in order to crow over our extraordinary possessions. And of course, our knowing means the public's knowing—means museum display. Rather than to display only a few works which symbolize what we consider at any one moment the major achievements, we display that range of material which we believe represents the continuing complexity of the varied experiences in American art.[35]

Collections Management

For many years the Smithsonian art collections had been divided into three categories according to different functions: a study collection, a lending collection, and a collection for exhibition purposes, the first two groups consisting of works considered to be of lesser quality than those assigned to the latter. Under Taylor's concept of the entire collection as a record of American art in its cultural diversity and as evidence of American taste, these divisions were eliminated as serving no useful purpose.

Through the 1970s acquisitions numbered close to 1,000 each year through government transfers, gifts, and purchases. By 1980 the collection totaled more than 26,000 paintings, sculptures, and works on paper. Through an agreement with the Government Services Administration, NCFA received works originally created as part of the New Deal programs of the 1930s and subsequent government contracts, including maquettes, drawings, and studies for art in federal buildings. Noteworthy gifts also came from private donors; the S. W. and B. M. Koffler Foundation collection of contemporary Chicago art featuring works by Roger Brown, Ellen Lanyon, Gladys Nilsson, Jim Nutt, Ed Paschke, and Ray Yoshida, among others; paintings from the Vincent Melzac collection included canvasses by Willem DeKooning, Franz Kline, Morris Louis, and Clyford Still. A cache of materials from Joseph Cornell's studio was given by the artist's sister and her husband, Mr. and Mrs. John A. Benton; this gift became the basis of the Joseph Cornell Study Center, opened in 1979. Eighteenth- and nineteenth-century works were added, landscapes, genre subjects, portraits, and still-lifes by Albert Bierstadt, David Gilmour Blythe, Asher Brown Durand, Ralph Earl, Rembrandt Peale, John Peto, and other artists. Charles Willson Peale's miniature painting *Matthias and Thomas Bordley*, a combined museum purchase and gift from Mr. and Mrs. Murray Lloyd Goldsborough Jr., joined an outstanding collection of over 400 ivories, 291 by American painters and 135 by artists of other national origins.[36]

Most unusual of NCFA's acquisitions during this decade, *The Throne of the Third Heaven* does not fit into conventional curatorial categories. Not a professional artist, James Hampton, an African American government employee, gave form to a compelling inner vision by transforming the commonplace (old furniture, light bulbs, and aluminum foil) into the sacred, creating a personal, glittering spectacle that continues to stun museum visitors. *The Throne* helped to initiate a major area within the collection: works by untrained artists, many of whom, like Hampton, use ordinary objects to create images that range from the amusing to the spiritual.

While new acquisitions increased the museum's holdings in American art, NCFA's permanent collection still resided within motley gatherings from the past: European works, decorative arts and furnishings of the Gellatly collection, historical memorabilia from the Harriet Lane Johnston bequest, and other objects not of American origin or definable as art. Questions about the scope and nature of the collection emerged once again: how should the "national collection of fine arts" be properly defined? Early in the course of its development the collection had been directed toward the nation's own art, particularly the "fine arts" of painting and sculpture—but not exclusively so. Directives of the 1930s mandated concern for American art and living artists. During the 1970s many works that seemed less related to that goal were transferred from NCFA's collection to other Smithsonian museums or government agencies, the largest group—116 paintings and sculptures and 8,000 portrait prints—to the newly established National Portrait Gallery.

Another possibility for refining the collection at this time was deaccessioning. Smithsonian deaccession procedures were now in place (after having been an issue for the museum in the 1960s), and the practice had become more common throughout the museum world in the United States. In European institutions deaccessioning typically is not a viable possibility, and curators there often look aghast at such connivings in this country. Perhaps a difference in the historical origin of collections here—where museum donations often arrive fresh from the marketplace—results in fewer qualms about such methods. But the process at best involves financial risk and questions about public interest.

With limited funds for the purchase of art, the question of deaccessioning at NCFA rose again. Selling certain European paintings and decorative pieces could be justified by using the resulting funds to buy American works. Taylor, however, did not consider deaccessioning an acceptable option for a national collection that had been gathered over more than a century; it constituted a record of the nation's past and should be preserved in its integrity. He explained his approach at length to the secretary:

> To go back and eliminate works from the collection on the basis of modern taste would be to falsify history and to weaken seriously the value of the collection. Because someone in the past acting according to his best judgment made what we feel now was an embarrassing choice, is not a matter to be

> eliminated but rather to be recorded, to be preserved. We are quite content that other collections might wish to eliminate these errors of past judgment, but it is the peculiarity of this museum that it is content to harbor both the errors and the successes of the past. We are quite aware that the definition of error and success may indeed at any time change.[37]

Thus delighting in the museum's quirky past, Taylor organized an exhibition designed as a glimpse into the collection's rambling history. It was "a painless way to learn how a well-organized modern museum emerges from a disparate group of 19th century art collections," observed a reviewer who could remember the gallery in the Natural History Building.[38]

A definition of the National Collection was now projected into another dimension—the larger context of the American hemisphere. An interest in and knowledge of the arts of Mexico and Latin America led to the director's role as adviser to art museums in South American nations. Even though the director did not suggest that NCFA should collect art outside the fifty states, he stressed the importance of being aware of shared historical circumstances in the development of art traditions in the New World. In keeping with this interest, NCFA in 1974 sponsored a symposium, "The Common Situation: Colonialism to Independence," on the art traditions of Mexico and the United States, with papers presented by scholars from both nations.

Distinctive Exhibitions

Taylor's maverick approach to American art attained its highest visibility in NCFA's exhibition program. Tremendous confidence in his own vision enabled him to present the kind of art that most museum directors would not have touched: sentimental paintings of the mid-nineteenth century—not only questionable subject matter but also by a female artist, Lily Martin Spencer; biblical subjects and works expressive of faith and spirituality, at the time almost completely ignored as a presence in American art; and an exhibit centered on a type universally denigrated and stereotyped, academic art. These were convincingly presented as dealing with significant issues in the nation's cultural traditions. And before such studies became de rigueur, NCFA presented exhibitions of works by artists who were women, Native Americans, African Americans, and Hispanics. Memorables examples include the work of Romaine Brooks, featured in a gallery setting keyed to her paintings with expanses of empty spaces and stark contrasts of black and white; contemporary works of Native American painters Fritz Scholder and T. C. Cannon; the art of African American artist William H. Johnson; and an exhibit of contemporary Western works that included Hispanic artists, "The First Western States Biennial Exhibition."[39]

With a commitment to American art throughout the nation, NCFA made geographic breadth another factor in its exhibition policy through a series of regional shows featuring American art from Chicago to the Pacific Northwest to Alaska. Monographic shows dealt with well-known artists such as Robert Rauschenberg and Mary Cassatt, the lesser-known nineteenth-century painter Charles Bird King, and the early twentieth-century modernist Arthur Wesley Dow. The most ambitious event in a strenuous program that presented more than twenty exhibits a year (including those in the Renwick Gallery, a curatorial department of the National Collection of Fine Arts) was NCFA's bicentennial exhibition, "America as Art." This sweeping view of art in the United States within specific themes of its cultural history was unconventional—as is suggested by the catalogue's cover illustration, a woodcut from *Davey Crockett's Almanack of 1838, A Woman Rescued from the Jaws of a Catamount and Fangs of a Serpent*.[40]

Publications related to the museum's exhibitions had evolved from typescripts in the 1910s and 1920s, merely listing the names of artists and titles of works, to printed brochures that added facts about an artist's career or descriptive material about a particular craft where that was appropriate. In the 1960s, publications began to be based on original research and often included chronologies of an artist's career or an interpretive summary of a particular era or group of artists. Many of the catalogues that accompanied NCFA exhibitions in the late 1960s and 1970s represented major scholarly endeavors that remain significant resources in the field of American art—a convincing sign that scholarship in art museums had reached a level of achievement and recognition formerly associated only with university scholars.

Taylor's concepts of the collection and exhibitions were not applauded by everyone throughout the Smithsonian—or even within NCFA. Some curators favored a deaccession policy in order to obtain more works by major artists; they would have welcomed the opportunity "to crow" about the museum's possessions. Having a director who took an active role in everything from collections management to exhibition policy to the color of walls and carpets seemed overpowering at times. Designer Val Lewton recalled Dr. Taylor's presence when exhibitions were being mounted, his often voiced opinions—and unerring sense of design. The Smithsonian Office of Development complained about exhibitions that featured names of artists nobody had previously heard of, stating a definite preference for exhibits that would draw crowds. Taylor, however, would not give an inch on any of his principles. He refused to let popularity determine the subjects of exhibitions in place of what he saw as the museum's responsibility to present the breadth of American art and new aesthetic and educational experiences for the public.

Rethinking International Exhibitions and Lending Programs

Unlike David Scott, Taylor could not endorse NCFA's involvement in the Venice and São Paulo biennials and other exhibitions abroad—a conclusion he reached before problems erupted in planning for the Venice Biennale of 1970. Harry T. Hopkins of the Fort Worth Art Center acted as director for that event, planned as an exhibition of prints and a setting for an experimental graphic arts workshop organized by Lois Bingham. But on the national scene in May of that year (the month before the Venice exhibit opened), one calamity followed another: American troops invaded Cambodia; the National Guard fatally shot four students at Kent State University; two African American students were killed at Mississippi State College. By early June nearly half the artists selected for representation in Venice had requested to withdraw their works, stating their refusal to allow the United States government to employ art as a "cultural veneer" over such deplorable acts (figure 35 shows their protest poster). Taylor respected the wishes of the artists, and Charles Blitzer, assistant secretary for History and Art, gave the protesters permission to distribute at the pavilion a statement about their reason for not participating. In the short time before the scheduled opening, not much could be done at the American Pavilion except to produce a truncated display, described by one reviewer as "a non-exhibition, nothing more than a messy printshop, full of empty crates, some presses . . . and some prints on the wall."[41] Prints produced in the workshop at the American exhibit were shown at NCFA in 1971 and afterward sent on tour to venues in Europe and Africa.

Objections of NCFA's director to the operations of the International Art Program concerned the disproportionate amount of staff time and budget that it consumed, which he saw as "the tail wagging the dog." Although a 1971 agreement released NCFA from sponsorship of the international biennials, the museum agreed

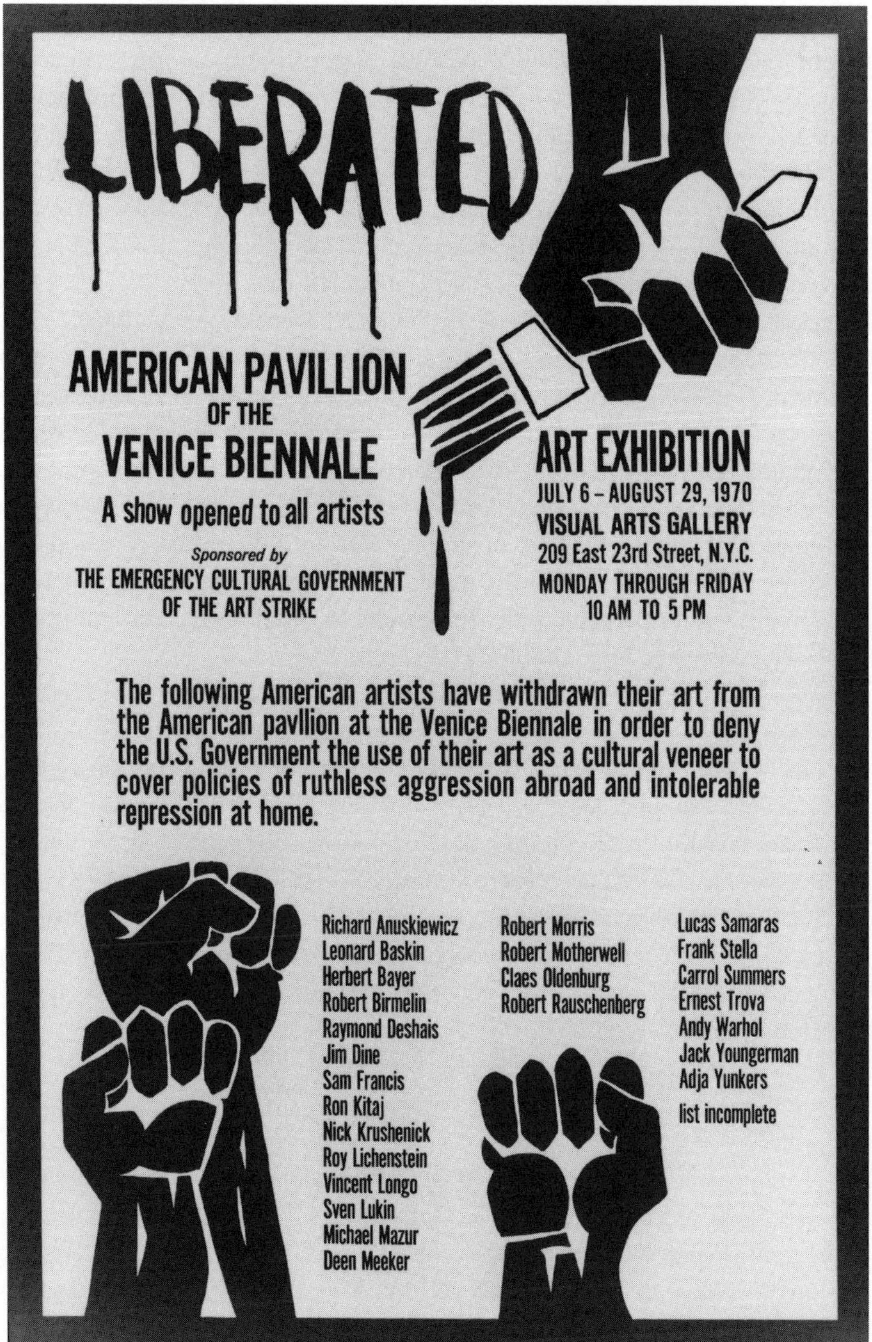

Figure 35. *Liberated.* Poster by Artists Protesting the Venice Biennale of 1970. Courtesy of Margaret P. Cogswell.

to mount the U.S.A. exhibit at the Venice Biennale of 1972, and to coordinate the American section of the São Paulo Bienal in 1973. Six artists were featured in Venice, selected by Walter Hopps, director of the Corcoran Gallery. For the São Paulo event, Don Baum, a professor at Roosevelt University, together with the Museum of Contemporary Art in Chicago, organized the exhibition "Made in Chicago" (shown the following year at NCFA). International exhibits other than the biennials continued to be sent out by the NCFA office through 1975.

Discussions with representatives of the State Department, the National Endowments, USIA, and the American Federation of Arts culminated in 1976 in the establishment of an International Exhibition Committee formed under the American Federation of Arts to coordinate exhibitions abroad. Administrative costs were to be paid by grants from the Endowments for the Arts and Humanities, with additional support from the State Department and USIA—reorganized as the International Communications Agency, ICA. A further agreement in 1979 placed responsibility for content with a joint endowment panel and implementation with ICA. The important aim was to perpetuate the separation of artistic judgment and political bureaucracy established under NCFA's operation.

The Lending Program that Thomas Beggs had proudly viewed as fulfilling an aspect of the museum's raison d'être was also perceived anew—as a major headache. At any one time as many as 1,000 works were on loan to government offices. Keeping track of such a number located in many different places, and periodically checking on them, constituted an onerous task for the registrar's office, but even more disturbing were problems that occurred on site: the removal of artworks to areas of harmful climatic conditions and their occasional disappearance. After a systematic inventory and the retrieval of many works, the program continued but with considerably fewer objects on loan to a very select group of cabinet members and the White House staff.

Raising the Status of Education and Research

Off to a running start under David Scott, education programs continued apace with the establishment of a department of education at NCFA, replacing staff members from the Smithsonian's central office assigned to the National Collection. The new arrangement resulted from the decentralization of certain aspects of the Smithsonian bureaucracy, efforts energetically pushed by Taylor.

In most museums, education departments at this time were headed by education specialists—customarily viewed as beneath the curators in importance, thus subordinating educational to curatorial activities. Such a hierarchy of values was unacceptable to Taylor, who insisted on appointing an art historian to head the department as Curator of Education with full curatorial status. His first appointment for this role was Darrell Sewall, followed by Peter Bermingham. As in other museum education departments, the curator engaged in training docents, producing materials for elementary and secondary schools, and presenting public lectures, films, videos, and occasional concerts and dance performances.

Several other activities were less conventional. Programs for children built upon two activities first organized in 1969: Children's Day, an annual day-long series of events for children and their families; and the Children's Museum, a special exhibition room. Originally, this special area contained material for both children and adults, but the reorganized and retitled concept emerged in 1974 as the Explore Gallery—exclusively for children. Small visitors entered through a hole in the door (too small for parental passage) to find a variety of materials and shapes and forms—some realistic, some fantastic—all of which they could touch or walk through or crawl under for a variety of sensory and kinesthetic experiences. Taylor pointed out that the aim of the gallery was to "create an awareness of the wonders of sense and the associated reaches of the imagination. Rather than serving as a child's alternative to the galleries, it sets out to stimulate those perceptions that will make the works displayed throughout the museum accessible. Much of what the docents do with the children is closely related to experiences like those provided by the Explore Gallery, and many of the prepared 'self-tours,' especially popular with families, carry further this kind of exploration throughout the museum."[42]

A Discover Graphics program brought high school students into the museum to learn printmaking from an artist-in-residence, and a summer program offered training in printmaking for teachers. One consequence of these efforts was that printmaking became a major activity in the art programs of area schools. Other results were the quality of work often attained by the novices and their pride in seeing prints they had made displayed in a juried exhibition of high school graphics shown at NCFA every two years. In an additional program designed for high school students, "Junior Interns" or "Future Scholars" worked directly with staff members at various assigned museum tasks, excited to be "behind the scenes" while becoming familiar with potential vocational fields.

NCFA's Department of Education maintained a gallery called "Discover" where temporary exhibits focused on particular aspects of art not dealt with in the major shows. Here about four exhibits each year presented a variety of themes: for example, "A Future for Our Past," a display of methods used in the conservation of paintings and sculptures (produced in part by museum interns); and "Raíces y Visiones / Roots and Visions," featuring works by artists of the United States whose Latin American background formed the basis of their artistic expression.[43]

Museums in the United States could not operate in their customary style without contingents of volunteers to augment the hired staff. The docent program at NCFA in the 1970s numbered about seventy volunteer members—only slightly fewer than the total of museum professionals. In an extensive training program they studied art history, aesthetic theory, and communication techniques. As with all aspects of the museum, the director took a personal interest in their work and in frequent sessions with them helped to shape their approach to works of art and to the public. Though some museums prefer to employ professional scholars and educators to deal with visitors, NCFA's director saw positive advantage in the trained volunteers. "He felt that the docents could relate to the questions of the visitors because they were essentially on the same level," Nora Panzer, then manager of the docent program, recalled. The point was not first to try to fit a particular art work into a preexisting historical scheme, or describe it in "someone else's language," declared Taylor but to consider "how differently the mind works because of the encounter. The viewer should first question himself, not the expert."[44]

One of the attractions for Joshua Taylor in leaving the university world to become director of NCFA was the opportunity to bridge the gap he perceived between academic scholarship and the study of art as carried on in museums. He questioned whether many professors of art history realized that paintings had a back side, so confined were they to images of slides on a screen; museum curators, on the other hand, captivated by the care and history of individual items, could rarely back off to see the forest—objects gathered together in a context of meaning.

At that time, advanced study in American art, not yet widely offered in universities, was regarded by some art historians as less intellectually viable than the Italian, French, German, or other European traditions. A scholar of both European and American art, Taylor could speak authoritatively: "The study of art in the United States makes its own demands as to method and intellectual preparation, not provided simply by the general preparation in European material." Elaborating, he pointed out that

> the nicety of relating art from the United States to that of Europe is no simple matter. It requires wide and specific knowledge, and a constant critical re-examination of judgments. Furthermore, the interplay between art and other aspects of culture seems much more real and of undeniable importance in looking at our own national past. Certainly the demands put on the conscientious historian are different and probably greater here than for any other field, in which disinterest is a less problematic ingredient.[45]

Before leaving Chicago, he had worked out a plan for a research program in which pre- and postdoctoral fellows, as a resident community at the museum, could pursue their studies in the midst of works of art and, with their questions and ideas, stimulate members of the museum staff toward new patterns of thought. He appointed a scholar and former teacher as Curator of Research in charge of the program (this was my role). In keeping with the director's concept of the proper scope of studies in American art as well as taking advantage of opportunities afforded by the breadth of resources at the Smithsonian, NCFA's program for Smithsonian fellows was interdisciplinary.

The former Museum Assistants program for college students then became an Intern Program. Selected through an annual competition, college students were assigned to staff offices for practical experience in a variety of museum vocations. Program director Patricia Chieffo reported that Taylor took an active role in developing intern policies; he suggested tuition-sharing with universities and other ideas that were to define internships into future years.

One of the impressive developments resulting from the move into the Patent Office Building was the growth of library resources. The prediction of Edgar Richardson at the opening of NCFA in 1968 came true within a decade: the National Collection of Fine Arts / National Portrait Gallery Library, initially under the leadership of librarian William Walker, was well on its way to becoming a major resource for scholars of American art and history.

NCFA began to forge research tools. As the museum's project to mark the bicentennial of the nation, Taylor proposed making an inventory of American paintings created before 1914, including the title, date, size, and location of each work.

This seemingly impossible task was organized and made ready for use in 1976, the celebratory year, by Abigail Booth Gerdts. At the opening date a computerized list, "The Bicentennial Inventory of American Paintings before 1914," included 150,000 paintings representing the works of 12,800 American artists and became an invaluable resource for study of the art of the United States, where works are located throughout an immense geographic expanse.

Beyond the Patent Office Building

In the midst of planning the move from the Natural History Building to the Patent Office, NCFA in 1967 had another building dropped into its administrative lap: the original Corcoran Gallery on Pennsylvania Avenue, used since 1899 as the United States Court of Claims. Designed in 1859 by the architect of the Castle, James Renwick, this building—like the Patent Office—had survived several reincarnations and just barely escaped destruction by the wrecker's ball. Its distinctive mansard roofline, adapted by Renwick from the leading style of his day, the architecture of France's Second Empire (figure 36), was subsequently carried out also in the extraodinary Executive Office Building directly opposite, designed by A. B. Mullett and constructed in 1871–88. Through efforts of First Lady Jacqueline Kennedy in 1962, Renwick's Corcoran Gallery and other historic structures on Lafayette Square were preserved from the demolition mania of development interests in the capital city. Dillon Ripley could envision the dilapidated building—with its interior of false ceilings and office partitions slathered in the green paint that certified former government occupancy—as a Smithsonian museum and made a convincing proposal to President Lyndon B. Johnson for its use as a gallery "to exhibit American arts and crafts drawn from our own resources as well as the Traveling Exhibition Service and other museums."[46]

A five-year restoration project begun under David Scott was still under way when Joshua Taylor came to NCFA in 1970. The interior renovation proceeded, directed by architect Hugh Newell Jacobsen, with work on the exterior of the building supervised by the John Carl Warnecke architectural firm. Once again dedicated to its original purpose, the building opened in 1972 as the Renwick Gallery.

The function of NCFA's newest gallery was broadly defined to deal with crafts, decorative arts, architecture, and industrial design, primarily of the United States but also including work from other countries—thought to be appropriate because

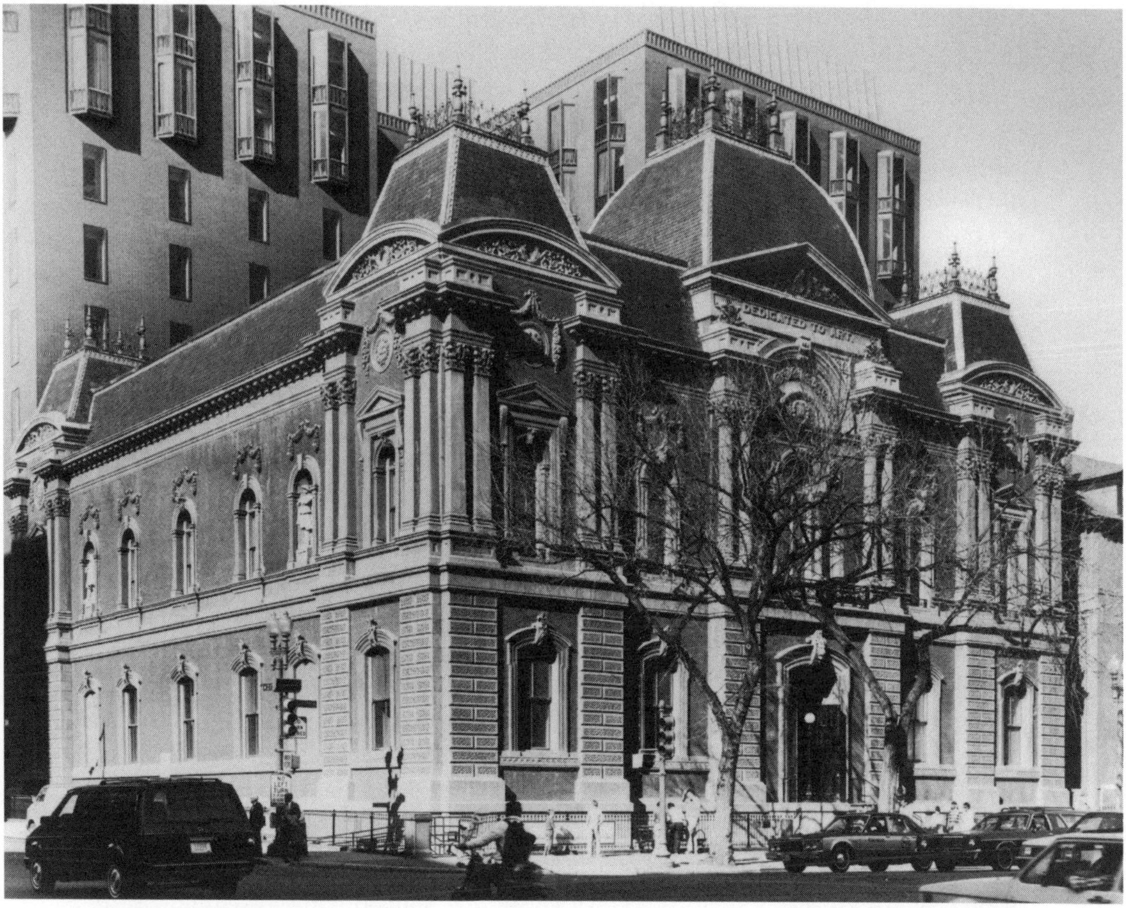

Figure 36. *Renwick Gallery (exterior), 1978. Washington, D.C.* Smithsonian American Art Museum, Staff Photographer.

the Renwick's next-door neighbor, Blair House, served as the federal government's official guesthouse for foreign dignitaries. Though at the founding the intent was not to maintain a permanent collection, works that related to the Renwick's particular areas of interest were occasionally purchased by NCFA. Permanent installations in the handsomely restored Grand Salon and Octagon Room consisted of nineteenth-century American and European paintings, sculptures, and *objets d'art* on loan from the Corcoran and NCFA collections.

Lloyd E. Herman, a staff member in the office of Frank Taylor, who was director-general of Smithsonian museums, submitted a proposal for programs at the new gallery that impressed NCFA's director and led to his appointment as director of the Renwick. Under Herman's leadership the Renwick embarked on a lively schedule of exhibitions that earned a glowing reputation in the crafts field, nationally and internationally. Of fifty-three exhibitions from 1973 through 1979, forty consisted of crafts or decorative arts of the United States and thirteen of foreign works. The Renwick's bicentennial exhibit featured Latin American decorative arts and related to NCFA's concern for making aesthetic and intellectual connections with art traditions throughout the hemisphere. Events with U.S. themes ranged from the contemporary designs of Raymond Loewy (which included putting an automobile in the gallery) to an exhibition of crafts titled "The Object as Poet."

Ideas and sources for exhibits at the Renwick came from collections in other Smithsonian museums, especially the wealth of Native American ceramics and other materials in the anthropological collections of the Museum of Natural History. "Murals in the Round," for example, featured tipi paintings of the Kiowa and Kiowa-Apache Indians as reproduced in models made for James Mooney of the Smithsonian during his field studies at the turn of the century. Exhibit materials from the Museum of History and Technology included items as diverse as western saddles and musical instruments.

Objects originally studied as cultural artifacts in the science collections could be viewed in these exhibits with the same sense of appreciation and enjoyment as works of art in the painting galleries, for the modes of display and the nature of modern art and theory had eroded distinctions between contrasting definitions of these two types of objects. An especially popular Renwick exhibit, "Signs of Life," exemplified the ambiguity of the terms. Produced in association with the architectural firm of Venturi and Rauch, it involved visitors with contemporary industrial art/artifacts such as neon signs and other images of urban sprawl, which shone forth with monumental beauty in the unlikely setting of an exhibition hall. Studies in cultural anthropology had also broadened. Originally developed by Western scholars to analyze exotic peoples across the globe, the methodology now turned to consider objects and patterns of culture in the industrialized societies of Europe and the Americas such as urban environments. The Loewy automobile, appreciated for its beauty of design, could also be approached much like a birchbark canoe, considering its material and manufacturing process and its relation to the values and life needs of a particular people.[47]

The historically accurate restoration on the exterior of the Renwick, completed in 1968, began crumbling less than ten years later. As scaffolding veiled the Renwick for another round of masonry replacement, a detailed plan for the repair and decoration of Barney Studio House (presented to the Smithsonian in 1960) was also put into place. By late 1979 the public could tour the renovated rooms and enjoy an active program of events in the arts that continued the tradition of Mrs. Barney's original use of her building on Sheridan Circle. In a setting of paintings and pastels by Alice Pike Barney and other works from her collection, "Evenings at Barney Studio House" presented programs of poetry reading, music, and dance, followed by receptions that honored the performing artists.

Although the Smithsonian's original mandate had charged "the increase and diffusion of knowledge," Taylor observed, the institution eagerly obeyed a much older admonition, to "increase and multiply." In the late 1970s the urge to multiply resulted in plans for two new museums in the South Yard behind the Castle. These buildings were designated for African art and Asian art, with most of their space below ground in order not to disturb the skyline of Renwick's Castle Building—once maligned as an architectural monstrosity but now become the institution's hallmark. As an antithesis to the traditional classic museum building, where a majestic staircase marks ascendancy to the higher plane of art, in these structures museum visitors descend into the depths of earth, where no natural light can enter. They are thus transported to another world, one that the collections of the Museum of African Art and the Sackler Gallery of Asian Art represent for most American visitors.

These latest projects brought the total of new Smithsonian art museums to five in less than two decades and, though science and technology interests still dominated, helped to make the art interests of the institution more visible.

Not long thereafter the importance of a name arose again. As early as 1973 the director and NCFA commissioners had discussed the possibility of changing "National Collection of Fine Arts" to a title that would specifically indicate the museum's primary concern with American art. Taking up the matter more seriously in the spring of 1980, the commissioners' development committee, headed by R. Philip Hanes Jr., proposed "National Collection of American Art," but it was the "National Museum of American Art" (NMAA) which, after approval by the Regents and Congress, became effective October 13, 1980—bestowing upon the collection its third official title.[48] Twenty years later in October 2000, the name would change again, this time to "the Smithsonian American Art Museum" (SAAM).

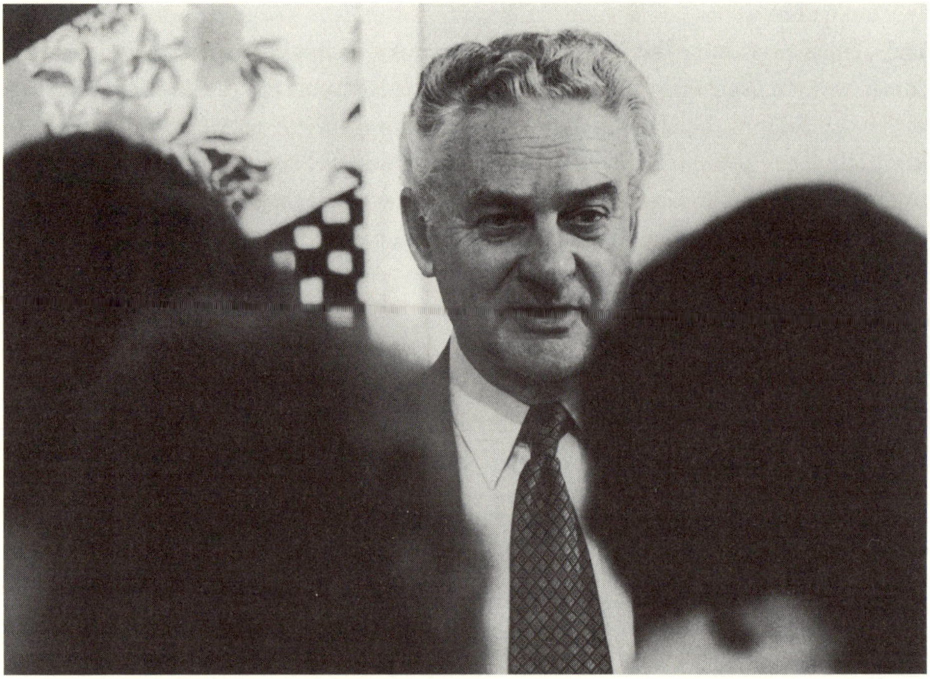

Figure 37. *Joshua C. Taylor with Gallery Visitors*. Still from film *A Sense of Discovery*. Smithsonian Institution Archives, neg. no. 2002-1079.

A Place of Discovery

The Smithsonian Office of Telecommunications made a film in 1980 to serve as orientation to the museum's collection and programs. Called *A Sense of Discovery*, it was "based on Dr. Taylor's feeling that each individual should form and trust his own responses to art," noted the WETA news release for its showing on Washington public television (figure 37, a still from the film, shows Taylor talking with gallery visitors).[49] The title also aptly described experiences of the first dozen years in the new building for NCFA/NMAA visitors and members of the staff, fellows, interns, and docents. Delight in experiences of the new and unfamiliar had not yet worn off in viewing the nation's art within one of the most beautiful—and oldest—buildings in Washington.

A sense of discovery also characterized the emergence of new approaches to the study of cultural phenomena. Critical theories of art history proposed new ways of seeing and understanding works of art. Traditional methods that traced careers of artists and the development of styles gave way to analyses of viewer response, aspects of political content, the seeking of underlying meaning by deconstructing a work. Originating in the fields of sociology, psychology, literature, and linguistics, and coming from perspectives of gender and race, these innovations invigorated methods of study but, at the same time, diminished the importance of historical research. More to the point at hand, they appeared to pose a potential threat to the programs of art museums. If the essential meaning of art could be found in aspects exterior to the work itself, then reproductions, or even verbal descriptions, might substitute for the real thing. In addition, new technology and possibilities of cyberspace offered "virtual" exhibitions in which entire museum collections could be explored via computer screens—with viewers comfortably sitting down instead of plodding through endless galleries.

Taylor considered the potential consequences of the verbal superceding the tangible, and the role of museums and their objects in a future era defined by technology:

> No matter how conceptualized learning becomes, man remains a sensuous creature, and the sensuous component in the learning process cannot long be bypassed without producing a debilitating separation between erudition and personal experience. . . . In spite of a particularly modish line of talk, the museum with its actual objects, whether of art or science, will not become an anachronism in an age of computerized learning, but an ever more necessary complement to the new techniques. I foresee the expansion of exhibitions as calling attention to specific objects and processes, rather than seeming the physical display of objects reduced to symbolic tokens. And in this, it is important ultimately that they not imitate the mechanized and multi-media capsules that are becoming the new standard texts. They should serve as the antidote. The *thing* must not be lost sight of in the scheme or the presentation if the museum is to survive.[50]

The year after the release of the *Discovery* film, on April 23, 1981, Joshua Taylor died, after a brief illness, at the age of sixty-three. Unanticipated and sudden, his loss produced a sense of shock throughout the NMAA staff and indeed, throughout the entire museum community, where he had been so strong a source of ideas and principles.

Reflecting on Taylor's impact on the Smithsonian, Thomas Lawton, director of the Freer Gallery wrote: "Josh Taylor was a scholar whose interest and expertise

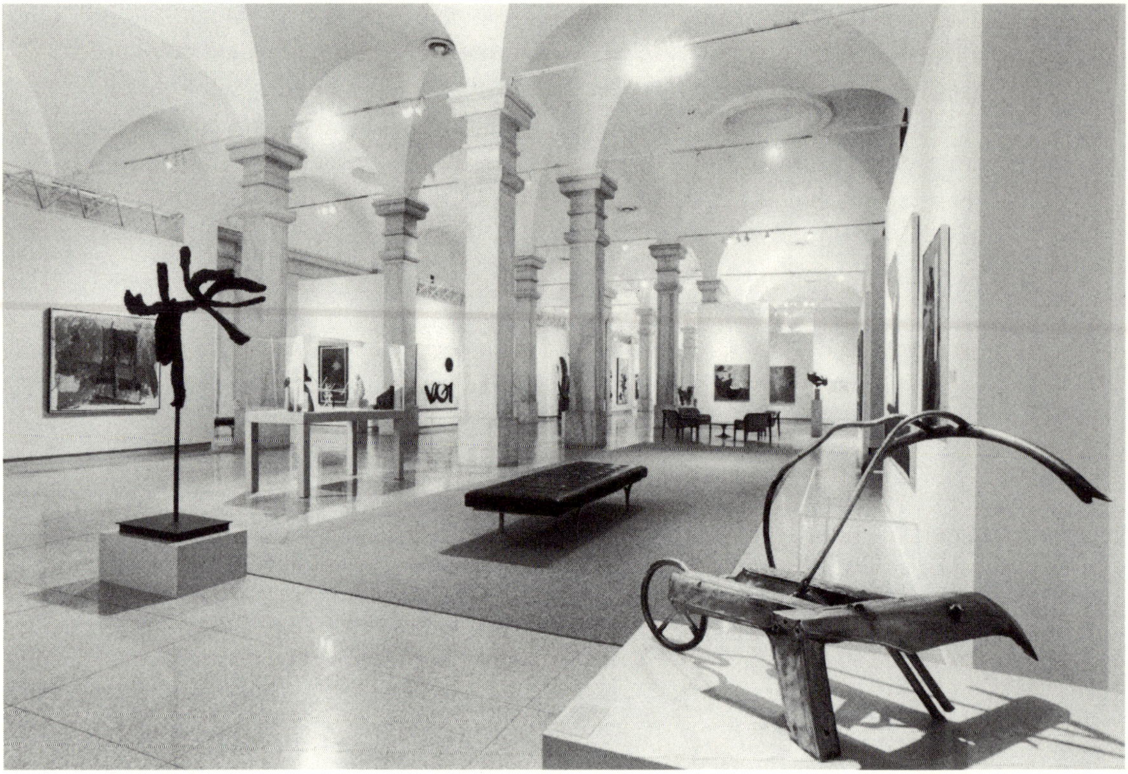

Figure 38. Robert Lautman, *Lincoln Gallery*, 1984. Sculpture at left: Fritz Bultman, *Azores I*, Gift of Mr. and Mrs. David K. Anderson, Martha Jackson Memorial; sculpture in foreground at right: Richard Hunt, from "Great Ideas" series, Gift of Container Corporation; painting in background facing chairs: Willem DeKooning, *The Wave*, Gift of the Vincent Melzac Collection. Smithsonian American Art Museum, Slide and Photo Archives.

transcended the usual limitations of country or culture. He was equally at home discussing the arts of America, Europe or the Far East. In everything he did, said or wrote, he insisted upon excellence. And, in retrospect, the results of his quest for excellence are Josh Taylor's bequest to all of us."[51]

Two dynamic directors had given the NCFA/MNAA new energy at the most formative stages of its circuitous history. David Scott provided the concepts and organizational skills that moved the collection—figuratively and literally—out of its doldrums of lethargy in the Natural History Building. Joshua Taylor forged the separate parts of the museum into a coherent program for scholars and the public. Both directors with their staffs brought the museum into an era of new possibilities for promoting the nation's own art and artists, the intended purpose of the art collection proposed at the founding of the Smithsonian.

As another beneficial development, scholarly prestige and popular interest in American art was rising to unprecedented levels. Activities flourished in all areas: research, exhibitions, symposia, university courses, publications. The National Museum of American Art played a significant role in this new appreciation and would continue to do so—along with the National Portrait Gallery, the Archives of American Art, and the American Art/Portrait Gallery Library—all together forming a peerless center for the study and enjoyment of American art and history within the architectural beauty of the Patent Office Building (figure 38).

CODA: LOOKING BACK TO BEGINNINGS

Washington residents of the early 1800s who first gathered the objects that became part of the Smithsonian would marvel at the displays of art, history, and science that today represent the national collections. Yet amid bewildering differences from their own time, they would be able to recognize a basic feature as unchanged: the tremendous importance attached to museums. Like the founders of the capital city, our generation reveres museums as essential cultural institutions. In Washington and throughout the country, museums continue to proliferate and attract crowds of visitors. Museum architecture is consistently among the most innovative as compared with that of buildings intended for any other purpose, a visible statement of the era's values.[1] Why this lively interest in collections of tangible objects when computerized information and images of virtual reality beguile with easier and faster methods of accessing materials?

Examining the museum phenomenon in the experience of our predecessors, Neil Harris has suggested that a crucial reason for the tremendous growth of museums during the life-changing economic and technical innovations of the nineteenth century was their potential to make various kinds of connections in an era imbued with a sense of historical discontinuity, "a feeling of interruption, of separation from thousands of years of human existence. The museum became a corrective, an asylum, a source of transcendent values meant to restore some older rhythms of nature and history. . . as settings to promote integration and solidarity, between social and economic classes, between humanity and nature, between mankind and time, or between human beings and the act of creation."[2]

Perhaps this helps to explain the popularity of museums within the unsettling and fragmenting experiences of our own era: we seek to restore some of our own lost connections—through encounters with the reality of things, and the renewing experiences of art.

APPENDIX

Pre-Smithsonian Sources of the SAAM Collection

Columbian Institute for the Promotion of Arts and Sciences, 1816–1838
The War Department's Indian Gallery, from 1817
John Varden's Washington Museum, 1829–1840
National Institute for the Promotion of Science, 1840–1862

Museum Titles

Smithsonian Gallery of Art or The Picture Gallery, before 1865
The National Gallery of Art (NGA), 1906–1937
The National Collection of Fine Arts (NCFA), 1937–1980
The National Museum of American Art (NMAA), 1980–2000
The Smithsonian American Art Museum (SAAM), 2000–

Buildings of the Museum

The Patent Office Building, 1840–57/58
Smithsonian Building (the Castle), 1857/58–1910
National Museum Building (Arts and Industries Building), 1881–1910
New Museum Building (National Museum of Natural History), 1910–1967
The Patent Office Building, 1968–2000; closed for renovation, 2000; reopened, 2006
The Renwick Gallery, 1972–

Proposed Designs for Buildings

Charles A. Platt, Architect: "The National Gallery of Art," 1924
Eero Saarinen, Eliel Saarinen, J. Robert F. Swanson, Architects: "The Smithsonian Gallery of Art," 1939

Smithsonian Secretaries

Joseph Henry, physicist, 1846–1878
Spencer Fullerton Baird, biologist, 1878–1887
Samuel P. Langley, astronomer and aeronautics pioneer, 1887–1906
Charles Doolittle Walcott, geologist and paleontologist, 1907–1927
Charles Greeley Abbot, astrophysicist, 1928–1944
Alexander Wetmore, biologist, 1945–1952
Leonard Carmichael, psychologist, 1953–1963
S. Dillon Ripley, ornithologist, 1964–1984
Robert McCormick Adams, anthropologist, 1984–1994
Ira M. Heyman, lawyer and law professor, 1994–1999
Lawrence M. Small, banker, 2000–

Directors of the Museum

William H. Holmes, curator NGA, 1906–1920; director NGA, 1920–1932
Ruel Pardee Tolman, acting director NGA/NCFA, 1932–1946; director NCFA, 1946–1948
Thomas Montague Beggs, director NCFA, 1948–1964
David Winfield Scott, acting director NCFA, 1964; director NCFA, 1964–1969
Robert Tyler Davis, acting director NCFA, 1969
Joshua C. Taylor, director NCFA/NMAA, 1970–1981
Harry Lowe, acting director NMAA, 1981–1982
Charles C. Eldredge, director NMAA, 1982–1988
Elizabeth Broun, acting director NMAA, 1988–1989; director NMAA/SAAM, 1989–

Smithsonian Board of Regents

Members are appointed from all three branches of the federal government—the Chief Justice of the Supreme Court and the Vice President of the United States (both ex officio), three members of the Senate (from different states), three members of the House of Representatives (from different states)—and nine private citizens from the District of Columbia and across the country.

NOTES

Introduction

1. The earliest and most influential publication for a class-based analysis of art museums, Pierre Bourdieu and Alain Darbel with Dominique Schnapper, *L'amour de l'art: Lés musées d'art européens et leur public* (Minuit, 1969), continues to be an important source for English-speaking scholars in Caroline Beattie and Nick Merriman's translation, *The Love of Art: European Art Museums and Their Public* (Stanford: Stanford University Press, 1991). A seminal article by American scholars Carol Duncan and Alan Wallach applies the theory to institutions in Europe and the United States: "The Universal Survey Museum," *Art History* 3 (December 1980). Michael S. Shapiro questions conclusions of these approaches, citing nineteenth-century sources that contradict the theory of early museums as attempting "to deprive an emerging middle-class audience of its cultural patrimony": "The Public and the Museum," in *The Museum: A Reference Guide* (New York: Greenwood Press, 1990), 233. From a non-Western point of view, Chengbo Feng, a scholar in the History Department of Nakai University, the People's Republic of China, asserts that museums function to liberate the human mind from feudal control and concludes that public libraries and public museums together constitute "the most important contributions ever made to the history of mankind": "A Chinese Perspective of American Museums and Their History," lecture presented January 19, 1991, at the National Museum of American History, Smithsonian Institution.

2. For a study of the institution's early programs of original research and international exchange, see Nancy E. Gwinn, "The Origins and Development of International Exchange in Nineteenth-Century America" (Ph.D. diss., George Washington University, 1996), 208–81. This activity expressed Secretary Henry's efforts to make the Smithsonian not just a national but an international institution.

3. Philip Kennicott, "Open Letter Berates Smithsonian's Small," *Washington Post*, January 17, 2002.

4. Some scholars have commented on the abundance of writings dealing with theories about museums as compared with historical studies. Steve Conn, *Museums and American Intellectual Life, 1876–1926* (Chicago: University of Chicago Press, 1998), 10, remarks that although they "serve as central landmarks in our cultural geography, museums have received remarkably little historical treatment." At the College Art Association conference in February 2001, a paper by Jeffrey Abt, "Museology and the Absence of History," questioned the lack of historical research in the extensive literature on museums, "this most historically oriented of institutions": *Abstracts, College Art Association Conference; CAA Chicago* (February 28–March 3, 2001), 225. Abt's own book, *A Museum on the Verge: A Socioeconomic History of the Detroit Institute of Arts, 1882–2000* (Detroit: Wayne State University Press, 2001), is a historical study informed by relevant theories. Daniel J. Sherman, *Worthy Monuments: Art Museums and the Politics of Culture in Nineteenth-Century France* (Cambridge: Harvard University Press, 1989), sets specifics of time and place within perspectives of political and social theory. Vera L. Zolberg, "The Art Institute of Chicago: The Sociology of a Cultural Organization" (Ph.D. diss., University of Chicago, 1974), provides another example of a sociological study of a particular institution within the context of its history.

1. Art as Knowledge

1. *National Magazine, or the Cabinet of the United States* (December 1, 1801).

2. Marcin Fabianski, "Iconography of the Architecture of Ideal *Musaea* in the Fifteenth to Eighteenth Centuries," *Journal of the History of Collections* 2, no. 2 (1990): 95, 127, 130, discusses use of the word "museum" with two meanings: as a place for study of the arts, sciences, and literature; and as a public collection of objects of artistic, scientific, or historical interest.

3. Charles Coleman Sellers, *Mr. Peale's Museum* (New York: Norton, 1980), 52.

4. Quoted in Joseph B. Varnum Jr., *The Seat of Government of the United States*, 2nd ed. (Washington, D.C.: R. Farnham, 1854), 19.

5. This collection, the Museum Wormianum, was reassembled for an exhibition in Copenhagen in 1988: H. D. Schepelern, "The Museum Wormianum Reconstructed," *Journal of the History of Collections* 2, no. 1 (1990): 81–85.

6. Eva Schulz points out that the history of collections is connected with the concept of the scholar as it developed during the Renaissance: "Notes on the History of Collecting and of Museums in the Light of Selected Literature of the Sixteenth to the Eighteenth Century," *Journal of the History of Collections* 2, no. 2 (1990): 205. For further discussion about the identification of knowledge with power, see John C.

Greene, "Science, Learning, and Utility: Patterns of Organization in the Early American Republic," in *The Pursuit of Knowledge in the Early American Republic*, ed. Alexandra Oleson and Sanford C. Brown (Baltimore: Johns Hopkins University Press, 1976).

7. For a philosophical background of the relationship between collections and encyclopedism, see Barbara Maria Stafford, "The Eighteenth-Century: Towards an Interdisciplinary Model," *Art Bulletin* 70 (March 1988): 12–14.

8. [Joel Barlow], *Prospectus of a National Institution to be Established in the United States*, quoted from Barlow's preface to *The Columbiad* in Arthur L. Ford, *Joel Barlow* (New York: Twayne, 1971), 75.

9. This crucial future development is noted by George Brown Goode, "The Origin of the National Scientific and Educational Institutions of the United States," *American Historical Association, Report of Proceedings at the Sixth Annual Meeting, 1889* (Washington, D.C.: U.S. Government Printing Office, 1890), 53–61, where the author discusses several proposals in addition to Barlow's.

10. Sidney Hart and David C. Ward consider as reasons for Peale's failure to obtain government support from local and state jurisdictions "changing cultural and intellectual values that focused on the specific and specialized rather than the general and universal," and for lack of success in winning approval from Congress the political ideology of Jeffersonianism "that rigidly circumscribed the area of society into which the national government would intervene": "The Waning of an Enlightenment Ideal: Charles Willson Peale's Philadelphia Museum, 1790–1820," *Journal of the Early Republic* 8 (Winter 1988): 392.

11. Joel R. Poinsett, *Discourse on the Objects and Importance of the National Institution for the Promotion of Science, Established at Washington, 1840, Delivered at the First Anniversary* (Washington, D.C.: P. Force, 1841), 45.

12. King's Indian subjects are described and documented by Andrew J. Cosentino, "Catalog of Known Works," *The Paintings of Charles Bird King (1785–1862)* (Washington, D.C.: National Collection of Fine Arts, Smithsonian Institution Press, 1977), 165–86.

13. Herman J. Viola and Carolyn Margolis, eds., *Magnificent Voyagers: The U.S. Exploring Expedition, 1838–1842* (Washington, D.C.: Smithsonian Institution Press, 1985), presents a comprehensive study of the Wilkes venture.

14. For reference to trips Varden took to gather materials and for additional information about his collection, see his "Daybook," John Varden Papers, 1829–1863, RU 7063, SIA.

15. For further information about the architecture of the Patent Office, see Daniel D. Reiff, *Washington Architecture, 1791–1861: Problems in Development* (Washington,

D.C.: U.S. Commission of Fine Arts, 1971); Douglas E. Evelyn, "A Public Building for a New Democracy: The Patent Office Building in the Nineteenth Century" (Ph.D. diss., George Washington University, 1997).

16. A catalogue by Alfred Hunter went into at least four versions, with titles that varied slightly from *A Catalogue of the Extraordinary Curiosities of the National Institute to be seen in the Patent Office Building* (Washington, D.C.: A. Hunter, 1855). John Varden sought to make his catalogue appear more official with the title *A Guide for Visitors to the National Gallery, Prepared in Accordance with the Instructions of the Commissioner of Patents* (Washington, D.C.: H. Polkinhorn, 1856).

17. Quoted in David A. Roos, "The 'Aims and Intentions' of *Nature*," in *Victorian Science and Victorian Values: Literary Perspectives*, ed. James Pardis and Thomas Postlewait (New York: New York Academy of Sciences, 1981), 162.

18. Reynolds is quoted in F. S. Pulling, *Sir Joshua Reynolds* (London: Sampson, Low, Marston, Searle, & Rivington, 1886), 103. The scientists' mode of illustration is discussed in Alexander Nemerov, *The Body of Raphaelle Peale: Still Life and Selfhood, 1812–1824* (Berkeley: University of California Press, 2002), 35–38.

19. For discussions of art academies in France and the United States, see Albert Boime, *The Academy and French Painting in the Nineteenth Century* (London: Phaidon Press, 1971); Lois Marie Fink and Joshua C. Taylor, *Academy: The Academic Tradition in American Art* (Washington, D.C.: National Collection of Fine Arts, Smithsonian Institution Press, 1975).

20. The belief that the experience of art elevated taste and morality in all classes of society, while especially important to a democratic nation, also figured in plans for an art museum in an absolutist monarchy. See Steven Moyano, "Quality vs. History: Schinkel's Altes Museum and Prussian Arts Policy," *Art Bulletin* 72 (December 1990).

21. Asher B. Durand's admonition is from his "Letters on Landscape Painting," *The Crayon* 1 (January 1855): 34. The practice at the Ecole des Beaux-Arts is noted in Philippe Grunchec, *The Grand Prix de Rome: Paintings from the Ecole des Beaux-Arts, 1797–1863* (Washington, D.C.: International Exhibitions Foundations, 1984), 27.

22. Durand, "Letters."

23. For further study of these beliefs, see Herbert Hovenkamp, *Science and Religion in America, 1800–1860* (Philadelphia: University of Pennsylvania Press, 1978), chap. 4; William Martin Smallwood with Mabel Sarah Smallwood, *Natural History and the American Mind* (New York: Columbia University Press, 1941). The importance of geology to American artists and theologians is discussed by Rebecca Bailey Bedell, *The Anatomy of Nature: Geology and American Landscape Painting, 1825–1875* (Princeton: Princeton

University Press, 2001), introduction and chap. 2. Joshua C. Taylor identifies cross-currents in American religiousity and art. Jane Dillenberger and Joshua C. Taylor, *The Hand and the Spirit* (Berkeley, Calif.: University Art Museum, 1972), 10–22.

24. The Will of James Smithson is included in Wiliam J. Rhees, ed. *The Smithsonian Institution, Documents Relative to Its Origin and History, 1835–1899* (Washington, D.C.: U.S. Government Printing Office, 1879, 1901) 1:5–6. "Farewell Address, to the People of the United States, September 17th, 1796," in *The Writings of George Washington,* ed. Jared Sparks (New York: Harper, 1847), 12:227.

25. George Brown Goode, ed., *The Smithsonian Institution, 1846–1896: The History of Its First Half Century* (Washington, D.C.: Smithsonian Institution, 1897), 55.

26. Rhees, *The Smithsonian Institution,* 1:635.

27. *Report of the Organization Committee of the Smithsonian Institution* (Washington, D.C.: Blair & Rives, 1847), 10.

28. In 1846 the city included 32 painters, 7 engravers, and 5 marble and stone cutters: Gaither and Addison, comps., *The Washington Directory* (Washington, D.C.: John T. Towers, 1846). Vendors of art supplies, engravings, lithographs, original paintings, and copies of paintings were also well established. For a comprehensive description of the art scene in Washington at this time, see Andrew J. Cosentino and Henry H. Glassie, *The Capital Image: Painters in Washington, 1800–1915* (Washington, D.C.: National Collection of Fine Arts, Smithsonian Institution Press, 1983), 39–71.

29. *Annual Report,* 1848, 26.

30. Charles Coffin Jewett, *Annual Report,* 1850, 30.

31. Quoted in *Harvard's Art Museums—100 Years of Collecting* (Cambridge: Harvard University Art Museums; New York: Harry N. Abrams, 1997), 16. For further confirmation of the importance of copies in Paris in the nineteenth century, see Boime, *The Academy and French Painting.*

32. *Annual Report,* 1854, 73. For a discussion of the contention over this issue between Secretary Henry and Assistant Secretary Jewett, see Joel J. Orosz, "Disloyalty, Dismissal, and a Deal: The Development of the National Museum at the Smithsonian Institution, 1846–1855," *Museums Studies Journal* 2 (Spring 1986): 22–33; followed in the same journal by S. Dillon Ripley and Wilcomb E. Washburn, "The Development of the National Museum at the Smithsonian Institution, 1846–1855: A Response to Joel J. Orosz's Article," 3 (Spring 1987): 6–11; and Joel Orosz, "In Defense of the Deal: A Rebuttal to S. Dillon Ripley's and Wilcomb Washburn's 'Response,'" 3 (Fall–Winter 1987): 7–12. Their controversy centered on interpreting the extent of Henry's objections to museum activities.

33. Gilmor's offer and its eventual failure to materialize is discussed in Lance Lee Humphries, "Robert Gilmor Jr. (1774–1848): Baltimore Collector and American Art Patron" (Ph.D. diss., University of Virginia, 1998, 1:429–37).

34. The Secretary's Report, *Annual Report,* 1856, 44–45.

35. *Annual Report,* 1861, 44. Orosz regards the crowds of visitors during the war as a factor in Henry's coming to a compromise position about collections presented to a general public: *Curators and Culture: The Museum Movement in America, 1740–1870* (Tuscaloosa: University of Alabama Press, 1990), 209.

36. Margaret Leech, *Reveille in Washington, 1860–1865* (Chicago: Time-Life Books, 1962), 295.

37. Lincoln's visit was recorded by John Varden in his Daybook, March 24, 1863, RU 7063, SIA. The proprietor of the Washington Museum, Varden had continued to work with the collections after the purchase of his gatherings by the National Institute and the subsequent transfer of works from the Patent Office Exhibition Hall to the Smithsonian Building. He performed all kinds of services, embalming birds, cleaning bones, repairing plaster busts, framing and hanging pictures. Varden worked at the Smithsonian until his death at the age of seventy-four on February 10, 1865. For obituaries, see *Washington Evening Star,* February 10, 1865; *Philadelphia Daily Evening Bulletin,* February 14, 1865.

38. *Annual Report,* 1865, 18. Julie Schimmel, "John Mix Stanley and Imagery of the West in Nineteenth-Century American Art" (Ph.D. diss., New York University, 1983), 143–49, discusses details of the loss of Stanley's works in the Smithsonian fire.

39. Alan Wallach, "William Wilson Corcoran's Failed National Gallery," in *Exhibiting Contradiction: Essays on the Art Museum in the United States* (Amherst: University of Massachusetts Press, 1998), includes a description of events relating to Corcoran's establishment of his gallery and also discusses other institutions in Washington. He incorrectly states that James Smithson's will "called for the creation of an art gallery" (24); it contained no reference to any kind of gallery or museum program. He asserts that "the Smithsonian was in effect forced upon a very divided American government" (130, note 2). John C. Calhoun and William C. Preston, senators from South Carolina, were leaders of a minority opposition to acceptance of the Smithson bequest on the grounds that the United States should not receive a gift from a foreigner, especially "a man of noble birth and lineage." Their objection to establishing the Smithsonian Institution centered on the claim that to do so usurped states' rights. Acceptance of Smithson's grant and the establishment of the institution were passed by Congress with majority votes in 1836 and 1846 respectively—not legislation forced upon a very divided government. See Rhees, *The Smithsonian Institution,* 1:138–39, 173.

40. Transferred items are listed or referred to in the Smithsonian's *Annual Report*, 1874, 65; 1878, 55–56; 1879, 60–61. Correspondence of the Corcoran Gallery between Spencer Baird and William McLeod from 1874 through 1880 also deals with these objects and subsquent deposits: Corcoran Correspondence, microfilm reels 246–47, 704, 705–6, AAA.

41. Prolonged attempts to persuade the government to purchase Catlin's paintings and negotiations between the Smithsonian and the Harrisons are described in William H. Truettner, *The Natural Man Observed: A Study of Catlin's Indian Gallery* (Washington, D.C.: Smithsonian Institution Press, 1979), 36–39, 135–38.

2. Exhibiting the Evolution of Culture

1. "*Hymne aux Etrangers*" by Placide Couly, music by Peter Cavallo, *Exposition Universelle de 1855, Explication des ouvrages de Peinture, Sculpture, Gravure, Lithographie et Architecture des Artists Vivants Etrangers et Français exposés au Palais des Beaux-Arts* (Paris, 1855), printed folded sheet in a copy of the catalogue at the Bibliothèque Nationale de France, Paris.

2. Robert C. Binkley makes this observation by contrasting the inaugural lecture at the 1851 exhibition by the British historian of science, William Whewell, with the introduction to jury reports of the 1867 Paris event by Michel Chevalier, a French economist: *Realism and Nationalism, 1852–1871* (New York: Harper, 1935), 19.

3. Gottfried Semper, "Science, Industry, and Art: Proposals for the Development of a National Taste," *The Four Elements of Architecture and Other Writings*, trans. Henry Francis Mallgrave and Wolfgang Herrmann (1852; Cambridge: Cambridge University Press, 1989), 137.

4. This manner of display still characterizes the Victoria and Albert Museum. For a study of its philosophy and collections, see Malcolm Baker and Brenda Richardson, eds., *A Grand Design: The Art of the Victoria and Albert Museum* (New York: Harry N. Abrams and the Baltimore Museum of Art, 1997).

5. For useful studies of industrial museums and conditions leading up to them, see Charles R. Richards, *The Industrial Museum* (New York: Macmillan, 1925), and Richards, *Industrial Art and the Museum* (New York: Macmillan, 1927); Nikolaus Pevsner, *Academies of Art, Past and Present* (Cambridge: Cambridge University Press, 1940); Francis D. Klingender, *Art and the Industrial Revolution*, ed. and rev. Arthur Elton (1947; New York: Schocken Books, 1970).

6. William Morris, *Hopes and Fears for Art* (London: Ellis & White, 1884), 35.

7. Winifred E. Howe, *A History of the Metropolitan Museum of Art* (New York: Columbia University Press, 1905–1941), 2:xi; John Cotton Dana, *The New Relations of Museums and Industry* (Newark, N.J.: Museum Association, 1919); Lloyd C. Engelbrecht, "The Association of Arts and Industries: Background and Origins of the Bauhaus Movement in Chicago," vol. 1 (Ph.D. diss., University of Chicago, 1973). Engelbrecht traces developments of this association to the founding of the independent School of Design and its subsequent affiliation with the Illinois Institute of Technology, where it still functions today. Susan M. Myers, Smithsonian Curator in the Division of Ceramics and Glass, made the point about collecting at the Smithsonian in a paper titled "Object Lessons: The Mixed Messages of Collections at the United States National Museum, 1880–1920," presented at the October 1994 Winterthur Conference at the Henry Francis du Pont Winterthur Museum, Winterthur, Del., "Perceptions of a Past."

8. The term "National Museum," in reference to the science, art, and history collections belonging to the federal government, was first used in a congressional act of 1842, which transferred government collections in the Patent Office exhibition hall from the care of the National Institute for the Promotion of Science to the Joint Library Committee of Congress. Natural history specimens gathered by Baird were first referred to as the "Museum of the Smithsonian Institution." Combining those items with the collections from the Patent Office brought about the common use of the title "the National Museum." See George Brown Goode, "The Genesis of the National Museum," *Annual Report*, 1881, 302.

9. Goode, "The Museums of the Future," *Annual Report*, 1889, 432.

10. Goode, "Report of the Assistant Director of the United States National Museum, for the Year 1881," *Annual Report*, 1881, 84.

11. Ibid., 85, 86.

12. Ibid., 89.

13. Frank Jewett Mather, "An Art Museum for the People," *Atlantic Monthly* 100 (December 1907): 729. See also Mather, "Art in America: A Question of Museum Policy," *Burlington Magazine* 9 (April 1906): 62. The author refers to Agassiz as an early proponent of this idea. Mather in the 1920s became a commissioner for the Smithsonian's National Gallery of Art.

14. Otis T. Mason, curator of ethnology, quoted in David Star Jordan, "Biographical Sketch of George Brown Goode," in *The Smithsonian Institution, 1846–1896* (Washington, D.C.: DeVinne Press, 1897), 508.

15. William J. Rhees, *Visitor's Guide*, 1891, 13, 16.

16. *Washington Star*, November 9, 1874. For the text of the petitions, see William J. Rhees, ed., *The Smithsonian Institution: Documents Relative to Its Origin and History, 1835–1899* (Washington, D.C.: U.S. Government Printing Office, 1879, 1901), 1309, 1574, 1662, 1814. A petition of 1880 (829) requested that the Congressional Library, the Smithsonian Institution, and the Medical Museum be open on Sundays and in the evenings.

17. Sylvester Rosa Koehler, "Report on the Section of Graphic Arts in the U.S. National Museum, 1889," *Annual Report*, 1889, 301–2. For a brief history of the Division of Graphic Arts, see Elizabeth Harris and Helena E. Wright, *G.A. 100: The Centenary of the Division of Graphic Arts* (Washington, D.C.: National Museum of American History, Smithsonian Institution, 1996). For a more complete history of the Smithsonian Graphic Art collection, including a discussion of Koehler, other curators, and important patrons and donors, see Helena E. Wright, *Prints at the Smithsonian: The Origins of a National Collection* (Washington, D.C.: National Museum of American History, Smithsonian Institution, 1996).

18. Koehler, "Report on the Section of Graphic Arts," 301.

19. Maynard Solomon, introduction to *Marxism and Art* (Detroit: Wayne State University Press, 1979), 6, refers to Mikhail Lifschitz as constructing a model of Marx's philosopy of art that focuses on "art as a form of the labor process," among other points. William Adams relates Marx's aesthetics to his central concerns for labor and production, and the creative powers of human beings: "Aesthetics: Liberating the Senses," *The Cambridge Companion to Marx*, ed. Terrell Carver (Cambridge: Cambridge University Press, 1991), 248–58.

20. Wallach, "The American Cast Museum: An Episode in the History of the Institutional Definition of Art," in *Exhibiting Contradiction*, 56, suggests the importance of patrons of art as agents in the change of taste that caused the removal of casts from exhibition galleries.

21. For details of these proposed bills, see Rhees, *The Smithsonian Institution*, 1:949, 981–82; 2:1131, 1279.

22. Franklin Webster Smith, *National Galleries of History and Art: The Aggrandizment of Washington* (Washington, D.C.: U.S. Government Printing Office, 1900), v; "A National Art Gallery," *Boston Daily Evening Transcript*, November 16, 1892.

23. The "National Academy of Art" was authorized by Congress, July 28, 1892; a typescript of the act is in the AA/PG Library. For the exhibition record, see *Catalogue of the First National Loan Exhibition of the National Art Association . . . in the Chapel of the Smithsonian Institution* (Washington, D.C., 1892).

3. Defining Art for the Nation

1. See "Back Home Again: The Impact of the Salon Experience," in Lois Marie Fink, *American Art at the Nineteenth-Century Paris Salons* (Washington, D.C.: Smithsonian Institution; Cambridge: Cambridge University Press, 1990), chap. 6.

2. Langley Letter-Books, RU 7003, box 18, SIA.

3. Reported by Cyrus Adler (librarian during Langley's tenure) at the court proceedings concerning the Harriet Lane Johnston Collection, June 8, 1906. Harriet Lane Johnston Collection Papers, Office of Registration and Collections Management, SAAM.

4. *Annual Report*, 1896, xiii–xiv.

5. Langley to S. H. Kauffman, president of the Corcoran Board of Trustees, May 23, 1896, asked for the return of all the works and included a list: Correspondence of the Corcoran Gallery of Art, microfilm 714, AAA. The return of the objects, the destruction of certain works, and the curator's inability to locate others are discussed in a letter from Corcoran curator F. S. Barbarin to Langley, July 18, 1896, Letterpress Books, Corcoran Gallery of Art, microfilm 251, AAA.

6. The will of Harriet Lane Johnston, on file in the Court House of the District of Columbia, was signed on June 1, 1895, and has five codicils. Mrs. Johnston died July 3, 1903. Relevant provisions of the will are found in Richard Rathbun, *The National Gallery of Art* (Washington, D.C.: U.S. Government Printing Office, 1916), 88.

7. S. P. Langley to the Honorable James T. McCleary, Washington, D.C., March 26, 1904, Office of the Secretary (Samuel P. Langley), Outgoing Correspondence, 1887–1907, microfilm no. 48, vol. 1, 48, SIA. Correspondence between Corcoran trustees and the executors of the estate is recorded in Corcoran Correspondence, microfilm 719, AAA.

8. Conditions of the conveyance of Freer's gift, which included $500,000 for the construction of a building to house the collection, were executed May 5, 1906—just a month before the trial concerning the Johnston bequest took place. For a study of Freer's collection and gift, see Thomas Lawton and Linda Merrill, *Freer: A Legacy of Art* (Washington, D.C.: Freer Gallery of Art, Smithsonian Institution; Harry N. Abrams, 1993).

9. Theodore Roosevelt, "Fourth Annual Message," *The State of the Union Messages of the Presidents, 1790–1966*, vol. 2, *1861–1904*, ed. Fred L. Israel (New York: Chelsea House with R. R. Bowker, 1967), 2125. Roosevelt's statement is quoted in *Annual Report*, 1905, 20.

10. Court case filed October 28, 1905, in the Supreme Court of the District of Columbia; copy of case in Registration and Collections Management Office, SAAM.

11. Ibid., testimony of June 6–8, 1906.

12. Richard Rathbun Papers, 1870-1918 and undated, RU 7078, box 1, SIA. Rathbun collected materials on the National Institute and planned to write a history of that organization but did not complete his project.

13. For more information about Holmes's career as an artist, see Clifford M. Nelson, *William Henry Holmes: Beginning a Career in Art and Science* (Washington, D.C.: Columbia Historical Society, 1980); Cosentino and Glassie, *The Capital Image*, 210–18; Amy Batson Strange, "William Henry Holmes, Artist: The Smithsonian's Nineteenth-Century Renaissance Man" (Master's thesis, University of Florida, 1992), vols. 1–2.

14. "Proposed Meeting of the Advisory Committee on the National Gallery of Art," Cyrus Adler to Richard Rathbun, March 20, 1908, NCFA, Office of the Director, Records 1895–1975, RU 311, box 1, folder 8, SIA.

15. William H. Truettner, "William T. Evans, Collector of American Paintings," *American Art Journal* 3 (Fall 1971): 57.

16. "The President Gratified, Expresses Thanks to William T. Evans for His Donation of Pictures," *Washington Star*, April 10, 1907, Smithsonian News Clipping File, 1852–1968, RU 96, box 1, SIA.

17. Charles D. Walcott to P. A. B. Widener, January 18, 1910, Office of the Secretary (Charles D. Walcott), 1903–1924, RU 45, box 79, SIA; Charles D. Walcott to John Gellatly, February 8, 1924, RU 45, box 24, SIA.

18. Charles D. Walcott, Address to the American Federation of Arts, in *Supplement to Art and Progress: The Proceedings of the First Annual Convention of the American Federation of Arts* I (July 1910): 38–40.

19. *Washington Sunday Star*, March 13, 1910. A brief description is recorded in James Henry Moser, "The National Gallery of Art," *Art and Progress* 1 (April 1910): 148–54. The works shown in the inaugural exhibition are listed in *Catalogue of Paintings and Other Art Objects Exhibited on the Occasion of the Opening of the Gallery in the New Building of the United States National Museum, March 17, 1910* (Washington, D.C.: National Gallery of Art, 1910).

20. For a history of the Natural History Building and additional details about the art gallery there, see Ellis Yochelson, *The National Museum of Natural History: 75 Years in the New National Museum* (Washington, D.C.: Smithsonian Institution Press, 1985), 40–45.

21. An early group of works purchased by the Ranger Fund is recorded in *The National Gallery of Art, Catalogue of an Exhibition of Paintings by Contemporary American Artists Purchased by the Council of the National Academy of Design from the Henry Ward*

Ranger Fund in Accordance with the Provision of the Ranger Bequest dated January 21, 1914 (Washington, D.C.: Smithsonian Institution, 1930). Charles Henry Phelps, *The Meaning of the Will of Henry W. Ranger* (New York: National Academy of Design, 1929) discusses the conditions of the bequest.

22. For a description of the collection, see George B. Rose, "The Ralph Cross Johnson Collection," *Art and Archaeology* 10 (September 1920): 110.

23. The paintings in the collection are listed in Thomas M. Beggs, *Catalog of American and European Paintings in the Gellatly Collection* (Washington, D.C.: Smithsonian Institution, 1954).

24. *Catalogue of a Loan Collection of Forty-five Paintings illustrating Scenes Mainly in the National Parks and Monuments of the United States, Assembled by the Department of the Interior* (Washington, D.C.: National Gallery of Art, 1917).

25. *Exhibition of War Portraits of American Leaders and Other Allied Nations in the War with Germany* (Washington, D.C.: National Gallery of Art, 1921).

26. *Catalogue of an Exhibition of Painting and Sculpture by American Negro Artists at the National Gallery of Art, Smithsonian Institution* (Washington, D.C., 1929).

27. Leila Mechlin to the Rev. Dr. Anson Phelps Stokes, Washington, November 16, 1928, NCFA, Office of the Director, 1892–1975, RU 311, box 35, folder 3, SIA.

28. Hippolyte Adolphe Taine, "Art in the Netherlands. Permanent Causes," in *Lectures on Art*, trans. John Durand (New York: Henry Holt, 1875; AMS Press, 1971), 2:168. For further study of Taine, see Hippolyte Adolphe Taine, *The History of English Literature*, trans. H. Van Laun (New York: Henry Holt, 1879). Lyall H. Powers, *Henry James and the Naturalist Movement* (East Lansing: Michigan State University Press, 1971), 6–9, discusses the spread of Taine's ideas and *le scientisme* in the United States.

29. Henri Bergson, *The Creative Mind* (1907; New York: Philosophical Library, 1946), 71, 36; Wilhelm Worringer, *Abstraction and Empathy: A Contribution to the Psychology of Style*, trans. Michael Bullock (London: Routledge & Kegan Paul, 1953; originally *Abstraktion und Einfuhlung*, Munich: R. Piper, 1908); Roger Fry, "An Essay in Aesthetics," *New Quarterly* (London), 1909; Wassily Kandinsky, *Concerning the Spiritual in Art*, trans. Francis Golffing, Michael Harrison, and Ferdinand Ostertag (1912; 1st Eng. Trans. 1914; New York: Wittenborn, Schultz, 1947).

30. Susan Vogel, a curator of African art, describes such display strategies in "Always True to the Object in Our Fashion," in *Exhibiting Cultures: The Poetics and Politics of Museum Display*, ed. Ivan Karp and Steven D. Lavine (Washington, D.C.: Smithsonian Institution Press, 1991), 195; Francis Sparshott discusses ambiguities in Western responses to objects in "Art and Anthropology," *Journal of Aesthetics and Art Criticism* 55 (Summer 1997): 240; Susan M. Pearce deals with influences upon perception and

the nature of material objects in *Museums, Objects, and Collections: A Cultural Study* (Washington, D.C.: Smithsonian Institution Press, 1992). Pearce summarizes several scholarly models for the study of works of art and artifacts, including methods of Erwin Panofsky (1962), E. McClung Fleming (1974), Jules Prown (1982), R. Elliott et al. (1985), R. Batchelor (1986), and her own: Susan M. Pearce (1986), "Interpreting Museum Objects: An Outline of Theory," in *Proceedings of the International Conference on Anthropology and the Museum*, ed. Tson-yuan Lin (Taipei: Taiwan Museum, 1995), 297–311. Pearce points out (301) that all such approaches to the interpretation of objects involve the "the notion of balance between intuitive appreciation and knowledgeable understanding."

31. Statement of Dr. Charles D. Walcott, Secretary of the Smithsonian Institution, in "Sundry Civil Appropriations Bill, 1921," U.S. Senate, 66th Cong., sess. 2. I am grateful to Ellis Yochelson for this reference. For further information about Walcott, see three books by Yochelson: *Charles Doolittle Walcott, 1850–1927* (New York: Columbia Press for the National Academy of Sciences, 1967); *Charles Doolittle Walcott, Paleontologist* (Kent, Ohio: Kent State University Press, 1998); and *Smithsonian Institution Secretary, Charles Doolittle Walcott, 1850–1927* (Kent, Ohio: Kent State University Press, 2001).

32. Neil Harris discusses this expanded popularity in "Polling for Opinions," *Museum News*, September/October 1990.

33. Three years after this site was reserved, Mrs. John B. Henderson of Washington offered a large plot of land occupying a full block on Meridian Hill, Sixteenth Street, for use as a site for the National Gallery. An anonymous letter to the editor of the *Washington Star* reminded readers of the designated Mall site—and suggested that Mrs. Henderson sell her land and donate the funds toward a building there (which did not happen): *Washington Star*, March 8, 1926, NCFA, Director's Files, 1908–1965, RU 312, box 7, SIA.

34. Royal Cortissoz, "The National Gallery of Art," *American Magazine of Art*, 16 (March 1925): 119. The scope of the proposed building is defined in the sundry appropriations bill for the fiscal year ending June 30, 1924 (H.R. 13696, 67th Cong.) This bill authorized the Regents to prepare plans for the building but did not provide funds.

35. Keith N. Morgan, *Charles A. Platt: The Artist as Architect* (Cambridge: MIT Press, 1985), 172.

36. A transcript of William H. Holmes's radio address of November 5, 1923, is in RU 311, box 15, SIA. His earliest article on behalf of the building campaign, "The Story of the National Gallery of Art," *Art and Archaeology* 15 (June 1923), reviews the history of the museum and reproduces works from the collection.

37. Leila Mechlin, "National Gallery of Art Project," *American Magazine of Art* 15 (July 1924): 362. These men all sent Mechlin letters of support and encouragement for the building campaign; copies of the letters are in RU 311, box 13, folder 7, SIA.

38. "U. S. May Get Gift of National Gallery," *Chicago Evening Post*, December 18, 1926.

39. Clipping from *The Times* (city is unidentified), November 9, 1927, Holmes, "Random Records," vol. 2, AA/PG Library, rare books collection; "The New National Gallery," *Washington Star*, November 9, 1927.

40. The influence of Mellon on Abbot probably began in late October or early November 1929. Abbot requested the U.S. Civil Service Commission to establish a list of eligible candidates for the position of director of the National Gallery of Art on October 4 of that year, indicating the desire of Dr. Holmes to be relieved; in the same month he asked commission member Gari Melchers to suggest members for a committee to select a new director. Reversing this move on November 5, Abbot wrote to Melchers that he was "confidentially informed that circumstances have arisen which will make it advisable to delay somewhat the action of the Civil Service Commission in re the National Gallery" and requested him to "hold the impending appointment confidential for the present": RU 46, box 140, folder l, SIA.

41. F. A. Whiting, Washington, D.C., to J. H. Gest, President, Rookwood Pottery Company, Cincinnati, Ohio, March 6, 1934, RU 46, box 140, SIA.

42. J. H. Gest, Cincinnati, Ohio, to Dr. Charles G. Abbot, Smithsonian Institution, March 14, 1934, RU 46, box 140, SIA.

43. Secretary Abbot, Smithsonian Institution, to Mr. J. H. Gest, President, Rookwood Pottery, Cincinnati, Ohio, March 16, 1934, Office of the Secretary, 1925–1949, RU 46, box 140, SIA.

44. C. G. Abbot, Secretary, Smithsonian Institution, to The Honorable A. W. Mellon, Pittsburgh, Pa., March 20, 1935, RU 46, box 143, folder 2, SIA.

45. Andrew Mellon, Pittsburgh, Pa., to Dr. C. G. Abbot, Secretary, Smithsonian Institution, March 22, 1935, RU 46, box 143, folder 2, SIA. Abbot clipped to these letters a handwritten note, apparently to himself: "l. Fawcett says he is authorized by Mellon to say that his project *is not* [double underline] The National Gallery. That must be by *Congress* [double underline]. 2. I ask Mellon to confirm or deny this, so that I may be free to proceed to work for The National Gallery. 3. Mellon refuses to answer now. 4. Am I then to wait?"

46. Theodore W. Noyes, Editor, "Not the National Gallery," *Evening Star*, February 20, 1935.

47. Minutes of the Fifteenth Annual Meeting, December 10, 1935, RU 311, box 21, SIA.

48. Confidential Minute of an Interview with Mr. Mellon, January 8, 1936; letter from A. W. Mellon, 730 Fifteenth Street, Washington, D.C., to Dr. C. G. Abbot, Secretary, Smithsonian Institution, January 14, 1936; noting his return of the confidential minute with some corrections: RU 46, box 143, folder 2, SIA.

49. Telegram to Hon. A. W. Mellon, 1785 Massachusetts Avenue, Washington, D.C., from C. G. Abbot, January 3, 1937, RU 46, box 143, folder 2, SIA.

50. Office of the Attorney General [Homer Cummings], Washington, D.C., to President Franklin D. Roosevelt, January 15, 1937, Presidential Papers of Franklin D. Roosevelt, Records Relating to Establishment of the National Gallery of Art; copy in Record Group 31, A. W. Mellon, Gallery Archives, National Gallery of Art, Washington, D.C.; original papers, Franklin D. Roosevelt Library-Museum, Hyde Park, New York.

51. Ibid.

52. Memorandum, D. D. Shepard for the Honorable Kent E. Keller, Chairman, Committee on the Library, House of Representatives, re Proposed legislation to effect the acceptance of gift from Andrew W. Mellon (H.R. Doc. 139), RU 46, box 143, folder 2, SIA.

53. National Gallery of Art, "News Release," March 31, 1994, 2–3.

54. In a history of the Mellon National Gallery of Art, Philip Kopper writes (in a chapter titled, "Before the Creation"), "Before a national art gallery worthy of the name was founded and grew to genuine national prominence, a series of them—at least in name or variation thereof—littered the city's chronology for more than a century": *America's National Gallery of Art: A Gift to the Nation* (New York: Harry N. Abrams, 1991), 27. This inconsequential "litter" included the Corcoran Gallery of Art, the Phillips Collection, and, at the Smithsonian, the Freer Gallery, the Smithsonian's National Gallery of Art, and other collections.

55. For the significance of the Paris Salons for American artists, see Fink, *American Art*.

56. Lillian B. Miller, *Patrons and Patriotism: The Encouragement of the Fine Arts in the United States, 1790–1860* (Chicago: The University of Chicago Press, 1966), 8–14, discusses cultural nationalism during the first half of the nineteenth century.

57. Janet Cecelia Marstine, "Working History: Images of Labor and Industry in American Mural Painting, 1893–1903" (Ph.D. diss., University of Pittsburgh, 1993), discusses murals painted to promote the Americanization of immigrants.

58. In New York City the establishment of the Metropolitan Museum of Art in 1870 followed meetings of John Jay and other American citizens in Paris urging the founding of "a permanent national Gallery of Art and museum of historical relics": *New York Evening Post*, October 21, 1869. Although they did not incorporate the word "national" into their title, officials of the Metropolitan Museum sometimes considered their institution to represent the nation in the arts, as when accepting major gifts from private donors.

59. A Park Commission to plan for the future development of Washington was first established by the Senate in 1901; President Theodore Roosevelt by Executive Order appointed a Council of Fine Arts in 1909. Upon taking office, President William H. Taft annulled that organization and in 1910, with congressional approval, established the Commission of Fine Arts: Sue A. Kohler, *The Commission of Fine Arts: A Brief History, 1910–1976* (Washington, D.C.: U.S. Government Printing Office, 1977), 2–3.

60. Leila Mechlin, "The Evans Collection in the National Gallery at Washington," *Century Magazine* 75 (December 1907): 316.

61. Charles de Kay, "The Evans Collection of American Paintings at Washington," *International Studio* 48 (February 1913): 89.

62. Theodore Roosevelt, "Address before the American Academy and National Institute of Arts and Letters, New York City, November 16, 1916," in *Theodore Roosevelt Cyclopedia*, rev. 2nd ed., ed. Albert Bushnell Hart and Herbert Ronald Ferleger (Oyster Bay, N.Y.: Theodore Roosevelt Association and Meckler, 1989).

63. "German Art and the German Character," *Burlington Magazine* (November 1905): 78.

64. S. G. W. Benjamin, "Tendencies of Art in America," *American Art Review* 1 (1880): 106.

65. Brooks Adams, *International Review*, reprinted in the *Boston Daily Evening Transcript*, July 26, 1880.

66. *Annual Report*, 1923, 18–19.

67. Holmes, "The Story of the National Gallery of Art," 51. Holmes conveyed the same message in a paper read at the convention of the American Federation of Arts in May 1923, "Shall America Have a National Gallery of Art?" (published in *Art and Archaeology* 15 [June 1923]).

68. Quoted in "Art Museums Considered as Centers of Civic Activities," *Christian Science Monitor*, January 11, 1923.

69. [Alfred M. Frankfurter], "A Portfolio of the Andrew W. Mellon Collection," *Art News* 35 (May 1, 1937): 78.

70. On the occasion of the fiftieth anniversary of the Metropolitan Museum of Art in 1920, the *New York Times* referred to an earlier statement by one of the founders, James Jackson Jarves, who pointed out that the Metropolitan "enjoys in Europe the reputation of being a national institution. . . . Its cosmopolitan reputation . . . overshadow[s] the other American museums." Quoted in Conn, *Museums and American Intellectual Life*, 193.

71. Youtz is quoted in Edward Alden Jewell, "New York Times," *Magazine of Art* 30 (February 1937): 73. Mellon's concern for national prestige is reported in D. D. Shepard, "Representing the Hon. A. W. Mellon Educational and Charitable Trust," RU 46, box 143, SIA.

72. Bernard Berenson, *Italian Painters of the Renaissance* (New York: Meridian Books, 1960), vi.

73. Ralph M. Pearson, Design Workshop, New York City, to President Roosevelt, February 15, 1937, Presidential Papers of Franklin Delano Roosevelt, Records Relating to the Establishment of the National Gallery of Art: copy, Record Group 31, A. W. Mellon, Gallery Archives, National Gallery of Art, Washington, D.C.; original papers, Franklin D. Roosevelt Library-Museum, Hyde Park, N.Y.

74. Thomas Hart Benton, "Art vs. The Mellon Gallery," *Common Sense* 10 (June 1941): 173.

75. Forbes Watson, "The Benefit of Great Art," *Magazine of Art* 34 (March 1941): 113.

76. *Art Digest* 11 (February 15, 1937): 29.

77. Herschel B. Chipp, ed., *Theories of Modern Art: A Source Book by Artists and Critics* (Berkeley: University of California Press, 1969), 474–83, quotes Adolf Hitler, speech in Munich inaugurating the "Great Exhibition of German Art 1937." Shortly after this event another exhibition arranged by Hitler opened in Munich, "*Entartete Kunst*" ("Degenerate Art"), designed to discredit and ridicule contemporary German artists working in expressionist and other modern modes. See also Matthew Baigell and Julia Williams, introduction to *Artists against War and Fascism: Papers of the First American Artists' Congress* (New Brunswick, N.J.: Rutgers University Press, 1986); Cécil Whiting, *Antifascism in American Art* (New Haven: Yale University Press, 1989).

78. Henry James, "The Madonna of the Future," in *The Tales of Henry James*, ed. Maqbool Aziz (Oxford: Clarendon Press, 1978), 2:203.

79. Cited by Donald D. Shepard, Mellon's attorney, as "Mr. Mellon's purpose in establishing the gallery": Memorandum for Kent E. Keller, Committee on the Library, House of Representatives, February 13, 1937.

80. Abbott Handerson Thayer to John Gellatly, Eastham, Mass., June 20, 1916, John Gellatly Papers, microfilm 4722, frame 770, AAA. Gellatly's statement in reference to Hassam's paintings is from an unidentified clipping, American Academy of Arts and Letters Collection, microfilm NAA 2, frame 282, AAA.

4. Rejecting Modern Art for Washington

1. Reported at a special meeting of the National Gallery of Art Commission (i.e., the Smithsonian's National Gallery of Art—the Commission still retained its original name at this point), April 6, 1937, NCFA, Office of the Director, Records 1895–1975, RU 311, Box 21, SIA.

2. House Joint Resolution 599 and Senate Joint Resolution 262, 75th Cong., 3rd sess., "To set apart ground for the Smithsonian Gallery of Art and for other purposes": RU 311, box 21, folder 4, SIA, contains copies of the bills; the full text is printed in *Art Digest* 12 (June 1, 1938): 19.

3. Art measures currently before the Congress that sought to promote links between the government and art included House Joint Resolution 79, proposed to establish a Department of Science, Art and Literature under a cabinet secretary, and H.R. 9102, to establish a Bureau of Fine Arts under a commissioner appointed by the president, introduced in January 1938. Leila Mechlin argued that such a measure would constitute "government control of the creative instincts of the people of this country": "Art Measures in Congress," *Washington Star*, February 13, 1938.

4. Summary of "National Competition . . . Program issued January 21, 1939 (prepared by Dean Hudnut in consultation with Mr. Edward Bruce, and later passed on by the Smithsonian Gallery of Art Commission)," RU 312, box 26, SIA. The program is published in "Competition," *Architectural Forum*, February 1939, 15.

5. Francis Henry Taylor, "Museums in a Changing World," *Atlantic Monthly* 164 (December 1939): 792.

6. As professional adviser, Professor Hudnut would have supervised the architectural requirements, leaving Bruce to write the program for the Gallery. Belisario R. Contreras, *Tradition and Innovation in New Deal Art* (Lewisburg, Pa.: Bucknell University Press; London: Associated University Presses, 1983), 64, relates the concepts behind this program to Bruce's "quest" to make the Federal Arts Program permanent by establishing federal support for contemporary American Art.

7. Holger Cahill in Chipp, *Theories of Modern Art*, 473.

8. "Approval Evinced for Art Gallery," *Washington Star*, February 23, 1938.

9. Letter from Jurors to Smithsonian Gallery of Art Commission, June 28, 1939, Office of the Director, NCFA, 1892-1975, RU 311, box 21, folder 5, SIA. The complete

report of the jury, with drawings from the Saarinen and Goodman designs, and the submissions of Paul P. Cret and the team of Albert Frey, Phillip L. Goodwin, and Louis C. Jaeger, are published in "The Smithsonian Gallery of Art Competition," *Architectural Forum* 71 (July 1939): 33–34. "Smithsonian Gallery of Art Competition," *Magazine of Art* 32 (August 1939), also carried an extensive report with reproductions of the Saarinen and Cret designs.

10. "The Smithsonian Gallery of Art Competition," *Architectural Forum.*

11. Glenn Dillard Gunn, "Smithsonian Art Gallery Stirs Critics," *Times-Herald* (clipping, city unidentified), August 20, 1939, RU 312, box 26, SIA. Travis McDonald discusses details of the architectural controversy in "The Smithsonian Gallery of Art Competition," in *Modulus: The University of Virginia School of Architecture Review* (March 1980).

12. Minutes of Meeting of the Commission of Fine Arts, September 15, 1939, Fine Arts Commission, microfilm no. 7, National Archives.

13. Minutes of the Annual Meeting of the Smithsonian Art Commission, December 5, 1939, RU 311, box 21, SIA.

14. A handwritten, unsigned manuscript reports both the Smithsonian Art Commission and the Fine Arts Commission as rejecting the prize-winning design, and adds that the Smithsonian Art Commission approved the architect—apparently referring to Clarke's suggestion as communicated to Abbot, "Smithsonian Gallery of Art, The House Resolution Bill No. 599," RU 311, box 21, SIA.

15. "Approval Evinced for Art Gallery," *Washington Star*, February 23, 1938.

16. Quoted in unsigned manuscript inserted in copy of House Joint Resolution 599, "Smithsonian Gallery of Art," RU 313, NCFA Administrative Files, series 1, box 2, 1908–1974, SIA.

17. "Report of the Secretary," *Annual Report*, 1946, 10, 12.

18. Appropriation figures are recorded in *Annual Report*, 1938, 37–38; 1952, 5.

19. For information about the *Ecole Américaine des Beaux Arts*, see Elizabeth Hutton Turner, *American Artists in Paris, 1919–1929* (Ann Arbor, Mich.: UMI Research Press, 1988), 28–31.

20. Thomas Beggs writing to William E. Huntington (Mrs. Barney's adviser), Washington, D.C., September 15, 1950, proposes that Mrs. Barney's collection be offered to the Smithsonian Institution for NCFA to use as the nucleus of a loan collection for federal buildings and short- or long-term loans to museums: RU 50, box 103, SIA.

21. For information on the collection, see Thomas M. Beggs, *Alice Pike Barney: Portraits in Oil and Pastel* (Washington, D.C.: National Collection of Fine Arts, 1957); Delight Hall, *Catalogue of the Alice Pike Barney Memorial Lending Collection* (Washington, D.C.: National Collection of Fine Arts, 1965). For a study of the artist's career,

see Jean L. Kling, *Alice Pike Barney: Her Life and Art* (Washington, D.C.: National Museum of American Art, 1994).

22. Lloyd Goodrich, "The Federal Government and Art," *Magazine of Art* 41 (October 1948): 237.

23. "Resolution Addressed to the President of the United States," with a six-page list of institutions from Alabama to Wisconsin and Hawaii that endorsed the Resolution: RU 312, box 6, SIA.

24. *Art and Government: Report to the President by the Commission of Fine Arts on Activities of the Federal Government in the Field of Art* (Washington, D.C., 1953).

25. The Committee on Government and Art, "Report Submitted to the President, May 17th, 1954," RU 312, box 6, folder 20, SIA. See also Lloyd Goodrich, "Government and the Arts," *Art in America* 42 (December 1954): 272–73. Criticisms of the Goodrich report and rebuttals by Goodrich appeared in a succession of issues of *American Artist*: 18 (October 1954): 32, 68–71; 18 (November 1954): 16, 18, 52–58; 19 (January 1955): 12–13, 55–56; 19 (April 1955): 18, 20; 19 (June 1955): 6.

26. The Committee on Government and Art, "Report Submitted to the President."

27. Lloyd Goodrich, Whitney Museum of American Art, to Thomas M. Beggs, July 17, 1953; Lloyd Goodrich, Chairman, Committee on Government and Art, to Hon. Charles R. Howell, Washington, D.C., July 10, 1953. Both letters are in RU 312, box 6, SIA.

28. Minutes of Meeting of Executive Committee, Smithsonian Art Commission, November 18, 1955, RU 312, box 27, folder 3, SIA.

29. *Washington Star*, March 1952 (date unclear); clipping, vertical files, AA/PG Library, under "Corcoran Gallery Clippings, 1950–1959."

30. Memorandum from Thomas Beggs, RU 312, box 6, SIA.

31. *Congressional Record*, Proceedings and Debates of the 84th Cong., 2nd sess., "UNESCO—Communism and Modern Art," speech of Hon. George A. Donderdo of Michigan in the House of Representatives, Friday, July 20, 1956, 1-7, RU 312, box 7, SIA. For further discussion of the activities of Representative Dondero and Senator McCarthy, see Jane De Hart Mathews, "Art and Politics in Cold War America," *American Historical Review* 81 (October 1976): 762–87; William Hauptman, "The Suppression of Art in the McCarthy Decade," *Artforum*, October 1973, 48–52.

32. Ben Shahn, "Artist and the Politician," *Art News* 52 (September 1953): 35.

33. Alfred M. Frankfurter discusses the maligning of the exhibit by the National Sculpture Society, "Vernissage, Graven Images," *Art News* 50 (February 1952): 11; *Art News* 51 (March 1952): 6 publishes the response of those members who protested their society's judgment.

34. Author's conversation with David Scott, November 29, 1984; Grace Glueck, "Washington Takes a Giant Step," *New York Times*, November 15, 1964. In 1967, art historian Francis V. O'Connor, while researching art of the New Deal era, encountered similar anxieties when he sent questionnaires to artists who had worked in the federal art programs. They were reluctant to respond because they suspected a government "trick": author's conversations with Francis V. O'Connor, September 1994.

35. *Annual Report*, 1957, 3.

36. Letters to the editor: J. Wilbur Potherby, "Modern Smithsonian Approved" and A Reader, "New Smithsonian Too Modern," both in *Washington Star*, October 22, 1953; Rossel Edward Mitchell, "New Smithsonian Too Modern," unidentified newspaper clipping with no date. All three are located in RU 312, box 26, SIA.

37. Quoted in Gary O. Larson, *The Reluctant Patron: The United States Government and the Arts, 1943–1965* (Philadelphia: University of Pennsylvania Press, 1983), 68. In her column, "My Day," Eleanor Roosevelt discussed the bill for a cultural center built as a national war memorial to include a theater, opera house, and the Smithsonian Gallery of Art: "We could have there [in the nation's capital] a center that would encourage modern art in all its branches. We might develop a place where young artists could feel they would receive a sympathetic and understanding opportunity." *St. Louis Post-Dispatch*, June 6, 1952, RU 311, box 25, SIA.

38. Memorandum for the Record, Summary of Meeting in Representative Howell's Office, May 19, 1953, RU 312, box 24, SIA.

39. Howell's first bill, House Resolution 452, calling for funds to establish the Smithsonian Gallery of Art as part of a national war memorial, was introduced January 3, 1953; Senator James E. Murray, a Democrat from Montana, supported it with a similar bill, Senate 1109. On May 26, Howell presented his revised version, House Resolution 5397; a subsequent and similar version was House Resolution 9111. These bills covered all the arts—architecture, fine arts, design, crafts, music, drama, ballet, literature, film, radio, and television—and provided for the establishment of a commission with powers to initiate and fund programs. Such complexities provoked controversy; Goodrich's critique of problem areas and his summary of the bill's provisions appear in Lloyd Goodrich, "Comments on H.R. 5397" and "Digest of H.R. 5397," RU 312, box 6, SIA. Goodrich commented on H.R. 9111 at a hearing before the House Committee on Education and Labor, June 8, 1954. In the 1950s, even while artists were being vilified on the floor of the House by Representative Dondero, a number of legislative proposals centered on the arts; between 1952 and 1957 more than a dozen of these related to the space problems of NCFA. One of the most promising, H.R.

7974, introduced by Representative Thompson of New Jersey in January 1956, was presented as an amendment of the joint resolution of May 17, 1938 (which set aside ground for the gallery (see note 2); among other provisions it would have changed the name of the proposed building to the "National Collection of Fine Arts Museum." A copy of H.R. 9988, introduced by Thompson on March 12, 1956, proposed providing space for NCFA in the National Gallery of Art—a measure not supported: RU 50, box 104, SIA. Leslie Judd Portner, "The U.S. Government and Art," *Washington Post and Times Herald*, July 15, 1956, describes a number of bills, introduced and pending, pertaining to the arts.

40. In order to draw attention to the plight of historic buildings threatened with destruction, Thompson introduced H.R. 7975 and 7976 to reactivate an incomplete survey of historic sites undertaken by the National Park Service. In the District of Columbia his efforts were directed at both the Patent Office Building and the Court of Claims Building (today the Renwick Gallery). The Court of Claims was briefly considered as a home for NCFA, but the condition of the structure seemed to make that suggestion impractical: Portner, "The U.S. Government and Art."

41. While a bill was pending for the destruction of the Patent Office Building (H.R. 4841, introduced June 2, 1956), as recommended by the General Services Administration (GSA), in a news release the same day GSA reversed itself and recommended retention of the building for Smithsonian use—not for NCFA but as a gallery of American portraiture "in accord with the views of Dr. Finley and other members of the Commission of Fine Arts": RU 312, box 7, SIA.

42. Minutes, Smithsonian Art Commission, December 4, 1957, RU 312, box 27, SIA. The preceding quotation from Goodrich is also from this source, folder 4.

43. Lloyd Goodrich, Chairman, Committee on Government and Art, to Frank Thompson Jr., House of Representatives, July 15, 1958, RU 312, box 7, SIA. Representative Thompson, Senator Clinton Anderson (a Democrat from New Mexico), and Goodrich exchanged views before the larger art community in *Arts* magazine. Senator Anderson, who supported moving NCFA into the Patent Office Building, responded in *Arts* 32 (May 1958): 7, to an editorial in *Arts* 32 (April 1958). Goodrich presented his case for a new structure on the mall in the May issue; Thompson's extended argument for the Patent Office Building appeared in June. A copy of Thompson's letter to Jonathan Marshall, editor of *Arts*, is in RU 312, box 7, SIA.

44. Benjamin Forgey, "Washington's Artful Edifice," *Washington Post*, March 16, 1991.

45. Lloyd Goodrich, "Rebirth of a National Collection," *Art in America* (June 1965): 79.

46. Walt Whitman, *Specimen Days* (1882; Meriden, Conn.: Meriden Gravine, 1971), 40.

47. "The Fire in the Patent Office," *Boston Daily Evening Transcript*, September 25, 26, 27, 1877. Evelyn, "A Public Building for a New Democracy," relates effects of the fire.

48. Wolf Von Eckhardt, "Fine Arts—Portrait Gallery: A Crude Blow to Culture," *Washington Post*, November 19, 1967.

49. For a brief history of the National Portrait Gallery, see Charles Nagel, "The National Portrait Gallery of the Smithsonian Institution, and C. K. Adams, "The Washington and London National Portrait Galleries: A Comparison, *Museums Journal* (London), March 1969, 156–59, 160–61. Marcia Pointon's discussion of the founding of the National Portrait Gallery in relation to politics of the time, "Imaging Nationalism in the Cold War: The Foundation of the American National Portrait Gallery," *Journal of American Studies* (December 1992): 357–75, contains several misconceptions. The Patent Office Building was transferred to the Regents of the Smithsonian Institution, not to the National Portrait Gallery Commission (as Pointon states, 362). She theorizes that "the National Collection of the Fine Arts and the Establishment cultural lobby produced imperatives, and negotiated territory. . . . Today the National Collection occupies the other half of the Patent Office building, an arrangement that reflects the relationship that underpinned the planning process for, if America was to exhibit a national school of historic painting, it must, by its very nature, encompass its national portraiture" (364). In fact, political compromise, not ideological purpose, determined the location of the two museums, side by side, in the Patent Office Building (see above, "Next Door to Dinosaur Bones and Totem Poles"). Pointon identifies the conservative nature of the National Collection of Fine Arts with its being a "State cultural institution" that "stood in opposition to the Left international avant-gardism" (364). When David Scott was appointed director in 1964, NCFA immediately began collecting and exhibiting modern contemporary art, as explained in chapter 5. This new direction, like the former stance of conservative art, was the result of internal decisions and actions, not NCFA's position as a "State cultural institution."

5. Opening a New Era for Art

1. John F. Kennedy, Speech at Amherst College, October 26, 1963, quoted in John Wetenhall, "Camelot's Legacy to Public Art: Aesthetic Ideology in the New Frontier," in *Critical Issues in Public Art*, ed. Harriet F. Senic and Sally Webster (New York:

HarperCollins, 1992), 153. Wetenhall discusses cultural policies of the Kennedy administration (142–57).

2. August Heckscher, *The Arts and the National Government: A Report to the President* (Washington, D.C.: U.S. Government Printing Office, 1963).

3. *Annual Report*, 1965, 245.

4. Hechscher, *The Arts*, 35.

5. David Winfield Scott, *The Arts: A Central Element of a Good Society* (Washington, D.C.: Arts Councils of America, 1965). His proposal, "Artmobile Project," is in RU 313, box 14, SIA. A resolution was introduced in the House in 1963 for NCFA to extend benefits by the use of artmobiles and other means.

6. This purchase and the disapproval it was expected to incur were recalled by Harry Lowe in a conversation with the author, November 16, 1994. Recalling commission meetings of the 1950s and 1960s, Commissioner Charles H. Sawyer confirmed the "very conservative" taste of the majority of members, with Gilmore Clarke as "the most vocal and eloquent opponent of the modernist trends": Sawyer, letter and draft of remarks for a luncheon session of the commission, to Elizabeth Broun, acting director, April 25, 1989. I am grateful to the late Mr. Sawyer for sharing this material. Animosity and indifference toward modern art, together with a lack of funding, storage, and exhibition space, drastically altered possibilities of what NCFA might have become early in its history.

7. Charles Blitzer, "Memo for the Record," December 22, 1969, RU 313, box 14, SIA. Charles H. Sawyer, then chairman of the NCFA Commission, shared with me his file of clippings and correspondence relating to this issue. Critical reaction was noted by Jack Anderson, "Smithsonian's Art Goof," *Washington Post*, July 12, 1970. The newly appointed director, Joshua C. Taylor, stated that it was not his intention to initiate any sales or exchanges of the collection.

8. Author's conversation with David Scott, November 19, 1984.

9. *Stuart Davis Memorial Exhibition, 1894–1964* (1965); Adelyn D. Breeskin, *Roots of Abstract Art in America, 1910–1930: A Survey of Trends toward Abstraction in American Art* (1965); *The Art of Stanton Macdonald-Wright*, intro. David W. Scott and "Treatise on Color" by Stanton Macdonald-Wright (1967); *The Drawings of Jasper Johns* (1966—a check list only); *Frederic Edwin Church* (1966).

10. Quoted in Benjamin Ives Gilman, *Museum Ideals of Purpose and Method* (Cambridge: Harvard University Press, 1923), xvii, found in Julius Langbehn, *Rembrandt als Erzieher* (Leipsig, 1890), 17.

11. Germano Celant, quoted in Emma Barker, ed., *Art and Its Histories: Contemporary Cultures of Display* (New Haven: Yale University Press, 1999), 14.

12. *Annual Report*, 1943, 2. Precedents can be traced from the 1920s when American investors sought economic and business opportunities in Latin America, efforts promoted by "Good Neighbor" programs of the 1930s. Another kind of exchange began in the period between the two world wars and continued afterward when hundreds of American artists traveled to Mexico, staying for weeks or months, or a lifetime. See James Oles, *South of the Border: Mexico in the American Imagination*, trans. Maria Ferrgut (Washington, D.C.: Smithsonian Institution Press, 1993).

13. The exhibitions, along with other temporary shows, are listed in the *Annual Reports* for these years. Eva Cockcroft, "Abstract Expressionism, Weapon of the Cold War," *Artforum* 12 (June 1974): 39–41, delves into political and private motives of the Latin American exhibition program and subsequent international cultural exchange, particularly through programs sponsored by the Museum of Modern Art.

14. Hugo Weisgall, introduction to *Advancing American Art, 1947* (Prague: United States Information Service). This exhibit was reprised in 1984 by the Montgomery Museum of Fine Arts and shown there and at the National Museum of American Art and other venues: *Advancing American Art: Politics and Aesthetics in the State Department Exhibition, 1946–1948* (Montgomery, Ala.: Montgomery Museum of Fine Arts, 1984). In the text Margaret Lynne Ausfeld writes on the history of the collection, and NMAA Curator Virginia M. Mecklenburg on the controversy over style.

15. Charlotte Devree, "The U.S. Government Vetoes Living Art," *Art News* 55 (September 1956): 34–35, 54–56, discusses situations leading to the 1956 decision of USIA. Larson, *The Reluctant Patron*, 23–29, 116–18, gives a summarized account of controversies centering on efforts of the State Department to send contemporary American art abroad. Max Kozloff, "American Painting during the Cold War," *Art Forum* 11 (May 1973), observes that by the late 1950s, modern art was losing its association with subversion and that radical artists in the 1960s were immersed not in politics but in the celebration of individual freedom (i.e., their own), though they were not entirely free from postwar anxieties.

16. Dwight D. Eisenhower in Robert L. Branyan and Lawrence H. Larsen, *The Eisenhower Administration, 1953–1961: A Documentary History* (New York: Random House, 1971), 1:462; 2:818.

17. "Friendship through Art Studied Here," *Washington Post*, February 19, 1957. Legislation for this ambitious endeavor was passed in 1956 as the International Cultural Exchange and Trade Fair Participation Act. For reports on these programs, see RU 312, box 20, SIA. See also Brian Wallis, "Selling Nations: International Exhibitions and Cultural Diplomacy," in *Museum Culture: Histories, Discourses, Spectacles*, ed. Daniel J. Sherman and Irit Rogoff (Minneapolis: University of Minnesota Press, 1994).

18. Margaret Price Cogswell, "The International Art Program of the Smithsonian Institution: Antecedents and Endings, 1960–1975" (Master's thesis, Georgetown University, 1989), 26–27.

19. Frank Getlein, "Roger and the Rabbits," *New Republic*, April 3, 1965, 28. The decision of USIA and subsequent sponsorship by NCFA is discussed by Representative Clement J. Zablocki of Wisconsin, "The USIA, Art, and Congress," in the Appendix to the *Congressional Record*, April 27, 1965. For a history of the Smithsonian's involvement in the biennials and other international art programs, see Cogswell, "International Art Program." Philip Rylands and Enzo di Martino, *Flying the Flag for Art: The United States and the Venice Biennale, 1895–1991* (Richmond, Va.: Wyldbore & Wolferstan, 1993), 159–66, discusses the 1966 and 1969 Venice exhibitions.

20. S. Dillon Ripley, foreword to *XXXIII International Biennial Exhibition of Art, Venice 1966, United States of America* (Washington, D.C.: National Collection of Fine Arts, 1966), 3.

21. The São Paulo Bienal of 1969 is discussed in Cogswell, "International Art Program," 47–51. See also Mary Wiegers, "Artists Boycott Brazil Show," *Washington Post*, July 15, 1969.

22. *Ten Negro Artists from the United States: First World Festival of Negro Arts, Senegal, 1966* (Washington, D.C.: National Collection of Fine Arts, Smithsonian Institution, 1966).

23. Author's conversation with David Scott, November 19, 1984. In Scott's opinion, the subsquent history of the two museums discloses that neither developed a sense of direction or emphasis.

24. David W. Scott to Mrs. Dorothy Phillips, May 5, 1966, and David W. Scott to Richard A. Madigan, January 18, 1966, both in RU 313, box 13, SIA; Leonard Carmichael to Hon. Omar Burleson, Chairman, Committee on House Administration, April 23, 1962, RU 50, box 103, SIA.

25. Adelyn D. Breeskin, *The Graphic Art of Mary Cassatt* (Washington, D.C.: Museum of Graphic Art and Smithsonian Institution Press, 1967).

26. David Winfield Scott, introduction to *Highlights of the National Collection of Fine Arts* (Washington, D.C.: National Collection of Fine Arts, Smithsonian Institution Press, 1968).

27. *Annual Report*, 1968, 189.

28. Lyndon B. Johnson, "Remarks at the Dedication of the Smithsonian Institution's National Collection of Fine Arts, May 3, 1968," in *Public Papers of the Presidents*

of the United States: Lyndon B. Johnson (Washington, D.C.: U.S. Government Printing Office, 1970).

29. Edgar P. Richardson, "The Opportunities and Needs for Research in American Art" (typescript), 4, 7, E. P. Richardson Papers, AAA.

30. Frank Getlein, *Sunday Star*, May 5, 1968.

31. Editorial, *Sunday Star*, May 4, 1969.

32. Influential writings on this topic include Bourdieu and Darbel, *The Love of Art*; Paul J. DiMaggio, Michael Useem, and Paula Brown, *Audience Studies of the Performing Arts and Museums: A Critical Review* (Washington, D.C.: National Endowment for the Arts, 1978); Vera L. Zolberg, " 'An Elite Experience for Everyone': Art Museums, the Public, and Cultural Literacy," in Sherman and Rogoff, *Museum Culture*; Carol Duncan, *Civilizing Rituals* (London: Routledge, 1995); and Duncan and Wallach, "The Universal Survey Museum." See also Karl E. Meyer, *The Art Museum: Power, Money, Ethics* (New York: William Morrow, 1979), esp. chaps. 1–2.

33. Quoted in S. Dillon Ripley, "Joshua Taylor: 'A Museum Is a Bridge That Should Be Well-Traveled,'" *Art News* (Summer 1981): 119.

34. Joshua C. Taylor, "Why Should Anyone Go to a Museum Any More?" *New York Times*, September 30, 1973.

35. Memorandum, Joshua C. Taylor to S. Dillon Ripley, "Notes on Collecting," July 28, 1976, RU 322, box 7, SIA.

36. See Robin Bolton-Smith, *Portrait Miniatures in the National Museum of American Art* (Chicago: University of Chicago Press, 1984).

37. "A Report on the Activities of the National Collection of Fine Arts, 1973–1979," 25–26, RU 438, box 8, SIA.

38. "Museum Evolution Outlined in Current Show," *Smithsonian Torch* (July 1978). The catalogue featured a summary history of the collection: Joshua C. Taylor, *National Collection of Fine Arts: Smithsonian Institution* (Washington, D.C.: Smithsonian Institution Press, 1978.)

39. With two exceptions that are noted, the catalogues for these exhibitions were published in Washington by NCFA and the Smithsonian Institution Press: Robin Bolton-Smith and William H. Truettner, *Lilly Martin Spencer: 1822–1902, The Joys of Sentiment* (1973); Jane Dillenberger and Joshua C. Taylor, *The Hand and the Spirit: Religious Art in America, 1700–1900* (Berkeley, Calif.: University Art Museum, 1972); Lois Marie Fink and Joshua C. Taylor, *Academy: The Academic Tradition in American Art* (1975); Adelyn D. Breeskin, *Romaine Brooks, "Thief of Souls"* (1971); Adelyn D. Breeskin, *Two American Painters: Fritz Scholder and T. C. Canon* (1972); Adelyn D.

Breeskin, *William H. Johnson, 1901–1970* (1971); *The First Western States Biennial Exhibition* (Denver: Western States Foundation, 1979).

40. Catalogues for these exhibitions were published in Washington by the National Collection of Fine Arts and the Smithsonian Institution Press: Donald Baum, Whitney Halstead, and Dennis Adrian, *Made in Chicago* (1974); Rachel Griffin and Martha Kingsbury, *Art of the Pacific Northwest, from the 1930s to the Present* (1974); Peter Bermingham and Pat Austin, *Contemporary Art from Alaska* (1978); Walter Hopps and Lawrence Alloway, *Robert Rauschenberg* (1976); Adelyn D. Breeskin, *Mary Cassatt: Pastels and Prints* (1978); Andrew J. Cosentino, *The Paintings of Charles Bird King 1785–1862* (1977); Frederick C. Moffatt, *Arthur Wesley Dow, 1857–1922*, (1977); Joshua C. Taylor, with a contribution by John G. Cawelti, *America as Art* (1976).

41. Emily Genauer, "Art and the Artist—Venice," *New York Post*, August 8, 1970. The Venice Bienale of 1970 is discussed in Cogswell, "International Art Program," 52–62.

42. Joshua Taylor, "A Report on the Activities of the National Collection of Fine Arts, 1973–1979," RU 438, Box 8, SIA.

43. Marc Zuver and Rebecca Kelley Crumlish, *Raíces y visions / Roots and Visions*, originated by Fondo Del Sol, Spanish American Media Center (Washington, D.C.: Smithsonian Institution, National Collection of Fine Arts, 1977).

44. Joshua C. Taylor, *To See Is To Think: Looking at American Art* (Washington, D.C.: Smithsonian Institution Press, 1975), 8.

45. Joshua C. Taylor, "Scholars' Program at the National Collection of Fine Arts," 1970, RU 322, box 61, SIA.

46. S. Dillon Ripley to President Lyndon B. Johnson, April 1, 1965; the president's reply, June 23, 1965: copies of both letters are in RU 313, box 109, SIA.

47. With one noted exception, these catalogues were published in Washington by the Renwick Gallery of the National Collection of Fine Arts and the Smithsonian Institution Press: Elizabeth Wilder Weismann, *Americas, the Decorative Arts in Latin America in the Era of the Revolution* (1976); Lloyd E. Herman and Lois Frieman Brand, *The Designs of Raymond Loewy* (1975); *The Object as Poet*, with an essay by Rose Slivka (1977); William C. Sturtevant, Ira S. Jacknis, and Bill Holm, *Boxes and Bowls: Decorated Containers by Nineteenth-Century Haida, Tlingit, Bella Bella, and Tsimshian Indian Artists* (1974); John C. Ewers, *Murals in the Round: Painted Tipis of the Kiowa and Kiowa-Apache Indians* (1978); *Signs of Life: Symbols in the American City* (New York: Aperture, 1976).

48. Public Law 96-441, 96th Cong., H.R. 8103 and S.R. 3107, was approved October 13, 1980 (*Congressional Record*, 126 [1980]). The same act renamed the

National Museum of History and Technology as the "National Museum of American History."

49. The script for *A Sense of Discovery* was written by Jean Quinnette and Paul Johnson of the Smithsonian Institution's Office of Telecommunications, with Steve York of York/Wiley Productions; cinematographers were Foster Wiley and Steve York. The film was awarded an Emmy by the Washington chapter of the National Academy of Television Arts and Sciences.

50. Joshua Taylor, "The Smithsonian in Thirty Years," August 3, 1970, RU 322, box 7, SIA.

51. Thomas Lawton, "Tribute to Joshua Taylor," *Calendar of the National Museum of American Art and Its Renwick Gallery*, June 1981.

Coda

1. See Douglas Davis, *The Museum Transformed; Design and Culture in the Post-Pompidou Age* (New York: Abbeville Press, 1990).

2. Neil Harris, "Museums: The Hidden Agenda," in *Cultural Excursions: Marketing Appetites and Cultural Tastes in Modern America* (Chicago: University of Chicago Press, 1990), 134–35, 137.

BIBLIOGRAPHY

This list includes both cited works and others that were helpful to me in forming my ideas or providing further context for the material in the text. Newspaper references, exhibition catalogues, and specific archival sources are fully cited in the notes and are not included here. All referenced archives are located in Washington, D.C.

Archival Records

Archives of American Art, Smithsonian Institution
Gallery Archives, National Gallery of Art
The National Archives
Smithsonian American Art Museum, Registration and Collections Management Office
Smithsonian Institution Archives

Books and Periodicals

Abt, Jeffrey. *A Museum on the Verge: A Socioeconomic History of the Detroit Institute of Arts, 1882–2000*. Detroit: Wayne State University Press, 2001.

Adam, T. R. *The Museum and Popular Culture*. New York: American Association for Adult Education, 1939.

Adams, C. K. "The Washington and London Portrait Galleries: A Comparison." *Museums Journal* (London, March 1969).

Adams, Williams. "Aesthetics: Liberating the Senses." *The Cambridge Companion to Marx*, ed. Terrell Carver. Cambridge: Cambridge University Press, 1991.

"American Art." *Illustrated Magazine of Art* 3 (1854).

Anderson, Clinton. Response to *Arts* editorial. *Arts* 32 (May 1958): 7.

Annual Report of the Board of Regents of the Smithsonian Institution. Washington, D.C., from 1846. Titles vary; cited in Bibliography and Notes as *Annual Report* with year.

Ansbacher, Ted. "John Dewey's Experience and Education: Lessons for Museums." *Curator* 41 (March 1998).

Art in America 69 (July/August 1971). Issue devoted to museums.

Baigell, Matthew, and Julia Williams. Introduction to *Artists against War and Fascism: Papers of the First American Artists' Congress.* New Brunswick, N.J.: Rutgers University Press, 1986.

Baker, Malcolm, and Brenda Richardson, eds. *A Grand Design: The Art of the Victoria and Albert Museum.* New York: Harry N. Abrams and Baltimore Museum of Art, 1997.

Barker, Emma, ed. *Art and Its Histories: Contemporary Cultures of Display*. New Haven: Yale University Press, 1999.

[Barlow, Joel]. *Prospectus of a National Institution to be Established in the United States.* Washington, D.C.: Samuel H. Smith, 1806.

Bedell, Rebecca Bailey. *The Anatomy of Nature: Geology and American Landscape Painting, 1825–1875*. Princeton: Princeton University Press, 2001.

Beggs, Thomas M. *Alice Pike Barney: Portraits in Oil and Pastel.* Washington, D.C.: National Collection of Fine Arts, 1957.

———. *Catalog of American and European Paintings in the Gellatly Collection.* Washington, D. C.: Smithsonian Institution, 1954.

Bello, Mark, et al. *The Smithsonian Institution, a World of Discovery: An Exploration of Behind-the-Scenes Research in the Arts, Sciences, and Humanities.* Washington, D.C.: Smithsonian Institution, 1993.

Benjamin, S. G. W. "Tendencies of Art in America." *American Art Review* 1 (1880).

Benton, Thomas Hart. "Art vs. The Mellon Gallery." *Common Sense* 10 (June 1941).

Berenson, Bernard. *Italian Painters of the Renaissance.* New York: Meridian Books, 1960.

Bergson, Henri. *The Creative Mind.* 1907; New York: Philosophical Library, 1946.

Binkley, Robert C. *Realism and Nationalism, 1852–1871*. New York: Harper, 1935.

Boime, Albert. *The Academy and French Painting in the Nineteenth Century.* London: Phaidon Press, 1971.

Bolton-Smith, Robin. *Portrait Miniatures in the National Museum of American Art.* Chicago: University of Chicago Press, 1984.

Bourdieu, Pierre, and Alain Darbel with Dominique Schnapper. *The Love of Art: European Art Museums and Their Public.* Trans. Caroline Beattie and Nick Merriman. French ed., 1969; Stanford: Stanford University Press, 1991.

Branyan, Robert L., and Lawrence H. Larsen. *The Eisenhower Administration, 1953–1961: A Documentary History*, vols. 1–2. New York: Random House, 1971.

Brigham, David R. *Public Culture in the Early Republic: Peale's Museum and Its Audience.* Washington, D.C.: Smithsonian Institution Press, 1995.

Brown, J. Carter. "The American Museum Experience: Patrons, Patronage, and the Federal Role." *In Quest of Excellence*, ed. Jan Van der Marc. Miami: Center for the Fine Arts, 1984.

Bruce, Robert V. *The Launching of Modern American Science, 1846–1876.* New York: Knopf, 1987.

Bryan, Wilhelmus Bogart. *A History of the National Capital, from Its Foundation through the Period of the Adoption of the Organic Act.* Vol. 1, 1790–1814. New York: Macmillan, 1914.

Buettner, S. "John Dewey and the Visual Arts in America." *Journal of Aesthetics* 33 (Summer 1975).

Bürger, Peter, and Christa Bürger. *The Institutions of Art.* Trans. Loren Kruger. Lincoln: University of Nebraska Press, 1992.

Carver, Terrell, ed. *The Cambridge Companion to Marx.* Cambridge: Cambridge University Press, 1991.

Chipp, Herschel B., ed. *Theories of Modern Art: A Source Book by Artists and Critics.* Berkeley: University of California Press, 1969.

Cockcroft, Eva. "Abstract Expressionism, Weapon of the Cold War." *Artforum* 12 (June 1974).

Cogswell, Margaret Price. "The International Art Program of the Smithsonian Institution: Antecedents and Endings, 1960–1975." Master's thesis, Georgetown University, 1989.

Commission of Fine Arts. *Art and Government: Report to the President by the Commission of Fine Arts on Activities of the Federal Government in the Field of Art.* Washington, D.C.: Commssion of Fine Arts, 1953.

"Competition." *Architectural Forum*, February 1939.

Conaway, James. *The Smithsonian: 150 Years of Adventure, Discovery, and Wonder.* Washington, D.C.: Smithsonian Books; New York: Knopf, 1995.

Conn, Steve. *Museums and American Intellectual Life, 1876–1926.* Chicago: University of Chicago Press, 1998.

Contreras, Belisario R. *Tradition and Innovation in New Deal Art.* Lewisburg, Pa.: Bucknell University Press; London: Associated University Presses, 1983.

Cortissoz, Royal. "The National Gallery of Art." *American Magazine of Art* 16 (March 1925).

Cosentino, Andrew J. *The Paintings of Charles Bird King (1785–1862).* Washington, D.C.: National Collection of Fine Arts, Smithsonian Institution Press, 1977.

Cosentino, Andrew J., and Henry H. Glassie. *The Capital Image: Painters in Washington, 1800–1915*. Washington, D.C.: National Collection of Fine Arts, Smithsonian Institution Press, 1983.

Dana, John Cotton. *The New Relations of Museums and Industries.* Newark, N.J.: Museum Association, 1919. Microfilm N37, frames 845–58, Archives of American Art, Smithsonian Institution.

Davis, Douglas. *The Museum Transformed: Design and Culture in the Post-Pompidou Age.* New York: Abbeville Press, 1990.

De Kay, Charles. "The Evans Collection of American Paintings at Washington." *International Studio* 48 (February 1913).

Devree, Charlotte. "The U.S. Government Vetoes Living Art." *Art News* 55 (September 1956).

Dewey, John. *Art as Experience.* New York: Minton, Balch, 1934.

Dillenberger, Jane and Joshua C. Taylor. *The Hand and the Spirit.* Berkeley, Calif.: University Art Museum, 1972.

DiMaggio, Paul J. *Nonprofit Enterprise in the Arts.* New York: Oxford University Press, 1986.

DiMaggio, Paul J., Michael Useem, and Paula Brown. *Audience Studies of the Performing Arts and Museums: A Critical Review.* Washington, D.C.: National Endowment for the Arts, 1978.

Duncan, Carol. *Civilizing Rituals: Inside Public Art Museums.* London: Routledge, 1995.

Duncan, Carol, and Alan Wallach. "The Universal Survey Museum." *Art History* 3 (December 1980).

Durand, Asher B. "Letters on Landscape Painting." *The Crayon* 1 (January 1855): 34.

Editorial. *Art Digest* 11 (February 15, 1937): 29.

Editorial. *Arts* 32 (April 1958).

Engelbrecht, Lloyd C. "The Association of Arts and Industries: Background and Origins of the Bauhaus Movement in Chicago." Ph.D. diss., University of Chicago, 1973.

Evelyn, Douglas E. "A Public Building for a New Democracy: The Patent Office Building in the Nineteenth Century." Ph.D. diss., George Washington University, 1997.

Fabianski, Marcin. "Iconography of the Architecture of Ideal *Musaea* in the Fifteenth to Eighteenth Centuries." *Journal of the History of Collections* 2, no. 2 (1990).

Field, Cynthia, Richard E. Stamm, and Heather P. Ewing. *The Castle: An Illustrated History of the Smithsonian Building.* Washington, D.C. and London: Smithsonian Institution Press, 1993.

Findlen, Paula. "The Museum: Its Classical Etymology and Renaissance Genealogy." *Journal of the History of Collections* 1, no. 1 (1989).

Fink, Lois Marie. *American Art at the Nineteenth-Century Paris Salons.* Washington, D.C.: Smithsonian Institution; Cambridge: Cambridge University Press, 1990.

Fink, Lois Marie and Joshua C. Taylor. *Academy: The Academic Tradition in American Art.* Washington, D.C.: National Collection of Fine Arts, and Smithsonian Institution Press, 1975.

Ford, Arthur L. *Joel Barlow.* New York: Twayne, 1971.

Frankfurter, Alfred M. [A. M. F.]. "A Portfolio of the Andrew W. Mellon Collection." *Art News* 35 (May 1, 1937): 78.

———. "Vernissage, Graven Images," *Art News* 50 (February 1952): 11.

Fry, Roger. "An Essay in Aesthetics." *New Quarterly* (London), 1909.

Gaither and Addison, comps. *TheWashington Directory and National Register for 1846.* Washington, D.C.: John T. Towers, 1846.

"German Art and the German Character." *Burlington Magazine*, November 1905: 78.

Getlein, Frank. "Roger and the Rabbits." *New Republic*, April 3, 1965.

Gilman, Benjamin Ives. *Museum Ideals of Purpose and Method.* Cambridge: Harvard University Press, 1923.

Goode, George Brown, "The Genesis of the National Museum." *Annual Report*, 1881.

———. "The Museums of the Future." *Annual Report*, 1889.

———. "The Origin of the National Scientific and Educational Institutions of the United States." *American Historical Association, Report of Proceedings at the Sixth Annual Meeting, 1889.* Washington, D.C.: U.S. Government Printing Office, 1890.

———. "Report of the Assistant Director of the United States National Museum for the Year 1881." *Annual Report*, 1881.

———, ed. *The Smithsonian Institution, 1846–1896: The History of Its First Half Century.* Washington, D.C.: Smithsonian Institution, 1897.

Goodrich, Lloyd. "The Federal Government and Art." *Magazine of Art* 41 (October 1948).

———. "Government and the Arts." *Art in America* 42 (December 1954).

———. "Mall Site for NCFA Building." *Arts* (May 1958).

———. "Rebirth of a National Collection." *Art in America* (June 1965).

Greene, John C. "Science, Learning, and Utility: Patterns of Organization in the Early American Republic." *The Pursuit of Knowledge in the Early American Republic; American Scientific and Learned Societies from Colonial Times to the Civil War*, ed. Alexandra Oleson and Sanborn C. Brown. Baltimore: Johns Hopkins University Press, 1976.

Grunchec, Philippe. *The Grand Prix de Rome: Paintings from the Ecole des Beaux-Arts, 1797–1863.* Washington, D.C.: International Exhibitions Foundations, 1984.

Gwinn, Nancy E. "Origins and Development of International Exchange in Nineteenth Century America." Ph.D. diss., George Washington University, 1996.

Hall, Delight. *Catalogue of the Alice Pike Barney Memorial Lending Collection.* Washington, D.C.: National Collection of Fine Arts, 1965.

Harris, Elizabeth, and Helena E. Wright. *G.A. 100: The Centenary of the Division of Graphic Arts.* Washington, D.C.: National Museum of American History, Smithsonian Institution, 1986.

Harris, Neil. *Cultural Excursions: Marketing Appetites and Cultural Tastes in Modern America.* Chicago: University of Chicago Press, 1990.

———. "Polling for Opinions." *Museum News*, September/October 1990.

Hart, Albert Bushnell, and Herbert Ronald Ferleger, eds. *Theodore Roosevelt Cyclopedia*, rev. 2nd ed. Oyster Bay, N.Y.: Theodore Roosevelt Association and Meckler, 1989.

Hart, Sidney, and David C. Ward. "The Waning of an Enlightenment Ideal: Charles Willson Peale's Philadelphia Museum, 1790–1820." *Journal of the Early Republic* 8 (Winter 1988).

Harvard's Art Museums—100 Years of Collecting. Cambridge: Harvard University Art Museums; New York: Harry N. Abrams, 1997.

Hauptman, William. "The Suppression of Art in the McCarthy Decade." *Artforum*, October 1973.

Heckscher, August. *The Arts and the National Government: A Report to the President.* Washington, D.C.: U.S. Government Printing Office, 1963.

Henderson, Amy, and Adrienne L. Kaeppler, eds. *Exhibiting Dilemmas: Issues of Representation at the Smithsonian.* Washington, D.C.: Smithsonian Institution Press, 1996.

Holmes, William H. *Catalogue of Collections.* 1922; reprint, Washington, D.C.: U.S. Government Printing Office, 1926.

———. "Shall America Have a National Gallery of Art?" *Magazine of Art* 24 (July 1923).

———. "The Story of the National Gallery of Art." *Art and Archaeology* 15 (June 1923).

Hovencamp, Herbert. *Science and Religion in America, 1800–1860.* Philadelphia: University of Pennsylvania Press, 1978.

Howe, Winifred E. *A History of the Metropolitan Museum of Art*, vol. 2, 1905–1941. New York: Columbia University Press, 1946.

Humphries, Lance Lee. "Robert Gilmor, Jr. (1774–1848): Baltimore Collector and American Art Patron." Ph.D. diss., University of Virginia, 1998.

James, Henry. "The Madonna of the Future." *The Tales of Henry James*, vol. 2, *1870–74*, ed. Maqbool Aziz. Oxford: Clarendon Press, 1978.

Jewell, Edward Alden. "New York Times." *Magazine of Art* 30 (February 1937): 73.

Jewett, Charles Coffin. *Annual Report*, 1850, 30.

Johnson, Lyndon B. *Public Papers of the Presidents of the United States: Lyndon B. Johnson.* Washington, D.C.: U.S. Government Printing Office, 1970.

Jordan, David Star. "Biographical Sketch of George Brown Goode." *The Smithsonian Institution, 1846–1896*, ed. George Brown Goode. Washington, D.C.: DeVinne Press, 1897.

Kandinsky, Wassily. *Concerning the Spritual in Art.* Trans. Francis Golffing, Michael Harrison, and Ferdinand Ostertag. 1912; New York: Wittenborn, Schultz, 1947. (First English translation 1914.)

Karp, Ivan, and Steven D. Lavine, eds. *Exhibiting Cultures: The Poetics and Politics of Museum Display.* Washington, D.C.: Smithsonian Institution Press, 1991.

Kimball, Fiske. "Le Programme Moderne des Musées en Amérique." *Cahiers de la République des Lettres des Sciences et des Arts*, vol. 13, *Musées.* Paris, ca. 1930.

Kingsbury, Martha. "Hung in Guilt Frames." *Art Journal* 51 (Fall 1992).

Kling, Jean L. *Alice Pike Barney: Her Life and Art.* Washington, D.C.: National Museum of American Art, 1994.

Klingender, Francis D. *Art and the Industrial Revolution.* Ed. and rev. Arthur Elton. 1947 New York: Schocken Books, 1970.

Koehler, Sylvester Rosa. "Report on the Section of Graphic Arts." *Annual Report*, 1889.

Kohler, Sue A. *The Commission of Fine Arts: A Brief History, 1910–1976.* Washington, D.C.: U.S. Government Printing Office, 1977.

Kohlstedt, Sally. "A Step toward Scientific Self-Identity in the United States: The Failure of the National Institute, 1844." *Isis* 62, part 3 (September 1971).

Kopper, Philip. *America's National Gallery of Art: A Gift to the Nation.* New York: Harry N. Abrams, 1991.

Kozloff, Max. "American Painting during the Cold War." *Artforum* 11 (May 1973).

Larson, Gary O. *The Reluctant Patron: The United States Government and the Arts, 1943–1965.* Philadelphia: University of Pennsylvania Press, 1983.

Lawton, Thomas. "Tribute to Joshua Taylor." *Calendar of the National Museum of American Art and Its Renwick Gallery*, June 1981.

Lawton, Thomas, and Linda Merrill. *Freer: a Legacy of Art.* Washington, D.C.: Freer Gallery of Art, Smithsonian Institution, Harry N. Abrams, 1993.

Lee, Sherman E., and Edward B. Henning. "Works of Art, Ideas of Art, and Museums of Art." *On Understanding Art Museums*, ed. Sherman E. Lee. Englewood Cliffs, N.J.: Prentice-Hall, 1974.

Leech, Margaret. *Reveille in Washington, 1860–1865*. Chicago: Time-Life Books, 1962.

Libbey, Edward Drummond. "The Need of a National Gallery of Art." *American Magazine* 16 (March 1925).

Lin, Tsong-yuan, ed. *Proceedings of the International Conference on Anthropology and the Museum*. Taipei: Taiwan Museum, 1995.

Maas, John. *The Glorious Enterprize*. Watkins Glen, N.Y.: American Life Foundation, 1973.

March, Benjamin. "La vie des Musées d'Art en 1930 aux Etats-Unis." *Cahiers de la République des Lettres des Sciences et des Arts*, vol. 13, *Musées*. Paris, ca. 1930.

Marstine, Janet Cecilia. "Working History: Images of Labor and Industry in American Mural Painting, 1893–1903." Ph.D. diss., University of Pittsburgh, 1993.

Mather, Frank Jewett. "Art in America: A Question of Museum Policy." *Burlington Magazine* 9 (April 1906).

———. "An Art Museum for the People." *Atlantic Monthly* 100 (December 1907).

Mathews, Jane De Hart, "Art and Politics in Cold War America." *American Historical Review* 81 (October 1976).

McClellan, Andrew. *Inventing the Louvre: Art, Politics, and the Origins of the Modern Museum in Eighteenth-Century Paris*. Cambridge: Cambridge University Press, 1994.

McClelland, Donald R. *Where Shadows Live: Alice Pike Barney and Her Friends*. Washington, D.C.: National Collection of Fine Arts, Smithsonian Institution, 1978.

McDonald, Travis. "The Smithsonian Gallery of Art Competition." *Modulus: The University of Virginia School of Architecture Review*, March 1980.

Mechlin, Leila. "National Gallery of Art Project." *American Magazine of Art* 15 (July 1924).

———. "The Evans Collection in the National Gallery at Washington." *Century Magazine* 75 (December 1907).

Meyer, Adolf Bernhard. *Studies of the Museums and Kindred Institutions of New York City, Albany, Buffalo, and Chicago, with Notes on Some European Institutions*. Washington, D.C.: Smithsonian Institution, 1905.

Meyer, Karl E. *The Art Museum: Power, Money, Ethics*. New York: William Morrow, 1979.

Miller, Lillian B. *Patrons and Patriotism: The Encouragement of the Fine Arts in the United States, 1790–1860*. Chicago: University of Chicago Press, 1966.

Mills, Robert. *Guide to the National Executive Offices and the Capitol of the United States.* Washington, D.C.: P. Force, 1842.

Morgan, Keith N. *Charles A. Platt, The Artist as Architect.* Cambridge: MIT Press, 1985.

Morris, William. *Hopes and Fears for Art.* London: Ellis & White, 1884.

Moser, James Henry. "The National Gallery of Art." *Art and Progress* 1 (April 1910).

Moyano, Steven. "Quality vs. History: Schinkel's Altes Museum and Prussian Arts Policy." *Art Bulletin* 72 (December 1990).

"Museums in a Changing World." *Atlantic Monthly* 164 (December 1939).

Nagel, Charles. "The National Portrait Gallery of the Smithsonian Institution." *Museums Journal* (London, March 1969).

National Collection of Fine Arts. *Catalog of American and European Paintings in the Gellatly Collection.* Washington, D.C.: National Collection of Fine Arts, 1933, 1940, 1945, 1954.

———. *Preliminary Catalogue Listing of Paintings, Drawings, and Sculpture.* Washington, D.C.: National Collection of Fine Arts, Smithsonian Institution, 1963.

National Collection of Fine Arts, National Portrait Gallery: Museums of the Smithsonian Institution. Washington, D.C.: U.S. Government Printing Office, 1968.

A National Competition to Select an Architect for the Proposed Smithsonian Gallery of Art, Washington, D.C. Washington, D.C.: United States Smithsonian Gallery of Art Commission, 1939.

National Museum of American Art. *Descriptive Catalogue of Painting and Sculpture in the National Museum of American Art, Washington, D.C.* Boston: G. K. Hall, 1983.

National Museum of American Art: Smithsonian Institution. Washington, D.C.: National Museum of American Art, 1995.

"National Sculpture Society Response." *Art News* 51 (March 1952).

Nelson, Clifford M. *William Henry Holmes: Beginning a Career in Art and Science.* Washington, D.C.: Columbia Historical Society, 1980.

Nemerov, Alexander. *The Body of Raphaelle Peale: Still Life and Selfhood, 1812–1824.* Berkeley: University of California Press, 2002.

Oles, James. *South of the Border: Mexico in the American Imagination.* Trans. Maria Ferrgut. Washington, D.C.: Smithsonian Institution Press, 1993.

Oleson, Alexandra, and Sanborn C. Brown, eds. *The Pursuit of Knowledge in the Early American Republic: American Scientific and Learned Societies from Colonial Times to the Civil War.* Baltimore: Johns Hopkins University Press, 1976.

Oleson, Alexandra, and John Voss, eds. *The Organization of Knowledge in Modern America, 1860–1920.* Baltimore: Johns Hopkins University Press, 1976.

Orosz, Joel J. *Curators and Culture: The Museum Movement in America, 1740–1870.* Tuscaloosa: University of Alabama Press, 1990.

———. "Disloyalty, Dismissal, and a Deal: The Development of the National Museum at the Smithsonian Institution, 1846–1855." *Museum Studies Journal* 2 (Spring 1986).

———. "In Defense of the Deal: A Rebuttal to S. Dillon Ripley's and Wilcomb Washburn's 'Response.'" *Museum Studies Journal* 3 (Fall–Winter 1987).

Paradis, James, and Thomas Postlewait, eds. *Victorian Science and Victorian Values: Literary Perspectives.* New York: New York Academy of Sciences, 1981.

Pach, Walter. *The Art Museum in America.* New York: Pantheon, 1948.

"Patently Suited to Art: National Collection of Fine Art." *Museum News* 59 (September 1980).

Pearce, Susan M. *Museums, Objects, and Collections: A Cultural Study.* Washington, D.C.: Smithsonian Institution Press, 1992.

———. "Interpreting Museum Objects: An Outline of Theory." *Proceedings of the International Conference on Anthropology and the Museum*, ed. Tsong-yuan Lin. Taipei: Taiwan Museum, 1995.

Pevsner, Nikolaus. *Academies of Art, Past and Present.* Cambridge: Cambridge University Press, 1940.

Phelps, Charles Henry. *The Meaning of the Will of Henry W. Ranger.* New York: National Academy of Design, 1929.

Poinsett, Joel R. *Discourse on the Objects and Importance of the National Institution for the Promotion of Science, Established at Washington, 1840, Delivered at the First Anniversary.* Washington, D.C.: P. Force, 1841.

Pointon, Marcia. "Imaging Nationalism in the Cold War: The Foundation of the American National Portrait Gallery. *Journal of American Studies* 26 (December 1992).

Powers, Lyall H. *Henry James and the Naturalist Movement.* East Lansing: Michigan State University Press, 1971.

Pulling, F. S. *Sir Joshua Reynolds.* London: Sampson, Low, Marston, Searle, and Rivington, 1886.

Rathbun, Richard. *Catalogue of Paintings and Other Art Objects Exhibited on the Occasion of the Opening of the Gallery in the New Building of the United States National Museum, March 17, 1910.* Washington, D.C.: National Gallery of Art, 1910.

———. *The Columbian Institute for the Promotion of Arts and Sciences.* Washington, D.C.: U.S. Government Printing Office, 1917; U.S. National Museum, Bulletin 101.

———. *The National Gallery of Art, Department of Fine Arts of the National Museum.* Washington, D.C.: U.S. Government Printing Office, 1906; U.S. National Museum, Bulletin 70 (reprint with additions, 1916).

Reiff, Daniel D. *Washington Architecture, 1791–1861: Problems in Development.* Washington, D.C.: U.S. Commission of Fine Arts, 1971.

Report of the Organization Committee of the Smithsonian Institution, with the Resolutions Accompanying the Same, and Adopted by the Board of Regents; Also, the Will of the Testator, the Act Accepting the Bequest, and the Act Organizing the Institution. Washington, D.C.: Blair & Rives, 1847.

Rhees, William J. *An Account of the Smithsonian Institution, Its Founder, Building Operations, etc.* Washington, D.C.: Thomas McGill, 1861.

———. *The Smithsonian Institution: Documents Relative to Its Origin and History, 1835–1899* vols. 1–2. Washington, D.C.: U.S. Government Printing Office, 1879, 1901.

———. *Visitor's Guide to the Smithsonian Institution and United States National Museum in Washington.* Washington, D.C.: Judd & Detweiler, 1880–87, 1889; cited in notes as *Visitor's Guide* with year.

Richards, Charles R. *Industrial Art and the Museum.* New York: Macmillan, 1927.

———. *The Industrial Museum.* New York: Macmillan, 1925.

Richardson, Edgar P., Brooke Hindle, and Lillian B. Miller. *Charles Willson Peale and His World.* New York: Harry N. Abrams, 1982.

Ripley, S. Dillon. Foreword to *XXXIII International Biennial Exhibition of Art, Venice 1966, United States of America.* Washington, D.C.: National Collection of Fine Arts, 1966.

———. "Joshua Taylor: 'A Museum Is a Bridge That Should Be Well-Traveled.'" *Art News,* Summer 1981.

Ripley, S. Dillon, and Wilcomb E. Washburn. "The Development of the National Museum at the Smithsonian Institution, 1846–1855: A Response to Joel J. Orosz's Article." *Museum Studies Journal* 3 (Spring 1987).

Roos, David A. "The 'Aims and Intentions' of *Nature.*" *Victorian Science and Victorian Values: Literary Perspectives,* ed. James Paradis and Thomas Postlewait. New York: New York Academy of Sciences, 1981.

Roosevelt, Theodore. "Address before the American Academy and National Institute of Arts and Letters, New York City, November 16, 1916." *Theodore Roosevelt Cyclopedia,* rev. 2nd ed., ed. Albert Bushnell Hart and Herbert Ronald Ferleger. Oyster Bay, N.Y.: Theodore Roosevelt Association and Meckler, 1989.

———. "Fourth Annual Message." *The State of the Union Messages of the Presidents, 1790–1966*, vol. 2, *1861–1904*, ed. Fred L. Israel. New York: Chelsea House with R. R. Bowker, 1967.

Rose, George B. "The Ralph Cross Johnson Collection in the National Gallery at Washington, D.C." *Art and Archaeology* 10 (September 1920): 110.

Rylands, Philip, and Enzo di Martino. *Flying the Flag for Art: The United States and the Venice Biennale, 1895–1991*. Richmond, Va.: Wyldbore & Wolferstan, 1993.

Schepelern, H. D. "The Museum Wormianum Reconstructed." *Journal of the History of Collections* 2, no. 1 (1990): 81–85.

Schimmel, Julie. "John Mix Stanley and Imagery of the West in Nineteenth Century American Art." Ph.D. diss., New York University, 1983.

Schulz, Eva. "Notes on the History of Collecting and of Museums in the Light of Selected Literature of the Sixteenth to the Eighteenth Century." *Journal of the History of Collections* 2, no. 2 (1990).

Scott, David Winfield. *The Arts: A Central Element of a Good Society*. Washington, D.C.: Arts Councils of America, 1965.

———. Introduction to *Highlights of the National Collection of Fine Arts*, with contributions by Richard P. Wunder, William H. Truettner, Adelyn D. Breskin, Jacob Kainen, and Caril Dreyfuss. Washington, D.C.: National Collection of Fine Arts, Smithsonian Institution Press, 1968.

Sellers, Charles Coleman. *Mr. Peale's Museum*. New York: Norton, 1980.

Semper, Gottfried. "Science, Industry, and Art: Proposals for the Development of a National Taste in Art at the Closing of the London Industrial Exhibition." *The Four Elements of Architecture and Other Writings*, trans. Henry Francis Mallgrave and Wolfgang Herrmann. 1852; Cambridge: Cambridge University Press, 1989.

Senic, Harriet F., and Sally Webster, eds. *Critical Issues in Public Art: Content, Context, and Controversy*. New York: Harper-Collins, 1992.

Shahn, Ben. "Artist and the Politician." *Art News* 52 (September 1953).

Shapiro, Michael S. "The Public and the Museum." *The Museum: A Reference Guide*, ed. Michael S. Shapiro with Louis Ward Kemp. New York: Greenwood Press, 1990.

Sherman, Daniel J. *Worthy Monuments: Art Museums and the Politics of Culture in Nineteenth-Century France*. Cambridge: Harvard University Press, 1989.

Sherman, Daniel J., and Irit Rogoff, eds. *Museum Culture: Histories, Discourses, Spectacles*. Minneapolis: University of Minnesota Press, 1994.

Smallwood, William Martin, with Mabel Sarah Smallwood. *Natural History and the American Mind*. New York: Columbia University Press, 1941.

Smith, Franklin Webster. *National Galleries of History and Art: The Aggrandizement of Washington.* Washington, D.C.: U.S. Government Printing Office, 1900.

"The Smithsonian Gallery of Art Competition." *Architectural Forum* 71 (July 1939).

"Smithsonian Gallery of Art Competition." *Magazine of Art* 32 (August 1939).

Solomon, Maynard. *Marxism and Art: Essays Classic and Contemporary.* Detroit: Wayne State University Press, 1979.

Sparshott, Francis. "Art and Anthropology." *Journal of Aesthetics and Art Criticism* 55 (Summer 1997).

Stafford, Barbara Maria. "The Eighteenth-Century: Towards an Interdisciplinary Model." *Art Bulletin* 70 (March 1988).

Strange, Amy Batson. "William Henry Holmes, Artist: The Smithsonian's Nineteenth-Century Renaissance Man." Master's thesis, University of Florida, 1992.

Taine, Hippolyte Adolphe. *The History of English Literature.* Trans. H. Van Laun. New York: Henry Holt, 1879.

———. *Lectures on Art*, 2nd ser. Trans. John Durand. New York: Henry Holt, 1875; New York: AMS Press, 1971.

Taylor, Brandon. *Art for the Nation. Exhibitions and the London Public, 1747–2001.* New Brunswick, N.J.: Rutgers University Press, 1999.

Taylor, Francis Henry. "Museums in a Changing World." *Atlantic Monthly* 164 (December 1939).

Taylor, Joshua C. "The Art Museum in the United States." *On Understanding Art Museums*, ed. Sherman E. Lee. Englewood Cliffs, N.J.: Prentice-Hall, 1975.

———. *National Collection of Fine Arts, Smithsonian Institution.* Washington, D.C.: Smithsonian Institution Press, 1978.

———. *To See Is to Think: Looking at American Art.* Washington, D.C.: Smithsonian Institution Press, 1975.

———. "Two Visual Excursions." *Critical Inquiry* 1 (September 1974).

Thompson, Frank. "Argument for Patent Office Building." *Arts* 32 (June 1958).

Townsend, M. E. "Pittsburg's [*sic*] Annual Art Exhibition." *Brush and Pencil* 16 (December 1905): 199–205.

True, Frederick W. *An Account of the United States National Museum.* Washington, D.C.: U.S. Government Printing Office, 1898.

Truettner, William H. *The Natural Man Observed: A Study of Catlin's Indian Gallery.* Washington, D.C.: Smithsonian Institution Press, 1979.

———. "William T. Evans, Collector of American Paintings." *American Art Journal* 3 (Fall 1971).

Turner, Elizabeth Hutton. *American Artists in Paris, 1919–1929*. Ann Arbor, Mich.: UMI Research Press, 1988.

"United States Patent Office." *United States Magazine* 3 (October 1856).

[Varden, John]. *A Guide for Visitors to the National Gallery, Prepared in Accordance with the Instructions of the Commissioner of Patents.* Washington, D.C.: H. Polkinhorn, 1856.

Varnum, Joseph B., Jr. *The Seat of Government of the United States.* 2nd ed. Washington, D.C.: R. Farnham, 1854.

Viola, Herman J. "Washington's First Museum: The Indian Office of Thomas L. McKenney." *Smithsonian Journal of History* 3 (Fall 1968).

Viola, Herman J., and Carolyn Margolis, eds. *Magnificient Voyagers: The U.S. Exploring Expedition, 1838–1842*. Washington, D.C.: Smithsonian Institution Press, 1985.

Vogel, Susan. "Always True to the Object in Our Fashion." *Exhibiting Cultures: The Poetics and Politics of Museum Display*, ed. Ivan Karp and Steven D. Lavine. Washington, D.C.: Smithsonian Institution Press, 1991.

Wacquant, Loïc J. D. "Bourdieu in America: Notes on the Translantlantic Importation of a Social Theory." *Bourdieu: Critical Perspectives*, ed. Craig Calhoun, Edward Li Puma, and Moishe Postone. Chicago: University of Chicago Press, 1993.

Walcott, Charles D. Address to the American Federation of Arts. *Supplement to Art and Progress: The Proceedings of the First Annual Convention of the American Federation of Arts* 1 (July 1910).

Wallach, Alan. *Exhibiting Contradiction: Essays on the Art Museum in the United States.* Amherst: University of Massachusetts Press, 1998.

Wallis, Brian. "Selling Nations: International Exhibitions and Cultural Diplomacy." *Museum Culture: Histories, Discourses, Spectacles*, ed. Daniel J. Sherman and Irit Rogoff. Minneapolis: University of Minnesota Press, 1994.

Washburn, Wilcomb E. "The Influence of the Smithsonian Institution on Intellectual Life in Mid-Nineteenth-Century Washington." *Records of the Columbia Historical Society of Washington, D.C., 1963–1965* (1966): 99–121.

———. "The Museum and Joseph Henry." *Curator* 8, no. 1 (1965).

Washington, George. "Farewell Address." *The Writings of George Washington.* New York: Harper, 1848.

Watson, Forbes. "The Benefit of Great Art." *Magazine of Art* 34 (March 1941).

Watson, Jane. "News and Comments: A Nation in Search of a National Gallery." *Magazine of Art* 34 (March 1941).

Watterson, George. *A New Guide to Washington.* Washington, D.C.: Robert Parkham, 1842.

Wetenhall, John. "Camelot's Legacy to Public Art: Aesthetic Ideology in the New Frontier." *Critical Issues in Public Art*, ed. Harriet F. Senic and Sally Webster. New York: Harper-Collins, 1992.

Whiting, Cécil. *Antifascism in American Art.* New Haven: Yale University Press, 1989.

Whiting, Frederic Allen. "Art Museums Considered as Centers of Civic Activities." *Christian Science Monitor*, Jauary 11, 1923.

Whitman, Walt. *Specimen Days.* 1882; reprint, Meriden, Conn.: Meriden Gravine, 1971.

Worringer, Wilhelm. *Abstraction and Empathy: A Contribution to the Psychology of Style.* Trans. Michael Bullock. Munich: R. Piper, 1908; London: Routledge and Kegan Paul, 1953.

Wright, Helena E. *Prints at the Smithsonian: The Origins of a National Collection.* Washington, D.C.: National Museum of American History, Smithsonian Institution, 1996.

Yochelson, Ellis. *Charles Doolittle Walcott, 1850–1927.* New York: Columbia Press for the National Academy of Sciences, 1967.

———. *Charles Doolittle Walcott, Paleontologist.* Kent, Ohio: Kent State University Press, 1998.

———. *The National Museum of Natural History: 75 Years in the New National Museum.* Washington, D.C.: Smithsonian Institution Press, 1985.

———. *Smithsonian Institution Secretary, Charles Doolittle Walcott, 1850–1927.* Kent, Ohio: Kent State University Press, 2001.

Zolberg, Vera L. "The Art Institute of Chicago: The Sociology of a Cultural Organization." Ph.D. diss., University of Chicago, 1974.

———. "'An Elite Experience for Everyone': Art Museums, the Public, and Cultural Literacy." *Museum Culture: Histories, Discourses, Spectacles*, ed. Daniel J. Sherman and Irit Rogoff. Minneapolis: University of Minnesota Press, 1994.

INDEX

Lois Marie Fink, a native of Indiana, earned her BA from Capital University and her MA and PhD in art history from the University of Chicago. She taught at Lenoir Rhyne College, Midland College, and Roosevelt University before joining the curatorial staff of the National Collection of Fine Arts—later the National Museum of American Art and currently the Smithsonian American Art Museum—where she served for twenty-three years. She retired in 1993 with the title Research Curator, Emerita. In recognition of her distinguished career her alma mater, Capital University, has conferred on her the honorary degree of Doctor of Humanities. Dr. Fink's publications include (in addition to numerous scholarly articles, chapters in books, and book reviews) *American Art at the Nineteenth-Century Paris Salons* (1990) and *Academy: The Academic Tradition in American Art* (coauthor, 1978). She lives in Rockville, Maryland.